Leo Laporte's Guide to Mac OS X Tiger

Leo Laporte
Todd Stauffer

800 East 96th Street,
Indianapolis, Indiana 46240

D1305561

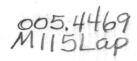

Leo Laporte's Guide to Mac OS X Tiger

Copyright ® 2006 by Que Publishing

International Standard Book Number: 0-7897-3393-5

Library of Congress Catalog Card Number: 2005922649

Printed in the United States of America

First Printing: August 2005

08   07   06   05   4   3   2   1

Trademarks

All terms mentioned in this book that are known to be trademarks or service marks have been appropriately capitalized. Que Publishing cannot attest to the accuracy of this information. Use of a term in this book should not be regarded as affecting the validity of any trademark or service mark.

Warning and Disclaimer

Every effort has been made to make this book as complete and as accurate as possible, but no warranty or fitness is implied. The information provided is on an "as is" basis. The author and the publisher shall have neither liability nor responsibility to any person or entity with respect to any loss or damages arising from the information contained in this book.

Bulk Sales

Que Publishing offers excellent discounts on this book when ordered in quantity for bulk purchases or special sales. For more information, please contact

> **U.S. Corporate and Government Sales**
> **1-800-382-3419**
> **corpsales@pearsontechgroup.com**

For sales outside the United States, please contact

> **International Sales**
> **international@pearsoned.com**

Associate Publisher
Greg Wiegand

Executive Editor
Rick Kughen

Development Editor
Todd Brakke

Managing Editor
Charlotte Clapp

Project Editor
Tonya Simpson

Production Editor
Benjamin Berg

Indexer
Heather McNeill

Technical Editor
Brian Hubbard

Publishing Coordinator
Sharry Lee Gregory

Designer
Anne Jones

Page Layout
Kelly Maish

Reviewers
Shelly Brisbin
Mark Frauenfelder
Brian Hubbard

Contents at a Glance

Table of Contents

About the Authors

Leo Laporte is the former host of two shows on TechTV—*The Screen Savers* and *Call for Help*. Leo is a weekend radio host on Los Angeles radio KFI AM 640 and co-hosts *Call for Help* on Canada's G4TechTV network. He also appears regularly on many other television and radio programs, including ABC's *World News Now* and *Live with Regis and Kelly*, as "The Gadget Guy." He is the author of four recent bestsellers: *Leo Laporte's 2005 Gadget Guide*, *Leo Laporte's Mac Gadget Guide*, *Leo Laporte's Guide to TiVo*, and *Leo Laporte's 2005 Technology Almanac*.

In January, 1991, he created and co-hosted *Dvorak On Computers*, the most listened to high tech-talk radio show in the nation, syndicated on more than 60 stations and around the world on the Armed Forces Radio Network. Laporte also hosted *Laporte on Computers* on KSFO and KGO Radio in San Francisco.

On television, Laporte was host of *Internet!*, a weekly half-hour show airing on PBS in 215 cities nationwide. He reported on new media for *Today's First Edition* on PBS, and did daily product reviews and demos on *New Media News*, broadcast nationally on Jones Computer Network and ME/U and regionally on San Francisco's Bay TV.

Todd Stauffer is the author or co-author of more than three dozen computing and technical books, a contributor to various technical magazines, a humor columnist, and a travel/automotive reviewer. He is the co-founder and publisher of *Jackson Free Press*, a news and culture weekly in Jackson, MS.

More than 500,000 copies of books by Todd Stauffer have been sold, including the best-selling *How to Do Everything with Your iMac* (Osborne), *Mac Upgrade and Repair Bible* (Hungry Minds/Wiley), *Small Business Office 2000 for Dummies* (Hungry Minds, with Dave Johnson), and *HTML By Example* (Que). He recently completed co-authoring *Leo Laporte's 2005 Mac Gadget Guide* for Que.

Todd is the former writer and co-host of the *Disk Doctors* television show on the Knowledge TV network from 1997 to 2000. He also hosted the *Peak Computing* radio show in Denver (with Dave Johnson) in the late 1990s. Before going freelance, Todd was editor of *Texas Computing Magazine* and an advertising writer. He graduated from Texas A&M University with a B.A. in English literature.

Acknowledgments

Todd would like to thank Leo, along with executive editor Rick Kughen, for the opportunity to work on this project; Todd Brakke for helping to shape the manuscript; and Tonya Simpson for managing the process. Todd would also like to thank technical editor Brian Hubbard and copy editor Benjamin Berg for their invaluable contributions to the finished product. On a personal level, Todd would like to thank the staff of the *Jackson Free Press* for their support during this project and, as always, huge thanks to Donna Ladd.

We Want to Hear from You!

As the reader of this book, *you* are our most important critic and commentator. We value your opinion and want to know what we're doing right, what we could do better, what areas you'd like to see us publish in, and any other words of wisdom you're willing to pass our way.

As an executive editor for Que Publishing, I welcome your comments. You can email or write me directly to let me know what you did or didn't like about this book—as well as what we can do to make our books better.

Please note that I cannot help you with technical problems related to the topic of this book. We do have a User Services group, however, where I will forward specific technical questions related to the book.

When you write, please be sure to include this book's title and author as well as your name, email address, and phone number. I will carefully review your comments and share them with the author and editors who worked on the book.

Email: feedback@quepublishing.com

Mail: Rick Kughen
        Executive Editor
        Que Publishing
        800 East 96th Street
        Indianapolis, IN 46240 USA

For more information about this book or another Que Publishing title, visit our website at www.quepublishing.com. Type the ISBN (excluding hyphens) or the title of a book in the Search field to find the page you're looking for.

Introduction

If you had to sum up the world of a Macintosh user in a single word, I'd probably go with "interesting." After all, the "mothership," as devout Mac fans call Apple, Inc., is run by none other than Steve Jobs, easily the most "interesting" executive in technology today, if not in all of corporate America. But there are other things that make working with the Macintosh interesting, such as the strong emphasis on the design of the machines, the power of the creative applications that Apple writes and (in many cases) gives away to its users, and, of course, the people like us who gravitate to the machines and use them for work and play—we may be the most interesting part of the whole darned thing.

Most central to making the Mac experience interesting, however, is undoubtedly the Macintosh operating system, which is what gives every Mac its interface, the core technology that makes up its toolset, and to a large extent its personality. Applications rely on the Mac OS for everything from the way you open and close documents, to how you manage the documents you create, to how movies and audio are played back within applications.

Mac OS X, now in its fifth significant version release, is the culmination of years of computer science and is designed to make using a Macintosh extremely interesting. In the version we discuss in this book, Mac OS X 10.4, Apple has released an extremely mature operating system, based on some of the latest computer science and technology know-how, but packaged in a user interface that looks pretty clean and futuristic even by Hollywood standards.

I guess another thing that makes us Mac users interesting is how much we can come to love the Macintosh and, by extension, the Mac OS. In many ways, this operating system can simply "get out of your way" and enable you to get some wonderful work done, as it works with the applications you run (word processing, Internet applications, video editing, professional tools) to seamlessly provide the experience you'll grow used to if you don't know it intimately. At the same time, the OS itself is a standout, with tools such as Automator to help you automate the tasks that you perform frequently, and the integration of Internet and networking tools to make your home or office a little more "connected" with relatively little configuration and effort.

If you're new to the Mac, new to Mac OS X, or simply new to this latest version, Mac OS X 10.4 "Tiger," I'm here to tell you, right now that you're in for an interesting—and hopefully extremely rewarding—experience.

Who Should Use This Book

Most of us aren't completely new to the world of computing, so I think it's time that books move from addressing the utter "newbie" and focus a little more on the rest of us—people who probably work a lot with computers and either live with them, too, or are close to buying a new machine. So I hope you'll find that the assumptions I make in the book are the right ones—you've got a passing familiarity with a mouse and have at least talked about word processing at parties (now there's an exciting party), even if you're not a devout fan yourself.

A lot of today's Mac users are people who have had Windows-based PCs in the past and are making a switch because they like Apple's other products, such as the iPod. I've tried to be sensitive to that throughout—if you're a "switcher" from Windows or if you have used a Mac in the past but aren't totally up on all the Mac OS X lingo, then you'll find a home with this book.

Most of all, I'd like to see you get through this book and feel like you've become an accomplished Mac user. So, throughout the book we're going to focus less on the type of instruction that takes you "menu by menu" through a topic and land more firmly on an accomplishment-based system—I'll show you *how* to use the contact management and scheduling tools, *how* to build a home network, *how* to use Mail and Safari for accessing the Internet, and so on. Call it a "success driven" model, unless that sounds too corny.

I also think that part of learning to use a Mac means learning a little about troubleshooting, so we'll spend some time on that, as well as on maintenance tasks and the utilities that make that maintenance a little easier.

So, if you're ready for a book that moves quickly from how things work to how you get them to work for you, I think you'll enjoy this one.

How This Book Is Organized

This book, too, is designed to be interesting—how could it not be? Here's a closer look:

- Part I. This part starts off with a chapter that takes a quick look at what makes Mac OS X version 10.4 different from Microsoft Windows and previous Mac versions. That includes a quick look at a number of the signature features of the OS—I'm assuming you've upgraded to Mac OS X 10.4, but if you haven't, you'll want to after this chapter. Chapter 2 takes a nuts-and-bolts look at managing your files in the Finder, including deep discussion of the way files are organized and how you can manage them using the special Finder window. Chapter 3 focuses on working with applications—that's the point, after all—including launching them and managing them in the Dock.

- Part II. Chapter 4 is one of those showcase chapters for a book like this (flip to it and show it to a friend in the bookstore if you're trying to sell this book to them). There I'll cover a ton of different and unique Mac OS X features, such as Exposé, Dashboard, System Preferences, and SpotLight, which is Mac OS X 10.4's brand new system for searching your entire Mac quickly for all sorts of documents and files. Chapter 5 takes a look at how you get various types of hardware configured to work with your Mac. Chapter 6 goes in-depth with Address Books, iCal, and your Mac's capability to synchronize such data with multiple computers. Chapter 7 is somewhat related, as we look at the iPod, iTunes, and iSync, which can be used with external devices to synchronize some of that same data to your handheld digital assistant or your smart phone.

- Part III. Chapter 8 is dedicated to disproving any notion you may have had that getting a high-speed connection to the Internet would require an advanced degree in physics—not with a Mac. I'll even toss in wireless coverage for the same price; it's easy. Chapter 9 delves into two deceptively powerful applications—Mail and iChat—which not only enable you to communicate with others, but to truly get a handle on that communication, from seemingly magic organizational techniques in Mail to ad-hoc audio (and video!) conferences and file sharing with iChat. Chapter 10 covers the ins and outs of Apple's Safari web browser, as well as introducing Sherlock, which is a specialized browser that offers certain "channels" of content in one simple window. Chapter 11 is a biggie—connecting, configuring, and working with a local area network in your office or home, complete with a discussion of getting Internet access to all those networked (wired or wireless) Macs—and PCs, if you've got 'em.

- Part IV. Chapter 12 takes a look at a number of the utility applications that are bundled with the Mac OS and how they can help smooth out your experience with the Mac; Chapter 13 takes a topical approach to some of the most common problems and issues you'll have with your Mac and how to correct them (sometimes referring you back to those utilities covered in Chapter 12). Chapter 14 ends things nicely with a discussion that's on the radar screen of a lot of today's PC and Mac users—security. The Mac has some exceptional security features that keep your data safe and your privacy intact while you're on the Internet, as well as security features that keep your data buttoned up with passwords and encryption so that if your Mac ever falls into "the wrong hands" (sorry if I sound like a Hollywood theatrical movie trailer here), you can be pretty secure in the notion that your private stuff is still private.

How to Read This Book

This book is arranged largely as a tutorial, with some of the material in later chapters building on earlier chapters. That said, most of the "building" is simply understanding some of the basic interface elements—and we've cross-referenced extensively, so I feel pretty confident that you can dive into a topic that interests you and get a good sense of what's going on from the outset. In particular, you can use Chapters 12 and 13 when you need them—I'd recommend at least skimming Chapter 14 pretty quickly, though, to get a sense of the security measures you want to take at the outset.

Otherwise, feel free to jump into the discussion of the iPod once you get yourself an iPod, or you can just skim the stuff about iCal if you use a different calendar or personal information management application.

In each chapter, you'll find a few common elements to help you navigate the chapter and to help me communicate what I'm trying to get across. Such elements include

NOTE

Notes are items that add to the current discussion but don't really fit in the steps or bullets that are being discussed in the main text. Most of the time you'll want to read these as you're reading the rest of the text and just notice that I'm offering a little advice or a caveat.

TIP

Tips are generally items that take what we're discussing to a different level, or show you how you can integrate the current topic with others we've discussed. Mostly they're just items I happen to be proud of and want to share with you—hopefully you'll find them mind-expanding at best and mildly amusing at worst.

CAUTION

We won't have too many of these, but a caution is a note that tells you something important about how you could either lose data, hurt your Mac, or conceivably hurt yourself. Take careful note of these when they pop up.

SIDEBARS OFFER TANGENTS OR THIRD-PARTY SOLUTIONS

If I put something in a sidebar, it's something that I hope you'll find interesting but that you can probably get away with not reading, unless you find the topic either interesting or important for your own personal situation. Sometimes I like to show off, too, dontcha know. I'll try to confine that to sidebars.

Get More Info

I hope you enjoy the book, and, as you'll find in the opening material, you can contact Que directly if you have questions or comments. If you'd like to keep up with what I'm doing or reach me via the Web, visit me at www.leoville.com. Todd also has a website where you can discuss things with him at www.macblog.com.

Thanks for reading and here's to making life a little more interesting with your Mac!

Part I

Chapter 1

What Makes Mac OS X Unique?

What's the big deal with Mac OS X? If you haven't been a Mac user all of your computing life, then you may very well be asking that question. In fact, even if you have been a Mac user, but you're used to the old "Classic" Macintosh operating system, then you may be wondering what all the fuss over Mac OS X is about. (And if you haven't been a Mac user, but you are familiar with operating systems such as Microsoft Windows, then you'll hopefully find Mac OS X both familiar enough to work with and different enough to appreciate and enjoy.) Put simply, it's a great-working, good-looking, modern operating system (OS) that has traded a good bit of the bad stuff in for some surprising capabilities. Mac OS X ain't perfect—if that were true, Apple wouldn't have to update it—but in this chapter I think you'll see why so many folks have such a soft spot in their hearts for something as dull as a computer operating system.

History of Mac OS X

This is kind of a funny story. Mac OS X probably began at least three different times. For years, from the late 1980s to the late 1990s, Apple had various projects going that were purported to be creating the next-generation operating system for the Macintosh.

For a long time, Apple had known that some such step was necessary—the original Macintosh operating system, while it had been updated and modernized in every way thinkable—wasn't going to last forever. Its basic problem was that it wasn't based on the latest computer science—there were some important underlying foundation thingies that needed to be reworked in order to make the Mac OS a modern operating system.

The problem was that you can't simply graft that stuff on to the bottom of your operation system and then head out for a cold soda—changing the fundamentals of an operating system meant, in most cases, that applications had to be rewritten to work with the new operating system. In the 1990s, that prospect scared the dickens out of some of Apple's higher-ups, because the Mac had a small market share and developers were already giving up on writing applications for the Mac. If the Mac OS changed, it might end up that nobody would rewrite their applications for the new OS because no one would care. And then Apple might be in big trouble as a platform and a company.

The other problem was that the internal projects to revamp the Mac OS weren't getting anywhere. Something would be announced every few years and, in some cases, some code would even get in the hands of evaluators and developers who write Mac applications. But delays and problems were getting to be the norm.

Around the time that Apple's last best internal hope died—a project called Copeland—CEO Gil Amelio and his vice president of development, Ellen Hancock, formerly of IBM, decided they need to go shopping for a new high-end operating system for the Mac. There were two central options on the table—a scrappy little bootstrapped OS named BeOS or the NextStep/OpenStep operating system that had been developed by NeXT Computers, which was owned by Apple founder Steve Jobs.

The rest, as they say, is history. Amelio decided to buy NeXT, getting its engineering talent, it's Unix-style operating system, and Steve Jobs as a special consultant. He later got Steve Jobs as something of a pain-in-the-rear, as Jobs engineered a takeover of Apple that left him chairman and "interim CEO," a title that was eventually shortened to "iCEO" and, ultimately, to just plain ol' CEO. Amelio was out of Apple within 500 days of his arrival, and Apple, with Steven Jobs now firmly at the helm, had the daunting task of reworking OpenStep (which ran on Intel-based PCs) into an operating system that would not only run on Macintosh hardware, but that also looked like the existing Mac OS (at least in outward appearance). It also had to run existing Mac software and, somehow, propel the Mac into the future, despite capturing only a small portion of the Mac market.

Somehow, Apple managed to pull it all off.

What's Different About Mac OS X?

From a computer nerd point of view, perhaps the most important thing about Mac OS X is that it's based on FreeBSD, an open-source Unix variant. No one but a nerd really cares about that, but it's cool anyway, because it gives the Mac OS a certain amount of computer science street credibility, along with tons of advanced technology that makes it, simply put, a fully modern operating system.

Compared to the "classic" Mac OS, Mac OS X is more *stable*, meaning it's less likely to come to a complete halt if an application encounters an error. It's also better at *multitasking*, which means running multiple applications at once. And it manages those multiple applications better, which allows it to perform better than earlier versions of the Mac OS under similar loads.

Think of FreeBSD as Mac OS X's foundation, then picture layers of technology on top of that foundation. Those layers include some great stuff that helps differentiate Mac OS X from any other type of computer operating system, including Microsoft Windows, other Unix variants, or even earlier version of the Mac OS itself. For example:

- Quartz—This is the technology that draws images and text on your screen. It's based on the Portable Document Format (PDF), which results in sophisticated handling of fonts, a very readable display, and the ability to "print" nearly any file to a PDF document for sharing with others. Quartz also incorporates some other high-end graphics technology that make the Mac OS pretty to look at.

- QuickTime—Apple's *multimedia* QuickTime technology exists as a layer in Mac OS X, making it possible to play back, translate, and generally work with and manipulate a wide variety of image, sound, and motion video formats. This technology makes a Mac particularly adept for working with photo, audio, and video editing.

- Aqua—Aqua is the name for the graphical interface that makes a Mac, well, *a Mac*. That interface—the windows, icons, menus, and so on—extends to applications as well, which is what makes for the Mac "user experience" and the similarities among the different applications that generally make them easier to learn and work with.

- Classic—The Classic environment allows Mac OS X to load, essentially, an "instance" of Mac OS 9.2.2, which can then be used to run older Mac applications within the Mac OS X environment. This is a handy way to run important Mac OS applications that either don't have newer Mac OS X "native" applications or that you prefer not to upgrade for some reason. However, Classic applications tend to run slower than native versions.

11

Of course, those are still *low-level* technologies that help to make Mac OS X different from other operating systems. The day-to-day stuff that makes a difference is less about "technology" and more about "features." After all, it's those features that make the Mac Experience what it is.

> **NOTE**
>
> By the way, I don't mean to be too casual about the fact that Mac OS X is based on FreeBSD, which is a variant of Unix. To a geek like me, that's almost too cool for words. While Microsoft Windows is an utterly *proprietary* system, Mac OS X has its feet in both worlds—the unique world of Macintosh applications and the well-supported landscape of Unix-like operating systems. The fact that FreeBSD helps make Mac OS X relatively bulletproof is a nice benefit, too.

Some of the features that set Mac OS X apart include

- The Finder—Mac OS X offers a unique application for managing the files and folders that you create during the course of working with your Mac. Called the "Finder," it's probably one of the major differentiators that makes the Mac experience unique.

- The Finder window—in particular, the Finder offers a special type of window, called a Finder window, that acts as sort of a "browser" for the contents on your hard disk and other storage devices that are connected to your Mac. The Finder window is designed to make it a little easier to access commonly used folders and files that you've stored on your Mac. (We'll discuss this in depth in Chapter 2, "The Finder and Your Files.")

- The Dock—To launch applications, switch between them, and manage your "minimized" windows, the Dock is again rather unique, and an important component that makes the Mac what it is.

- Exposé—Added in Mac OS X 10.3, Exposé enables you to view all of your open windows at once by pressing a special function key (see Figure 1.1). You can then choose a particular window to work in, or you can perform cool tricks such as dragging an icon from one window to another in one motion. (You can also use Exposé to reveal just the windows of your currently running application, or to move your windows out of the way and view just the Desktop area.)

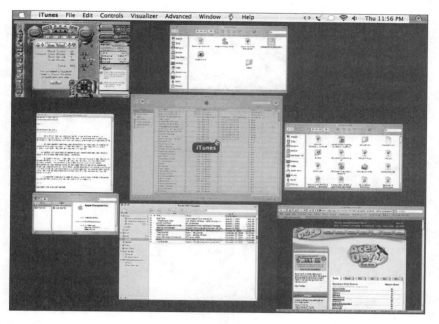

FIGURE 1.1

Exposé enables you to see all of your open windows by pressing a special function key.

- Bonjour—This is a special networking technology that Apple uses for a variety of applications. At its essence, it enables the Mac to automatically find other Macs or other resources on a network without requiring you to configure them. They just work—it's pretty cool.

- Spotlight—In Mac OS X 10.4, Apple has added a technology that builds on Mac OS X's already impressive searching capability. Spotlight enables you to simply begin typing a keyword in order to find all of the files on your Mac that are associated somehow with that keyword (including the contents of documents), including anything from Microsoft Word documents to email messages to graphics images and even stored web pages. And Apple has been working on this technology for a while, so it happens to be really fast.

- Dashboard—Also added in Mac OS X 10.4 is Dashboard (see Figure 1.2), a fun new feature that enables you to quickly access small "widgets" such as a calendar, clock, calculator, and even a small iTunes controller. As with Exposé, the widgets appear when you press a function key (F12 by default). In fact, third-party developers can write their own Dashboard widgets to add interesting features to Dashboard.

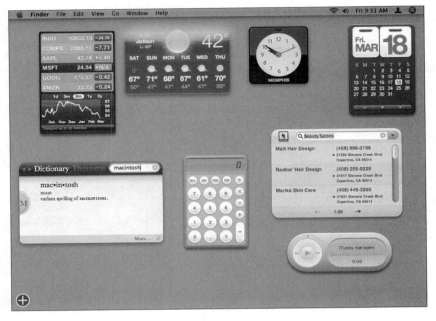

FIGURE 1.2
Like Exposé, Dashboard takes over your screen with an animated swoosh, giving you access to some handy "widgets."

- .Mac integration—Apple has its own online services, grouped under the name .Mac, which enable you to pull off a number of interesting tricks from within Mac OS X and Apple's iLife applications. While .Mac is an optional pay service, a number of its features are integrated into Mac OS X and its applications, making it possible to, for instance, access an Internet-based storage area (iDisk) directly within the Finder and drag files back and forth.

- Fast User Switching—Mac OS X in versions 10.2 (Jaguar) and higher offers a feature that allows you to change users quickly. Each user in Mac OS X can have his or her own desktop, settings, preferences, web bookmarks, email, and so on. You keep things separate by switching between user accounts. In the past this has been a more arduous process—you have to *log out* of your account, then your significant other or sibling or partner has to log in, which can take a few minutes for each process. With Fast User Switching, you simply head up to the menu in the top-right corner of your display and choose the user account that you want to switch to. Enter that user's password in the dialog box and the switching begins—

soon, that user will see his or her files and begin working in his or her own unique "space." Switching back is just as easy—choose an account name from the menu, then enter a password. (By default, Mac OS X even has a cool "rotating cube" animated effect for Fast User Switching.)

- Automator and AppleScript—For years the Mac OS has boasted AppleScript, a scripting language that makes it possible to automate tasks and share data between Mac applications. Mac OS X 10.4 adds to that Automator, a fun utility designed to help you create special scripts that perform repetitive tasks for you. See Chapter 4 for more on Automator.

- QuickTime—Apple's multimedia technology, QuickTime, is deeply integrated in the Mac OS, meaning many different applications are enabled to play back and translate various file formats for photos, digital videos, and digital audio. Even a Finder window can be used to play back a movie, for instance. Mac OS X 10.4 includes QuickTime 7, which features the latest high-quality playback technology for digital video.

And those are just a few of the special features. Along with those features, the Mac has interface guidelines for applications that make the windows look and work the way they do, formalize the structure for the menus in the menubar at the top of the window, and so on. All of those things come together to make the Mac OS the unique entity that it is—extremely powerful, sophisticated, stable, and user-friendly, all wrapped up in a pretty box and put on a shelf at your friendly electronics retailer.

The Mac OS X Metaphor

If you've used a computer in the past two decades then you're probably pretty familiar with the basics of how Mac OS X and its applications work. The mouse (or trackpad or similar pointing device) provides an entry point for you to manipulate the items on the screen, while the mouse *button* enables you to click and drag, select, or "activate" items on the screen.

Mouse-driven operating systems are called *graphical user interfaces* or GUIs, which is the sort of thing that Apple pioneered with the Macintosh when it was introduced in 1984. (There were GUIs prior to then, but Macintosh and, later, Microsoft Windows made the GUI a central part of many of our existences.) Because the GUI is so commonplace, there's probably not a huge reason to go through the basics of moving the mouse around and clicking.

All GUIs generally offer a metaphor based loosely on the idea of working at a desk. In Mac OS X, the colorful background behind everything else is called the Desktop, and you can store *icons* (small pictures) on that desktop that represent documents. Other icons represent applications, or "tools" that you use to accomplish things. In Mac OS X you have a special Trash icon for throwing away other icons that represent documents and applications.

Of course, that desk metaphor breaks down a little bit since there's so much other stuff going on. At the top of the Mac OS X screen is the *menu bar*, which holds the different *menus* that a particular application offers you for accomplishing tasks. In a way, those menus are sort of "drawers" in our "desk" metaphor. And in Mac OS X, the Dock is also sort of a drawer of sorts; kind of like that middle drawer on your desk where you store pencils and your calculator—stuff you need to get at quickly.

But, like I said, the metaphor is only a starting point, and the same basic approach is the most common of today's operating systems, including Microsoft Windows; Instead, what's more useful—particularly if you've spent, perhaps, more time on a Microsoft Windows-based computer, is to figure out some of the subtle differences between Mac OS X and other GUIs.

The Mac's Approach to Pointing and Clicking

Apple didn't invent the mouse and the concept of clicking around on a computer, but the Macintosh certainly made all of it popular. For that reason, it deserves a little respect for its idiosyncrasies. In fact, there's one in particular that comes to mind.

To this day, Apple ships its Macintosh mice with only one button; likewise, PowerBooks and iBooks have one button on their trackpads as well. That might be the thing that strikes Windows users the oddest, at least at the outset. (Even some long-time Mac users shake their heads a bit sometimes.) That's true despite the fact that Mac OS X supports mice with multiple buttons and can even take advantage of a second mouse button without any additional programming. More on that in a minute.

Aside from the one mouse button thing, using the mouse in Mac OS X should be familiar if you've ever done it before in any OS and if you bear in the mind the following rules of thumb:

- Single-click while pointing to an icon to select it (or highlight it, which is the same thing).
- Double-click (click twice fast) while pointing to an icon to activate or "launch" it.

- Click and hold the mouse button and then drag it around if you need to move an icon; release the mouse button to drop the icon.

Mouse behavior is only slightly different if you're working in an application window. In the case of text (in a word processor or page layout program) you'll click once to place the insertion point (or cursor) which then enables you to type. Double-clicking will generally select a word, while triple-clicking will select a sentence or sometimes a paragraph, depending on the application. And you click and drag to highlight a particular selection of text or other objects.

TIP

In many applications throughout the Mac OS, you can hold down the Control key and click in order to view a *contextual menu*, which is one that gives you commands that are appropriate for the current document or application. If you have a two-button mouse that is compatible with your Mac, then the second button should be automatically recognized by Mac OS X as equivalent to a Control+click.

Windows in Mac OS X

If you'll grant me another foray into the desktop metaphor I've been talking about, then windows on your screen are a little like the pieces of paper that you'd work with on a real desk. Windows can be stacked and dragged around; you'll write within them, make selections, and even play games or watch videos inside of those windows. (One day we might also watch movies on pieces of "paper" that we can move around on our real desks, although the closest we have so far are small LCD screens.)

If you've used any modern OS, then you're used to the concept of windows. In that case, what you're probably more interested in is what makes a window different in Mac OS X as compared to other OSes. Sounds like a good time for a figure; Figure 1.3 shows the top of a typical Mac window.

NOTE

Unlike Microsoft Windows and some versions of Unix and Linux, the Mac does not include menu commands within the windows of its applications. Instead, the menu commands change only when you change applications, as we'll discuss later in the section "Inside Mac Menus."

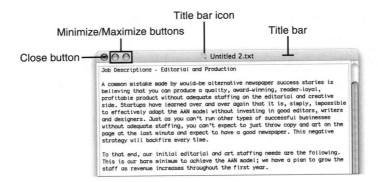

FIGURE 1.3

At the top of the typical Mac window you'll find some controllers.

The items in Figure 1.3 are used to change the position and size of the window or to otherwise make it a little easier to work with. Here's what each does:

- Close button—Used to close the window, which means store the document that the window represents until a later usage. A black dot showing in the Close button means that the contents of that window have changed since they were last saved.

- Minimize button—Click this button with the mouse and the window is "moved" to the Dock that resides (by default) at the bottom of the screen. (The window is actually visually compressed down to the size of an icon, which is then placed on the right side of the Dock.) This is a handy way to get a window out of the way but still have it open and quickly accessible.

- Maximize button—This button is poorly named, because what it actually does is *toggle* (switch back and forth) from the window's current size to its *optimum* size, as set by the programmers. Sometimes this is "maximized" in the sense that the window will fill your entire display; other times it will simply snap to a predetermined optimum size; clicking it again returns the window to its previous dimensions.

- Title bar—The title bar is mostly dead space that, as you may have guessed, holds the title for the window. This title is usually the name of the document or session or web page, or the subject of your email, or the name of whatever it is that you're viewing or working on. The title bar is significant because it's also where you can place the mouse pointer in order to click and drag the window around on the screen.

TIP

Often, double-clicking a window's title bar has the same effect as clicking the window's minimize button—the window is minimized to the Dock.

- Title bar icon—In some applications, this little icon can be handy for dragging to other windows—for instance, you can drag the icon of a document to the window of an open email message, thus "attaching" the document to the email so that you can send it to a friend or colleague. (In other applications, the icon is nothing more than a pretty decoration.)

So that's the top half of the window. The sides and bottom half offer their own intrigue. First, at the right side and bottom of many windows you'll find *scroll controllers*, which you can drag up and down or side to side within the *scroll bars*. Those are used to view the contents of a window when the entire contents aren't already visible—the bits that you can't see in a long or wide document can be revealed by scrolling. (See Figure 1.4; this is how you read long or wide documents.) And you don't have to drag the scroll controllers—you can also click the scroll arrows in the bottom-right corner of the window in order to scroll.

TIP

Some third-party mice have a special controller called a scroll wheel, generally situated between two mouse buttons. This scroll wheel can be used to scroll long documents so that you can continue to read them; you'll find that many word processing documents—as well as email messages, web pages and other documents—require a lot of scrolling. Fortunately, if you have one of these mice and it's already compatible with your Mac, then Mac OS X should recognize the scroll wheel and enable you to use it automatically.

As Figure 1.4 also shows, most windows have a resize box at the bottom right, which you can use to drag the window so that it's a different size. If you experiment a bit you'll sometimes find that resizing a window causes scroll bars to disappear—once all of the contents in a particular dimension are visible, you no longer need the scroll bars.

NOTE

There's something else interesting to notice about the scroll controls—the more content there is within the window, the smaller the scroll controls are. That's because they're designed to give you a visual approximation of where you are within a document and what percentage you're viewing at one time. In a long document, the scroll controls may be very small because you're only seeing a small portion of the document in the window's visible area at one time. In a shorter document, the scroll controls may take up nearly the entire scroll bar.

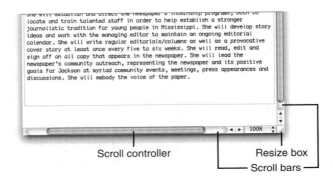

Scroll controller   Resize box
                           Scroll bars

FIGURE 1.4
The bottom and right sides of a typical Mac window.

You may have already noticed that not all Mac windows are made alike—in particular, there are two types of window that visually stand out from one another. Apple uses both its "Aqua" style windows and the "brushed metal" windows for different applications; *usually* the brushed metal windows are those that are designed for standalone use, such as in the iTunes and iMovie windows. That's not always the case, though; Apple sometimes seems to use brushed-metal windows because they're cool.

In any case, you'll find that both types of windows are largely the same in operation, with the exception that brushed-metal windows have more surface that can be used to drag the window around on the screen. A standard window can only be dragged by its title bar, while a brushed-metal window can be dragged by its sides and bottom as well.

Dialogs and Alert Boxes

There's another type of window that's worth mentioning quickly—the *dialog box*. A dialog box is a window that's specifically used for making choices—either about the next course of action or about an application's settings or options. Dialog boxes often appear as a result of a command that you've selected in an application's menus. For instance, you might select the Print command in one of the applications installed on your Mac. When you do, you'll see a special dialog box that's designed to retrieve settings and choices from you, including the choice to go ahead with the process of printing (see Figure 1.5). The dialog box does this by presenting a series of choices in menus, entry boxes, controllers, and buttons.

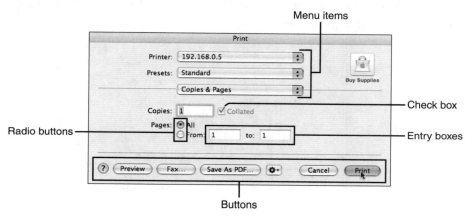

FIGURE 1.5

In this Print dialog box, I can choose from a number of options, and then click the Print button to begin printing.

The different types of controllers enable you to make different types of choices. *Radio buttons*, for instance, are used when a dialog box wants you to make one choice among many—either you're going to print all pages, a selection of pages, or a range of pages. By contrast, a *check box* control is used simply to get you to decide whether that particular option will be on or off.

Elsewhere, you'll see entry boxes that you can use for typing in information (for instance, entering the number of copies you want of a printed document) or menus which can be used for a variety of different selections. You'll also see tabs, disclosure triangles, and a few other unique controllers that will discuss in the next section.

In most dialog boxes you'll also see buttons, which are used to give yes or no answers. For instance, in the Print dialog box, you'll see buttons such as Print, Preview, Fax, and Cancel. In other dialog boxes, you'll often see buttons that say Apply or OK or otherwise are used to accept the changes you've made. (You might even see Accept

Changes.) In most cases, you'll also see the Cancel button, which is used pretty universally to give you the option of dismissing the dialog box without making any changes in it, if desired.

It's worth noting that Mac OS X has a special way of displaying some dialog boxes, called *dialog sheets*. In the case of a dialog sheet, the dialog looks like it's sliding out from under the window's title bar; you can then access it as you would a regular dialog box, but you can't directly alter anything in the attached window until the dialog sheet has been dealt with (see Figure 1.6).

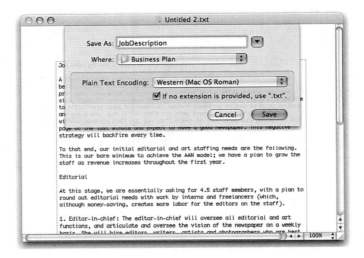

FIGURE 1.6
A dialog sheet appears from beneath a window's title bar to help make it clear which window or document will be affected by your choices.

There are some dialog box variations—for instance, you'll sometimes encounter a dialog box that doesn't have a Cancel button (or perhaps no such buttons at all) but instead has a Close button that can be used to dismiss the window. (Such dialogs may also have Minimize and Maximize buttons, although they may be "grayed out" and impossible to click.)

TIP

In many dialog boxes, you can hold down the ⌘ key and press the "." (period) key to choose Cancel from the keyboard.

Aside from those variations, there's another particular type of dialog box, called an *alert*. An alert is a dialog box that pops up for a very specific purpose—your Mac needs to tell you something or, in some cases, give you a simple choice. Often, it's a message that let's you know that something is going on in the background—a network disk you were working with has disappeared or a printer that you were printing to has run out of paper. Many alert boxes have only one controller—an OK button, which you can click to dismiss the alert after you've read it.

Special Selectors and Controllers

Since we're talking about what makes Mac OS X different in this chapter, we should take a quick look at some of the specialty controllers that you'll encounter in dialog boxes and elsewhere as you pursue excellence using your Mac. These controllers are generally items that you manipulate with the mouse pointer—items such as radio buttons and menus—but a bit more specialized.

One of the early Mac OS innovations was the *disclosure triangle*, which is used in a variety of circumstances and applications. If the triangle is pointing to the right, that means it's hiding something; click the disclosure triangle and it will point downward, revealing the items it was hiding. Usually what's shown is another level of a *hierarchy* of items. In Figure 1.7, for instance, the disclosure triangle reveals the subfolders inside the Library folder.

Another little innovative interface element that makes Mac OS X interesting are *tabs*, which enable one screen to show many screens' worth of information. A row of tabs works by sitting at the top of a window and enabling you to click a particular tab. When you do, that tab's information or options appear in the window, thus making a compact dialog box (or similar window) able to show many screens' worth of options and items. Figure 1.8 shows a window with tabs at its top.

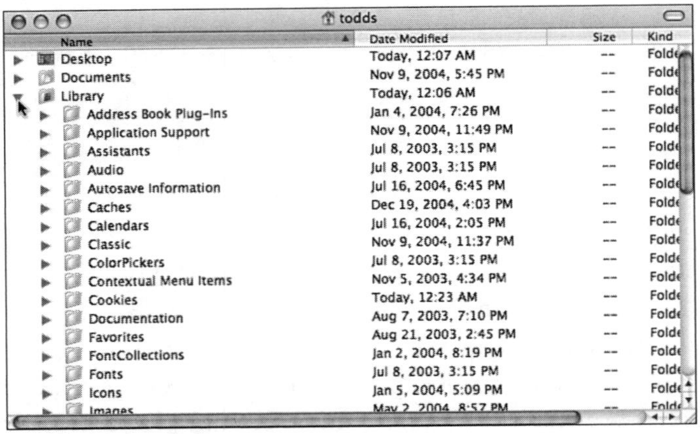

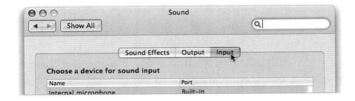

FIGURE 1.7
Disclosure triangles can be clicked to reveal additional options or items.

FIGURE 1.8
One thing worth noting about tabs in Mac OS X is that they don't really look like something you'd call a "tab." They used to look more like something you'd call a tab, though (trust me), and the name stuck.

Sliders are fun controllers, in that they're so obvious and elegant. When the Mac OS wants you to select from a linear range of options, it presents you with a slider. Sliders can be used for anything from changing colors within a spectrum to changing the amount of time your Mac waits before it goes to sleep or engages its screen saver (see Figure 1.9).

To use a slider, simply click and hold the mouse button while you're pointing at the slider's selector, then move the mouse left or right (or up and down) to change the slider's position. Release the mouse when you've got the slider's selector in the right spot.

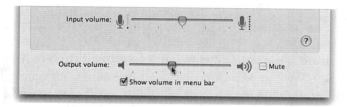

FIGURE 1.9
Sliders are fun. I can't help it.

One last controller that's worth touching on is the *combo box*, which is a combination entry box and menu. Usually these are useful because they allow you to either select a predetermined setting or item from the menu *or* they allow you to type it directly in the entry box. Sometimes typing is used to search the menu's contents for a match; other times, typing allows you to enter something that the menu didn't anticipate.

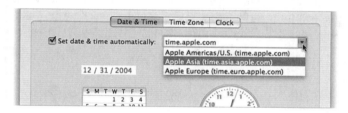

FIGURE 1.10
Using a combo box to select from a menu.

Inside Mac Menus

As I mentioned earlier, the menus on your Mac are a little like the drawers in your real-world desk—they're where you store the tools with which you create or calculate, and they're the places where you store labels for your little file folders...and so on. We stretch that metaphor a bit when working in Mac OS X because the menus really hold *commands*—different things we can do to the selected document, or the selected text within a document, or to certain pictures or pixels on the screen, and so forth.

Again, the part that's probably most disconcerting to non-Mac users is the fact that the menus always stay up in the menu bar at the top of the screen. In Windows and many Unix variants, the menus are in each window of an application. In Mac OS X, the menu bar at the top of the screen changes whenever you launch a new application or switch between applications that are currently open. But, otherwise, the menus don't move

25

from the menu bar—you've got to mouse up to them if you'd like to choose a command.

Another unique feature is the *application* menu; every application in Mac OS X, including the Finder, has its own application menu. In one sense, it's handy because it tells you what application you're currently working in. It also holds special commands that are specific to the application, including the Preferences command and Quit command, both of which should appear in any Mac OS X application. The application menu appears in every application right next to the Apple menu in the top left corner, and it's named for its application, as in Word (for Microsoft Word) or iTunes (for Apple's iTunes application); see Figure 1.11.

NOTE

To work with computer applications, they must be *launched* (which you can do by double-clicking the application's icon, single clicking its icon in the Dock, or via some other options we'll discuss later) in order for them to appear on the screen complete with windows and menus. When you're done using an application, you *quit* the application, which can be done via the application menu.

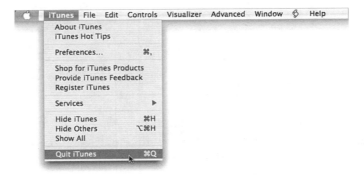

FIGURE 1.11
In Mac OS X applications, you'll find a special application menu that's named for the application itself.

Aside from its application menu, most applications have a Help menu, which you can use to access either the Apple Help system or any special help features or documents that the application's author has put together for you. Likewise, nearly all applications have a File menu, which is where some standard commands such as Open, Load, and

Save are found. And, most applications have an Edit menu, which is where Cut, Copy, and Paste are found, among others. We'll discuss some common application commands in more detail in Chapter 3.

Before we leave this section, however, we should look more closely at a type of menu that I mentioned earlier: the contextual menu. When you hold down the Control key and click the mouse button in most applications, you'll see a special menu appear. This menu contains commands that are relevant in the current *context*; for instance, if you Control+click a folder in the Finder then you'll see commands that have to do with Finder folders; if you highlight a paragraph in AppleWorks and then Control+click that paragraph, you'll see commands that are relevant to working with text selections in AppleWorks. In Figure 1.12, the contextual menu shows different choices you can make in the Finder when you click on a document icon.

FIGURE 1.12

A contextual menu shows you commands that are relevant to the item or items that you Command+click.

Contextual menus can be surprisingly handy—I encourage you to get in the habit of using them. Not only do they make accessing common commands easier, but a contextual menu can also help you make sense of a new application when you just get started exploring its capabilities.

> **NOTE**
>
> Mac OS X offers another unique type of menu, called the *menu bar icon*. You'll see these small icons on the (you guessed it!) menu bar, toward the top-right corner of your display. These menus are for quick access to systemwide options and settings, such as speaker volume, display settings, and things like turning on and off Airport and network configurations. We'll look at many of these options as they come up throughout the book.

Exploring Toolbars

One other Apple interface item is worth noting here before we move on, and that's the *toolbars* that you'll find in many applications. A toolbar is usually a collection of icons that appear at the top of some windows. Those *tools* are generally duplicates of menu commands, but they're a little more convenient when in icon form right there on the window. You'll see a prevalent toolbar in the Finder windows (which we'll discuss in much greater detail in Chapter 2), but you'll also find them in many other applications, such as in Apple Mail and Safari and so on.

To use a toolbar tool, simply click it once to activate it (you may need to select something in the active window first). That should put the command into motion, resulting in a dialog box or dialog sheet or some activity taking place.

In Apple Mail, for instance, you can change the order of toolbar icons, add others that you'd prefer to keep handy, or even remove those that are placed there by default. Simply choose View, Customize Toolbar.

In the dialog sheet that appears, you can drag icons up to the toolbar, or you can drag tools off of the toolbar; release them away from the toolbar and they disappear in a puff of smoke. If you end up doing more customizing than you wanted to, you can drag the Default Set from the bottom of the sheet up to the toolbar (see Figure 1.13). Notice also that you can use the Show menu to choose what form you would like the tools to take on the toolbar: text, icons, or both.

Dragging an icon to the toolbar

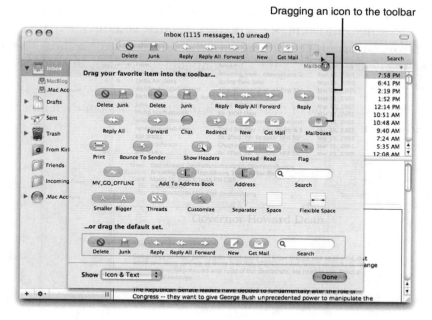

FIGURE 1.13
Customizing a Mac OS X toolbar is as easy as drag-and-drop.

Setting Preferences

Any computer operating system is likely to have a special tool or series of tools that enable you to set preferences and choose options that affect how that operating system is configured and customized. Mac OS X is no exception, with the System Preferences application designed to fill that function. Users familiar with the Classic Mac OS will note that the old Control Panels are no more—Mac OS X has a single application that it uses for settings, much like Microsoft Windows does. (Windows's preference application is called Control Panel, not to be confused with the older Mac OS's Control Panels. Ahem.)

To launch System Preferences, head up to the Apple menu (at the top-left; it looks like an Apple logo) and click it, then choose System Preferences. You'll see the System Preferences application appear once it loads. (You can also launch System Preferences by clicking its icon once in the Dock; it looks like an Apple logo with a light switch.)

Once you've launched System Preferences, you'll be greeted by a number of icons—each icon represents a different set of preferences that you can configure (see Figure 1.14). We'll cover many of them throughout the book, particularly those that deal with networking (Network, Sharing), Internet configuration (.Mac), and security (Security and Accounts).

When you click once on one of these icons, it brings up a System Preferences *pane* that includes those configuration options.

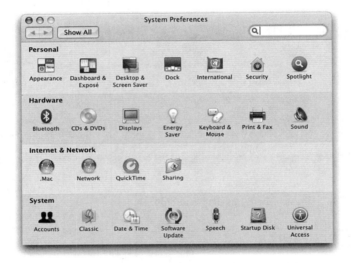

FIGURE 1.14
The System Preferences application gives you quick access to many of Mac OS X's settings, as well as some third-party additions if they've been installed.

Aside from those mentioned, there are a few different panes that you should experiment with yourself. For instance, the Appearance pane can be used to customize the colors that are used throughout the Mac OS, how the contents of your windows will scroll, and the size of font at which Font Smoothing is turned off. (Font Smoothing makes onscreen fonts look more like they will on paper, but it can make very small fonts tough to read.)

Here's a quick look at some of the panes that we won't go into in much detail about elsewhere, but that you may wish to configure and experiment with as you're getting started with Mac OS X (the panes that I skip are covered elsewhere in the book):

- Appearance—As mentioned, this pane is used to set certain aesthetic choices about text and windows throughout the Mac OS X interface. (Changes here should affect most Mac OS X applications as well as the Finder and any utility programs.)

- Date & Time—This pane is used to set the current time and date; if you have Internet access, the best way to do this is to choose Set Date & Time Automatically (that option is on the Date & Time tab if you don't see it after opening the Date & Time pane). The automatic feature consults an Internet Time Server in order to get an accurate setting. For it to be accurate to your location, you'll need to click the Time Zone tab and use the map and/or menu to choose your time zone. Finally, the Clock tab is used to customize the look of the clock that appears in your Mac's menu bar at the top-right of your screen.

- Desktop & Screen Saver—Here you can choose a pattern or color to customize your desktop; you can either select from Apple's default colors and patterns (see Figure 1.15), or you can click the Pictures Folder and then select from images that you have stored in your own Pictures folder on the hard disk. Click the Screen Saver button to choose from the different screen saver patterns that Mac OS X offers; click the Test button to see what the screen saver will look like at full screen. The slider enables you to choose how many minutes of inactivity the Mac will wait before activating the screen saver.

NOTE

Modern displays and screens don't "burn in" the way that older displays used to, so a screen saver is really more for fun these days. However, a screen saver can be used to keep prying eyes away from your screen after you've been away for a few minutes. In fact, in the Security pane you can opt to force a login name and password in order to disable the screen saver, which can add another layer of privacy and security. (More on security in Chapter 14.)

- Energy Saver—This pane enables you to choose settings that balance your Mac's performance with the amount of power it consumes. The easiest setting to choose is from the Optimize Energy Settings menu, where you can select from prior configurations. (Highest Performance consumes the most energy.) You can also customize the settings using the sliders to determine when your Mac goes to *sleep* (a low-power mode that it can "wake" from more quickly than being shut down) or when the display and/or hard disk are powered down. In all these cases, the Mac can usually be revived quickly by simply clicking the mouse button or pressing a key. The Energy Saver pane also has a Schedule tab, which can be used to schedule your Mac to either sleep or shut down at a specific time every day; likewise, you can set it to start up or wake automatically.

FIGURE 1.15
You set the desktop pattern by selecting one of the locations for patterns and pictures, then clicking one of the "thumbnail" images that appears.

NOTE

While any energy conscious person will appreciate Energy Saver, it's particularly important for PowerBook and iBook users who need to get the most battery life out of their portables. In the Optimization menu, you can choose Better Energy Savings if you have a portable; likewise, if you're using a portable Mac you'll see a Settings For menu where you can choose to customize the settings for your Mac when it's running on an AC adapter versus when it's running on battery power. Also, on the Options tab, note the Processor Performance option, which can be set to Reduced if you're willing to take a hit in performance in exchange for a longer-running battery.

- International—The International pane enables you to choose a different Language for the Mac OS (you can drag them around to sort them in order, so that applications that don't support a particular language have a second and third choice). Click the Formats tab to change the format of dates and times; on the Input menu, you can choose the type of keyboard layout you would like to use if your keyboard is different from a standard U.S. keyboard. (You can turn on the Show Input Menu in Menu Bar option if you'd like a small menu bar item that can be used for switching keyboard layouts.)

- Keyboard & Mouse—This is a deceptively simple pane that's mostly used to fine-tune the sensitivity of your keyboard, mouse, or trackpad; if you don't like the feel of any of these input methods, launch this pane and click the appropriate tab. You can then set the keyboard's Key Repeat Rate or the trackpad's Tracking Rate and so on. In Chapter 4, we'll discuss the Keyboard Shortcuts section of this pane, which is very powerful and can be fun to use.

- Sound—On the Output tab, you can choose an output method (if you have more than one attached) and set the volume for your Mac (which can also be done via the Volume menu bar item and, on most modern Macs, using keys at the top of the keyboard). On the input tab, you can select the device you would like to use for audio input, which can be important if you're recording something to your Mac using a recording application. The Sound Effects tab is used to select your Mac's *alert* sound, which is the sound your Mac makes when it wants your attention.

- Universal Access—Here you'll find options that Apple includes to help people who have difficulty using a Mac at its default settings. Universal Access offers settings for people who have trouble seeing their display (you can magnify text or change the contrast), hearing their Mac (you can have the screen flash when an alert is necessary), and various solutions if you have trouble manipulating the keyboard or mouse. If you fall into any of those categories, you might explore the Universal Access options to see if they're for you.

If you happen to check out any of the other panes in System Preferences, there's one thing you should watch out for—a small padlock icon (see Figure 1.16). That icon is used to lock "regular" users out of settings that can affect the Mac systemwide, which should be reserved for "Administrative" users. If you've recently installed Mac OS X or begun using your Mac, then you may be working in an administrative account anyway, which means you don't have to worry about the padlock. (In that case, you can just worry about making sure you don't mess up any important settings.)

FIGURE 1.16
A padlock icon means that settings on this page are accessible only by administrative users.

If you do encounter a padlock and you need to change that setting, you can click the padlock icon. A dialog box appears asking for an administrative user's name and password. If you don't have those then you can't make changes in that pane (or, at least, you can't make changes to the protected options). You'll need to ask your Mac's administrator or consult Chapter 4 for more on user accounts and Mac administration.

The Apple Menu and Basic Mac Commands

We'll look at one final menu and set of commands in this chapter—the Apple menu. The Apple menu is unique in that it never changes. It's always right there on the menu bar, waiting for you to access it. And that's a good thing, because the Apple menu holds items that you might want to access regardless of the application that you're currently working in—in fact, that's the idea.

NOTE

The Apple menu has been a part of the Mac OS since System 1, in the beginning, when it was used to allow access to Desk Accessories. Back before the Mac could *multitask*, the Desk Accessories were small tools that could pop up on top of the running application for quick access. These Desk Accessories included a calculator, Key Caps (used to locate special characters through key combinations), and the old-style Chooser, which was used to connect to and choose printers. Some of these utilities and functions live on, although these days the Apple menu is quite a bit simpler.

If you're familiar with the Classic Mac OS, you might notice that the Apple menu in Mac OS X isn't quite as jam-packed. While the Apple menu used to be a little like that junk drawer most of us have in the kitchen, these days it's a bit more svelte (see Figure 1.17).

FIGURE 1.17

The Apple menu is always accessible from most any application (with the exception of some games that hide the menu bar while you're playing).

Info, Updates, and Downloads

At the top of the Apple menu are three special commands. The About This Mac command is actually a bit more powerful than you might think—choose it and the About This Mac window appears. In that window, you'll learn what version of Mac OS X your Mac is running, your Mac's processor speed, and the amount of memory (this refers to *random access memory* or *RAM*) that is installed in your Mac.

> **NOTE**
>
> RAM is the "short-term" memory in your computer—it's used by the operating system and by currently running applications to display items on the screen, compute, and respond to commands. If you see a document up in AppleWorks, for instance, it's using RAM. That's as opposed to *storage*—hard disks, CDs, and so on—which is the equivalent of long-term memory. When you turn off your Mac, the contents of RAM are lost, which is why you "save" to a disk first.

Aside from these little tidbits of information, the About This Mac window has two buttons. The Software Update button can be used to launch Mac OS X's built-in upgrade utility. If you have an active Internet connection then Software Update can check with Apple's special Internet servers to see if any updates to the Mac OS or any of Apple's own applications are available for downloading and installation. More on that in a moment.

The other button is the More Info button, which launches the System Profiler, a special utility that can tell you tons of stuff about your Mac and the version of Mac OS X that you have installed. More on System Profiler in Chapter 5.

Back in the Apple menu, you'll find two more commands at the top of the menu. The Software Update menu item does the same thing that the Software Update button does in the About This Mac window: It launches the Software Update tool.

The Mac OS X Software command launches your default web browser (usually Safari) and connects to a special location on Apple's website where new Mac OS X applications of all kinds are announced, discussed, and presented for downloading. Some of these applications are *freeware*, meaning you don't have to pay to use them, while others are *shareware*, which is commonly thought of as "try before you buy" software. These servers are one of the key places to explore when you need a special utility, want to try a new application for work, or you want to check out some recent games and game demos.

Just below that command is the System Preferences command, which we discussed earlier in the section "Setting Preferences."

Recent Items and Force Quit

I'd like to skip the Dock and Location menus until we discuss them more directly in Chapters 3 and 8, respectively, but you should know that they're here.

The Recent Items menu is a fun one—by default, it remembers the last 10 applications and the last 10 documents that you've used. Open up the menu and select any of those items to immediately launch them again and begin working with them (see Figure 1.18). Or, if you don't want those items to show up in that menu anymore, choose the Clear Menu command at the bottom of the menu.

TIP

The number of recent items that are tracked can be changed via the Appearance pane of System Preferences.

The Force Quit command is something we'll get into a little later, in Chapter 13, but for now you can know that the command is here to help you get rid of applications that crash and/or won't respond to input. Mac OS X is resistant in the sense that an application that crashes doesn't necessarily affect others—usually, you can end the crashing application and continue to compute. However, applications *do* still crash, and when you have a problem with one, the Force Quit window can sometimes be useful in getting that application out of the way so that you can continue working in others.

FIGURE 1.18
The Recent Items menu gives you quick access to applications and documents you've been working with in the past few days.

Sleep, Shut Down, and Log Out

The last few commands we'll look at in the Apple menu are those that control power to your Mac. The Sleep command is used to send your Mac into a low-power mode; the display is shut down, as are the hard disk and other vital components. A trickle of power remains, however, which is used to keep RAM from clearing out and to watch for signs that you want the Mac to wake up (such as pressing a key or opening a PowerBook's lid). Sleep mode is a good idea when you'll be away from your Mac for more than a few minutes or when you're done for the day. It's especially nice in Mac OS X, because, most of the time, your Mac will wake up from sleep mode in just a few seconds, ready to work where you last left off.

> **NOTE**
>
> I'm a stickler for saving files that I'm working on, and I recommend that you save anything that's open and in progress before your put your Mac into Sleep mode. That way if it loses power somehow, you won't lose any changes you've made in open windows.

The Shut Down command is used to completely power down your Mac—something you'd want to do if you're going to spend more than a few days away from it, or if you want to disconnect it from wall power (in the case of a desktop Mac). The Shut Down command is very important to use, because the Mac goes through a series of steps in order to properly close down both any open applications and its many system files that are used in the background to make Mac OS X tick. Whenever possible, you should avoid simply "pulling the plug" or otherwise cutting off power to your (desktop) Mac before using the Shut Down command; on a PowerBook or iBook, similarly, you should use Shut Down before removing the battery.

To shut down your Mac correctly, choose Shut Down from the Apple menu. You'll then be asked if you're sure that's what you want to do—click Shut Down again or just wait about two minutes. Now the shutdown process will begin. The Mac OS attempts to close all open applications—if you have any unsaved changes, you may be prompted by those applications to save before the application quits. Once all applications have closed successfully, Mac OS X itself will go through a final shutdown phase and quit; when it's done, your Mac should automatically turn itself off.

> **NOTE**
>
> Shut Down doesn't always seem to work—if you have many applications open and some of those applications require that you save changes, the Shut Down command may "time out" before completing. If that happens, you can simply select the Shut Down command again and it should complete its steps.

So what's Restart? It's the same as Shut Down, except it immediately starts the Mac back up right after it's almost totally powered down. This is done after certain types of updates to the Mac OS and, in some cases, after you've installed peripheral devices. It can sometimes be a useful trick for troubleshooting, as well, as discussed in Chapter 13.

Finally, down at the bottom of the Apple menu is the Log Out command, which you can use to exit your user account and, if desired, switch to another one. This is one way to secure your Mac from prying eyes, and it's also a good way to share a Mac. To log out, choose Log Out {Your Account Name} from the Apple menu. You should see your applications quit as if you were shutting down, but the end result will be the Mac's login screen.

That's all it takes. To log back in, select your user account name, enter your password, and click the Log In button. If you're successful in entering the correct password, you'll see the login window disappear, your desktop will appear, and your workspace will load.

NOTE

Don't quite get the whole "multiple user account" thing? We'll discuss user accounts and switching between them in more depth in Chapter 4.

The Finder and Your Files

A big part of getting to know your Mac is getting to know the Finder—and, lo and behold, Apple changes the Finder in small ways every time it updates the Mac OS. Still, the concept of the Finder has a long and storied past going back to the original days of the Macintosh. It's the interface that generations of Mac users have used to file away their documents, create folders, install applications, and generally make their Macs their own.

In this chapter, we're going to take a look at the Mac OS X Finder, which is really a mix of the traditional Finder and metaphors that are familiar to anyone who has used a web browser in the past few years. As you'll see, the Finder is ultimately a *file-management* tool—it enables you to create and manage entire hierarchies of folders for storing documents, applications, and other types of icons. (If you're used to Microsoft Windows, you'll see that the Finder is similar to My Computer in Windows.)

Aside from file management, we'll also take a look at one of Mac OS X 10.4's most significant additions, a special tool designed specifically for finding files called Spotlight.

The Finder and the Home Folder Concept

Before we get started with the Finder, it's important to back up and talk about one important aspect of Mac OS X that you may not be familiar with if you haven't used it much in the past. That's the *home folder* organization that Mac OS X has for your personal documents and other important files.

Inside your Mac is a hard disk, where files—applications, documents, images, movies, email—are stored. The main way that you go about organizing all those items is by placing them in hierarchies of folders—folders and subfolders that can help you recall where you've put something. Some of these folders are created by the Mac OS itself; others you create using the Finder.

Every user account on a Mac that's running Mac OS X has its own *home* folder, and that's precisely because Mac OS X supports multiple users. The earlier Mac OS, because it didn't support multiple users, had only one desktop, one set of document folders, and a relatively accessible set of system files and other important items and documents. In Mac OS X, things are a bit more sophisticated and—in part because of the Unix-style foundation—a bit more rigid, at least when it comes to where files are supposed to be stored.

Because each Mac can have multiple users, each user has his or her own hierarchy of "personal" folders, which are stored in the special Users folder found on the main level of your hard disk. Within the Users folder are one or more home folders, depending on how many user accounts have been created (see Figure 2.1). When you log in to your Mac, the home folder associated with your unique username and password is accessed and the files and settings that are stored in that home folder become the foundation of your experience once the Mac OS loads and your desktop appears.

> **NOTE**
>
> By default, you probably aren't required to type your username and password to log in to your Mac, so what I'm saying may not make immediate sense. When there's only one user defined for a Mac OS X installation, then you tend to be logged in automatically, without requiring you to enter a name and password. They're still being entered, though, just behind the scenes. And if you'd like to log in, as an extra security step, that's an option even if only one user account has been defined. We'll discuss that in more depth in Chapter 4, "Conquer the Mac OS X Interface."

FIGURE 2.1

The home folders for all the users on your Mac are stored in the main Users folder; the active account actually has a little "home" icon.

Okay, so we each have a home folder on our Macs. Who cares? Well, it's not terribly important, but it's good to know three things in particular about your home folder:

- Your home folder is where the special document folders that a lot of applications use for storing files reside, such as the Documents, Movies, Music, and Pictures folders that a lot of Apple's applications use automatically.

- Your home folder has a special Desktop folder, which is where the items that appear on your desktop are stored. Each user on your Mac can have a different desktop (even a different color scheme or pattern) and whatever icons they choose to put on that desktop, in whatever arrangement they come up with.

- The Library folder in your home folder holds many of your personal settings and preferences, meaning that even the settings in applications—your bookmarks in Safari or your preferences in Microsoft Word—can be different from other users of your Mac.

In other words, each individual home folder stores a person's unique documents, Desktop layouts, and preferences; when you log in to your user account, those preferences are loaded and your personal workspace appears. It's actually pretty cool if you have to share your Mac with someone. And, as you'll see, the Finder and its special Finder windows are pretty well plugged into the idea of a home folder and all its special subfolders.

Introducing the Finder Window

Other disks can be connected to your Mac—such as external hard disks and removable drives—and you will, from time to time, insert CDs or DVDs into your Mac's built-in optical drive. Those disks also store files in folders and subfolders, and those files are also managed using the Finder—and, specifically, the *Finder window*.

In earlier versions of the Mac OS, the exact configuration of the Finder window wasn't as important as it is in Mac OS X. Mac OS X's Finder window is really a file *browser* of sorts, and if you have any experience with web browsers, you'll see that there's something of a similarity.

This move to a "browser" approach makes some sense for the following reason—in 1984, when the Mac was first released, people dealt with, at most, *tens* of files. Now we deal with thousands. Music files and photos and email messages and attached PDF documents and downloaded applications and presentation documents—as I said, *thousands*. Apple's solution to that, in part, is the Finder window's design, which makes it easy to traverse the hierarchy of folders on your Mac's hard disk, as well as any connected or inserted disks and even networked (and Internet-based!) storage options.

> **NOTE**
>
> *Traverse the hierarchy*...huh? In Mac OS X, as we saw with the home folder, the organization tends to be more top-down hierarchical. As you'll see, your hard disk is set up with a folder called Applications, one called System, one called Users, and so on. Within Users is your home folder, where you'll find folders called Movies, Documents, Music, and others. One reason for this, again, is the sheer number of files we're talking about; another is the multiuser nature of the Mac these days.

With the Finder application active (that is, if you see the word Finder at the top-left on the menu bar), you can open a Finder window by choosing File, New Finder Window or by pressing the ⌘ and N keys simultaneously. (You'll also automatically open a Finder window whenever you click the Finder's icon in the Dock if one isn't already open.) Figure 2.2 shows the Finder window and some callouts so that we can discuss some of its major characteristics.

Back and Forward buttons

Search box

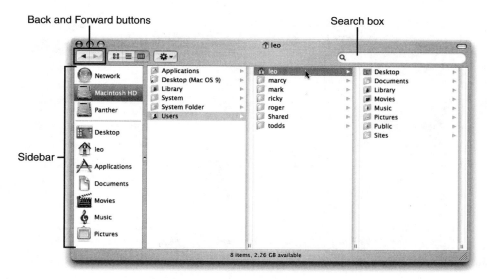

Sidebar

FIGURE 2.2

The Finder window acts as a browser (and has a certain similarities to a web browser) that helps you locate and manage files that are available on the storage devices in or connected to your Mac.

The Sidebar

The Sidebar is a relatively recent (Mac OS X 10.2) addition, but it's a darned handy one. At the top of the Sidebar is where the Mac automatically adds the storage devices—internal disks, inserted CDs/DVDs, and network volumes—that are available to your Mac. That makes it easy to get at your internal hard disk, but it also makes it easy to see when a new disk—say, an external FireWire disk or an inserted CD—has been recognized by the Mac. It's also how you'll access networking and Internet-based disks, which we'll get to in later chapters.

The Sidebar is separated top-from-bottom by a small gray bar. The bottom half of the Sidebar is used for convenient access to frequently used folders. By default, you'll see an Applications folder icon, an icon for your home folder, and icons for some of your important personal subfolders. Click one of those folders, and its contents are instantly revealed in the main portion of the Finder window (see Figure 2.3).

FIGURE 2.3

After clicking my home folder in the Sidebar, I see the subfolders in my home folder.

One thing that's nice about this bottom portion of the Sidebar is that you can add to it yourself, if you want to. I do this often when I'm working on a project and want quick access to a particular folder. All you have to do is drag the folder's icon from the Finder window's main portion to the Sidebar; you'll see a line appear between the existing icons and, when you release the mouse button, an icon for the new folder will be added.

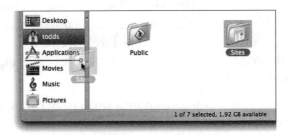

Now, click the folder's icon in the Sidebar and you'll instantly see its contents in the Finder window.

This doesn't *move* the folder, incidentally. The folder itself is still in its same place; this is just a representation of that folder on the Sidebar. (I call them Sidebar *shortcuts*;

Apple just calls them "items.") And that means you can remove it easily; simply drag the icon from the Sidebar to anywhere else on the screen and release the mouse button. The icon should disappear in an animated puff of smoke. Again, this doesn't affect the original folder or its contents; only the representation is, as the mobsters might say, *disappeared*.

TIP

You can also edit the contents of the Sidebar using the Sidebar section of Finder Preferences, if you like. To launch Finder Preferences choose Finder, Preferences from the menu.

One other thing is cool about those Sidebar shortcuts—they act as drag-and-drop targets. You'll find that most of the time when you want to move a file from one folder to another, you have to have two Finder windows open so you can drag from one folder to another. But if you have a particular folder on the Sidebar and you want to move a file to that folder, you can drag the file onto the Sidebar shortcut. You'll see it become highlighted; if you release the mouse button, that file will be moved (or, in some cases, copied) to the folder represented by that shortcut.

NOTE

For more on moving and copying and the distinction between the two, see the section "Selecting, Copying, and Moving Files," coming up shortly in this chapter.

Browsing Your Files

The Finder window enables you to view your files using three different "modes"—by icon, in a list, or using the Columns view. This third view is probably the most unique, particularly to users who are accustomed to the older Macintosh interface. But Columns view is also very handy, because it enables you to quickly see that hierarchy that I was talking about earlier. Using Columns view, you can get a sense of where on your Mac's disks (or elsewhere) a particular file is stored (see Figure 2.4).

To switch to Columns view, either choose View, Columns from the menu in the Finder or click the Columns button in any Finder window's toolbar.

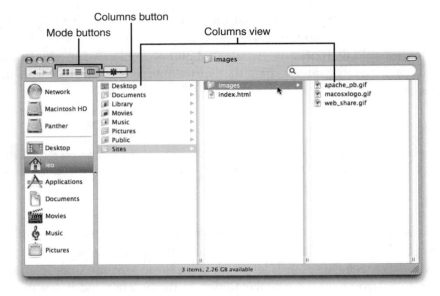

FIGURE 2.4

In Columns view, the Finder window lets you quickly dig through folders and subfolders to find items.

In Columns view, each level of folders is represented by a column within the main viewing portion of the window. The first column shows the contents on the item that you select in the Sidebar; in Figure 2.4, for instance, the home folder's icon has been selected. So, what we're seeing first are the folders on the main level—the Photos, Music, Document, and other first-level "home" subfolders—of my home folder, called Leo. (On most Macs, this the default name for the internal hard disk that shipped inside your Mac.)

To see the contents of one of those folders, you select it in that first column. The result is a second column of items that—as you might expect—displays the contents of the folder that you selected in the first column.

You can continue digging through subfolders this way until you find the item you're interested in. When you eventually do find the file that you're looking for, selecting it by clicking it once with the mouse highlights it in the Columns view and causes a final column to appear. This one will give you a good look at the item's icon (it'll be huge in the column) and information about the item you've selected. (You can click the More Info button to launch the Info window and learn more about that item; see more in the section "Get Info on Files.")

If the file happens to be a multimedia file the contents of which your Mac can display using its built-in technology, it will do that. For instance, image files are displayed automatically, as are some sorts of text documents. This can be very handy for viewing a folder full of images, for instance, to figure out the one that you're looking for.

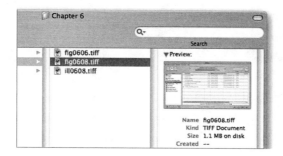

Finally, this one is really cool—many types of movies and audio (or song) files can be played back using the Columns interface. Select such a file and, if it can be played back, you'll see a player interface that has small buttons that look a little like VCR controls. Click the Play button and you'll see and/or hear the multimedia file play on your Mac.

Icon and List Views

The Columns view isn't the only way you can view items in the Finder window; you can also view items by Icon view or List view. Each is useful in its own ways.

To switch to Icon view, choose View, As Icons from the Finder's menu or click the Icon view button in the Finder window's toolbar. The result is a window that looks something like Figure 2.5.

Icon view is best used for dragging and dropping files between two different Finder windows, although some folks just like the way it looks. The larger icons make for better targets; it feels a bit more traditionally "Mac-like" than the columns view. I don't use Icon view much, but it has its place, particularly for making it easy to manage and manipulate the icons' names and characteristics directly.

When you're working in Icon view, you get two special commands that activate on the View menu: View, Clean Up and the View, Arrange By menu. Since icons can get messy in this view (which is less strict than the other two), you can use the View, Clean Up command for force the icons in the window to conform to a grid within the window, thus bringing about a bit more order.

Icons button   Mode buttons   Icons view

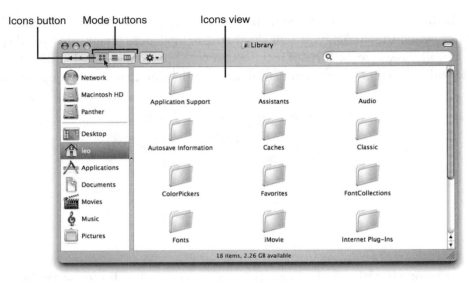

FIGURE 2.5
The Finder's Icon view gives you a different look at your files.

The View, Arrange By menu can be used to rearrange the icons by Name, the date that the items were created, or modified and so on. Selecting one of these commands also places the icons in a nice grid format.

TIP

While in Icon view, choose View, Show View Options and you can set some more permanent behaviors. For instance, turn on the Keep Arranged By option and choose a method from the menu; this is like having one of the View, Arrange By command turned on permanently. The View Options window is cool for other reasons—you can change the size of icons, the text size, and make other decisions as well about how your icons will look. Note that at the top of the window, you can choose This Window Only or All Windows, depending on whether or not you want these tweaks to be universal.

List view is another hold-over from the earlier Mac OS, and a lot of Mac users prefer to work in List view—I probably use it a bit more often than I use Icon view, but that's because I'm a Columns view junkie. To view a folder in list view, choose View, As List in the Finder's menu. Figure 2.6 shows List view in action.

List button

Mode buttons   List view

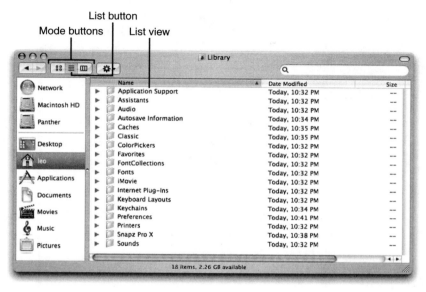

FIGURE 2.6
The Finder's List view shows you files as a series of small icons.

As shown in Figure 2.6, the List view offers its own method for viewing the hierarchy of folders and subfolders on your disks—click the disclosure triangle next to any folder icon and you'll see its contents appear below the folder. Click the triangle again to "close" the folder. You can dig as deep as you want by clicking the disclosure triangle for a subfolder, then an subfolder of that folder, and so on.

List view is particularly useful when you need to quickly know some extra info about the files and folder you're working with—their last-modified dates, the amount of space they require on your disk, the type of files, and many other tidbits of information.

In fact, you can customize what shows up in List view by choosing View, Show View Options and selecting the columns that you want to have appear. (Note, in Figure 2.7, the setting at the top of the View Options window, where you can choose This Window Only or All Windows.) Turn on the Calculate All Sizes option at the bottom of the window and you'll see the amount of disk space that all items—applications, documents, and folders—take up on your hard disk or other storage device.

FIGURE 2.7

The List view's View Options window lets you set up the columns that appear and determine some behavior in those columns.

The list view offers some other customization tricks:

- Click a column heading and you'll see it turn blue (or a shade of gray, depending on your color settings in the Appearance pane is System Preferences). That means that the list is now sorted by that column, such as the Size column or the Date Modified column. Click the heading again and you'll see the small triangle in the heading change directions—you've just changed the sort order from greatest to least or from A to Z or whatever ordering makes the most sense for that particular column.

- Other than the Name column, you can *reorder* the others, if you like, by clicking and dragging their column headings—click and drag the Date Modified column to the other side of the Size column, for instance, and they'll switch places when you release the mouse button.

- Can't read everything that's in a particular column? Move your mouse pointer to the line that separates two of the column headings and hold down the mouse button—you'll see the pointer change shape. It should look like two arrows pointing in opposite directions. While holding down the mouse button, drag left or right to change the size of the column that's to the left of your mouse pointer. Release the mouse button when things are the way you want them.

Selecting, Copying, and Moving Items

Now that you've seen the various ways you can look at your files in the Finder, let's do something with them. If the Finder is a file-management utility, then we need to learn how to manage said files.

Selecting Items

You know how to select one file in the Finder—click its icon. That's pretty straightforward. But what about two files at once? Here are some options:

- You'll often find that you want to select more than one file at a time for moving, copying, or labeling. To select more than one file, even if those files are non-contiguous, you can hold down the ⌘ key while clicking multiple icons and you'll see them all highlighted in the Finder window. Note that this works regardless of the view that you're using.

- In Columns view, you can select all of the files between one file and another by selecting the first file and then holding down the Shift key and clicking the last file. All of the files in the list between the two will become highlighted. (In Icon view, the Shift key works just like the ⌘ key.)

- In Icon view, you can select a group of icons by dragging a box *around* them, almost like you were roundin' up cattle. Click and hold the mouse button just above and outside of one of the icons, then click and drag diagonally to draw a box. When you've gathered in all of the icons you want, you can release the mouse button and they'll all be highlighted.

Drag and Drop

Once you have one or more items highlighted, you may find that you want to copy those items or move them elsewhere. This is usually done by dragging the items from one Finder window to another, or from a Finder window to the icon of a folder or disk that appears on your Desktop, in the Dock or in a Finder window's sidebar.

The classic approach to moving files is to use the mouse to drag a file from one Finder window to another. This, as you've probably gathered, requires two Finder windows to be open at once, as shown in Figure 2.8. You can then drag and drop from one window to the other and, if both windows represent folders that are on the same disk, the dragged items will be moved to the new folder. If the windows represent folders on different disks, then the items, by default, will be copied to the new location, meaning that they will still exist in the old location as well.

TIP

Want to copy files instead of move them between folders on the same disk? If the default action is a move, then you can change that by holding down the Option key while dragging. You'll see the pointer change so that a plus ("+") sign appears. That means when you release the mouse button, you'll copy the items to the new location instead of moving them.

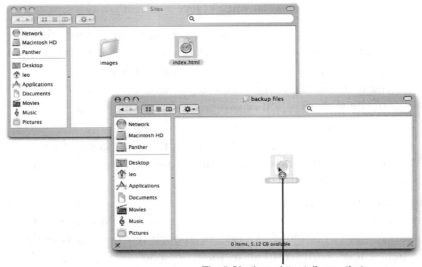

The "+" in the pointer tells you that
you're copying instead of just moving

FIGURE 2.8
You can drag items between Finder windows to move them from one folder to another.

A second Finder window isn't the only possible drag-and-drop target. You can also drag icons to another folder or disk icon, and, when you drop the items on the folder or disk icon, the items will be moved or copied, as appropriate. And the trick is that such disk or folder icons can be found in a lot of places—the Sidebar, in the Finder window itself, in another column (when using the columns view) in a subfolder (when using the list view) or even in the Dock. In nearly all cases, a folder icon that you see somewhere in the Finder is a valid drag-and-drop target.

Mac OS X has another cool option that you can use as you're dragging and dropping, called *spring-loaded* folders. Here's how it works. Say you want to drag something from the folder that you're currently viewing in the Finder window to a subfolder of your Documents folder. Usually, that would require opening the two Finder windows. Using the spring-loaded folders feature you would:

1. Select the item or items that you want to move or copy.

2. Click and hold down the mouse button, then drag the item(s) to the folder or disk icon where the destination subfolder will be found.

3. Keep holding down the mouse button while pointing at the target icon and hover for a few seconds. You should see the highlighting around the target icon blink twice, and then that folder or disk will (spring!) open on your screen.

4. Now, locate the next subfolder and, if necessary, drag to it and wait again for it to open.

5. When you reach your destination folder, you can drop the item on it and it will be moved or copied.

The coolest part is that when you release the mouse button, after the item is moved or copied, the folders will spring back closed and you'll be at the folder where you started this whole little operation.

Copy and Paste

You've got another option for copying files—the Copy and Paste commands. If you've used computer word processors or similar applications in the past, then you're probably familiar with the concept of copy and paste, but you may not have used it for files and other such items. Here's your chance:

1. In the Finder, you can select items that you'd like to move from one folder to another and then choose Edit, Copy x Items, where the x will be the number of items you've selected. (Mac OS X is pretty smart about this stuff.)

2. Next, navigate to the folder where you'd like the files to appear.

3. Choose Edit, Paste from the Finder menu. You should see the item's icons appear in the folder.

If you're not the drag-and-drop type, you'll find that this combination of the keyboard and some quick mousing can make it easy to copy files from one place to another, with the added advantage that you'll look like a serious pro. (Not to mention that this approach may be familiar if you're used to Microsoft Windows.)

Creating and Managing Folders

Now that you've seen some of what the Finder can do, you're ready to dig in and start organizing things. Step one is creating some subfolders.

While you *can* create subfolders within your home folder (alongside the Music and Pictures folder), it isn't necessarily recommended, if only for the clutter you can create that way. It's up to you, but most any subfolder that you're creating on your Mac is likely to be for personal documents, so it makes sense to create that subfolder within one of the existing folders, such as the Documents or Movies folders.

To create a folder, you should first navigate to the folder where you'd like the new subfolder to appear. Once you've got that folder open (or, if you want the subfolder to appear on the desktop, you can click the desktop background to select it) choose File, New Folder from the Finder's menu, or press ⌘+Shift+N. That should create a new, untitled folder.

 By default, the name of that folder will be highlighted so that you can immediately begin typing to rename it. When you're finished, just press Enter.

If you need to rename a folder (or, for that matter, any file) that's been named previously or that's still named Untitled Folder (whether or not you created it), click the folder to highlight it, then wait a moment and click it again. You'll see the name highlighted so that you can type to rename it.

> **NOTE**
>
> Occasionally you won't be able to rename a folder—usually that's because you don't have ownership or permission for that folder, which means it was created by the Mac OS itself or by another user on your system. We'll look into permissions in the next section.

To move a folder, you can drag-and-drop just as you would other items in the Finder. If you drag from one part of a disk to another part of that same disk, then you'll move the folder and its contents, including any and all subfolders. If you move the folder to another disk, you'll end up copying that folder.

To delete a folder, you can drag its icon to the Trash icon on the Dock, or you can select the folder and then choose File, Move to Trash or press ⌘+Delete. In each of these cases, both the folder and *any* subfolders or files within that folder will be moved to the Trash, where you can delete them permanently or retrieve them, as discussed later in the section "Trashy Issues."

Labeling Folders and Files

The Finder includes a special command that enables you to label a file or folder (or a group of either), giving it a particular color. Each color can be assigned a particular bit of label text, so that a red label can mean anything you want—that you're currently working on the file, that it's part of an important project, or even that it's no longer a file or folder that you use.

To define labels, choose Finder, Preferences. At the top of the Preferences dialog box, choose Labels. Now, on the Labels tab, you can see the different predefined labels and what they currently mean, as shown in Figure 2.9. (I should make it clear that the Finder doesn't *care* what they mean—that's basically for your own use and reference.)

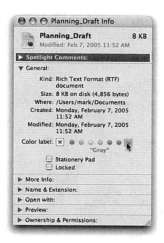

FIGURE 2.9

Applying a label to your files and folders can help you stay organized. You can also search based on the labels that you define.

To apply a label to an item, simply highlight it in the Finder and choose the File menu; then, at the bottom of that menu, choose the label that you'd like to apply to the item.

So what are labels good for? You'll see in a few different sections in this chapter and elsewhere. Aside from the visual label that can be nice when you see a file in the Finder, the label is particularly handy for automated tasks, such as backing up important files using Apple's Backup application (which comes with a .Mac membership—see Chapter 8, "Get on the Internet") or with the Finder's and other application's ability to search for items based on various criteria. One of those criteria can be a file or folder's label, making it easy to search for when necessary. (We'll discuss that a little in the section "The True Finder: Spotlight" later in this chapter.)

To remove a label, select the item and choose the File menu, then select the small X in the menu.

Learn More About Items and Understand Permissions

Feel like you just don't know your files well enough? The Get Info command is designed to let you dig a little deeper and learn more about your files and folders— anything you can access within the Finder has an associated Get Info profile.

Get Info

To get information about an item, highlight that item in the Finder and then choose File, Get Info from the Finder's menu, or press ⌘+I. The Get Info window then appears on your screen (see Figure 2.10).

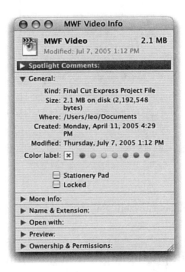

FIGURE 2.10
The Get Info window in the Finder tells you tons of stuff about the selected item.

The Get Info window is divided into little sections that use disclosure triangles for hiding and revealing all of the info you can see. By default, you'll see an area at the top of the window called Spotlight Comments, which you can use to add information that Spotlight will use when searching this file. (More on Spotlight later in this chapter.) Below that, you'll see the General information section that shows name, size, location on the disk and so on. You can also set a color label for the item in this section.

In the More Info section, you can learn a bit more about the file.

In the Name and Extension section, you'll see a small entry box that enables you to rename the file or folder if desired. For document files, you can also set or change the filename extension, which is a three- or four-letter code at the end of the filename that tells the Mac OS what sort of document the file is. (Folders don't have filename extensions.) You can also choose the Hide Extension option if you'd prefer not to see the filename extension for this item in the Finder. (More on filename extensions in Chapter 3, "Applications and the Dock.")

The Open With portion of the Get Info window is cool; this is where you can choose what application is used to launch the document that you're viewing currently. Again, we'll talk more about that in Chapter 3.

The Preview area is used to show a portion of the document, a "thumbnail" version (if the file is an image or movie), controls for playing back an audio file, or just a big ol' image of the icon. What you see in this section depends on what you're getting info about, but it's a handy little space to quickly check out the contents of a number of different types of documents.

The Ownership and Permission section of the Get Info window offers some deeper options. We'll talk about those in the next section, but first let me quickly mention the Spotlight Comments section of Get Info; open up this disclosure area and you can type a little something about the file, if desired. (Comments can be searched when you're using Spotlight or the Finder for the searches; other file management and backup applications can search the comments, too.)

Permissions and Users

If you read Chapter 1, "What Makes Mac OS X Unique," you know that Mac OS X is a multiuser operating system. "Users" in this context doesn't just apply to you and your brother or mother or best friend—the "system" is also a user, and there are things going on behind the scenes on your Mac that require special automated accounts.

Because of all these users, files and folders in the Mac OS are designed to keep track of two things—who owns a particular item (file or folder) and who has permission to access such files and folder.

For the most part, doling out these permissions is handled by the Mac OS. If you create a document and store it in your home folder, it's generally owned by you and only you have permission to see and work with it. If you save it elsewhere on your Mac's hard disk—in the Shared folder inside the Users folder or elsewhere on the main Macintosh HD disk—then you'll still be the owner, but others will have "read" access to the file (the ability to launch it and view it in an application) and, in many cases, "write" access as well (the ability to change and save the document).

So how does this translate to something practical? Like I say, most of the time the Mac OS handles this and, ideally, you'd leave it up to your Mac because it'll mess things up less often than you will. (Although, to be honest, it does sometimes mess things up, as do third-party applications.) But if you ever want to change permissions for whatever reason, you can, at least on files for which you are the owner. Just select one of those files and invoke the Get Info window. Reveal the Ownership & Permissions section, as shown in Figure 2.11.

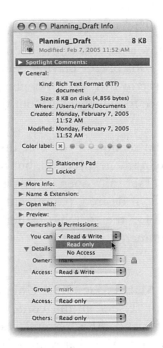

FIGURE 2.11
Setting Permissions for a file that you own.

In Figure 2.11, I've already revealed the Detail section, but you don't have to do that if you simply want to change the permissions to a file or folder for your *own* account. Just select what you'd like to be able to do to this file from the You Can menu. For instance, choosing Read Only would make it so that you can't accidentally change the file by saving over it, although you would be able to use the Save As command to make a copy and make changes to that copy. That might be a great idea for some fill-in documents or letterhead that you use often and want to make sure you don't save over.

In the Details section, you can dig in a little further. Here, you can change the owner of an item (click the padlock icon and enter your password first, if necessary). You can then change the access level for different types of users—the owner or a group (often it's the staff group, which means anyone with an administrator's account)—and you can set permissions for Others, which represents anyone who has an account on your Mac, regardless of the groups they belong to. Taken together, these permissions and options can be handy in particular for multi-use and networked Macs. So, I'll cover the "why" of setting some of these options in Chapter 5, "Work Those Peripherals" (for multi-user stuff) and Chapter 11, "Build a Home Office Network," (for networking stuff).

NOTE

There's one particular difference when you're looking at a folder as opposed to a document or application; the folder will have the option to Apply to Enclosed Items, which lets you set permissions for a folder and then set those same permissions to everything inside that folder. It makes sense, when you think about it—if you create a folder that you want others to have Read and Write access to, then you probably want them to be able to read and write to the files and subfolders inside that folder, too. Not every time, but most.

Once you've made the permissions changes (or any others in the Get Info window) you can click the Close button at the top of the window to dismiss it.

Disks and Discs

Clearly we've already been dealing with disks to some extent—a hard disk is installed in your Mac and automatically appears in Finder windows, at the top of the Sidebar. In fact, any hard disk that's automatically recognized by your Mac, including both internal disks and external hard disks (those that connect to the Mac via a FireWire or USB cable) will appear on the Sidebar, where you can click the drive's icon to access its contents.

The same is true of data CDs that you insert into your Mac's optical drive—they're automatically recognized (if you're dealing with a valid data CDs)—and placed on the Sidebar. You can then click the disc's icon in order to view it in the Finder window; you'll see icons appear according to the view that you've chosen for your Finder window.

But that's not the only place where you can see disks and discs appear on your Mac—you can also have them appear on your desktop, if desired. Choose Finder, Preferences and, on the General tab, choose the items that you'd like to see appear on the desktop (see Figure 2.12).

FIGURE 2.12
You can turn on the disks and external devices that you want to have on the desktop.

What's more, when you work with disks on the desktop, things actually go a little differently. First, to access a disk and its contents, you'll double-click the icon on the desktop. But what appears doesn't look like a typical Finder window, in that it won't have a Sidebar or even a toolbar. Instead it will be a plain window with items and folders in it. And when you double-click a subfolder, instead of seeing the window's contents change, another window will pop up to show you that subfolder's contents (see Figure 2.13).

TIP

You can click the oval button at the top-right of the window to return it to the typical Finder window and turn off the multi-window mode.

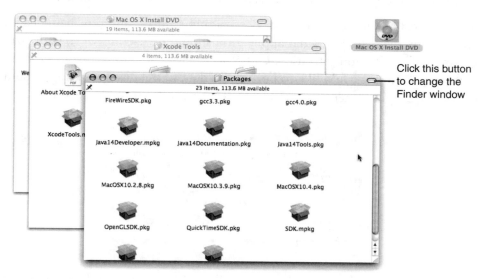

FIGURE 2.13

If you double-click a CD or DVD on the desktop, you can dig through the folders on your disks. (By default, double-clicking a hard disk icon will open a Finder window.)

If you've used Mac OS 9 or earlier, then you'll immediately recognize this as the way that the earlier Mac OS—the Classic Mac OS approach—worked with windows in the Finder. You were always pretty much in this "dig" mode, searching through subfolders by popping up windows. Things can get a bit cluttered this way, but as with the Classic Mac OS, you can hold down the Option key while you're double-clicking a folder and, as its window appears, the previous window will disappear, which helps to cut down on clutter. (You can also hold down the Option key while clicking the Close button on one of these windows in the Finder and, when you do, all open windows in the Finder will close.)

Now, not all discs are data discs—you'll probably feed your Mac at least the occasional audio CD or video DVD. And, of course, there are recordable CD and DVD discs on which you can actually store data. When your Mac detects any disc along these lines, it behaves a bit differently.

By default, when your Mac sees an audio CD, it'll launch iTunes so that you can play the CD and otherwise work with it using the tools in iTunes. If you insert a video DVD, it will be recognized by the Mac and the DVD Player will launch.

When you insert a blank recordable disc, something a little different happens—you'll see a dialog box that asks you what application should be used to work with that disc. For instance, if you're going to use a CD-R to record some music from iTunes, then you'd choose iTunes; if you'd like to burn some data to the disc for giving to someone else or for safekeeping, then you can choose Open Finder from the dialog.

If you choose to use the Finder, a disk icon will appear on your Desktop (unless you've turned off that preference) and in the Sidebar of a Finder window. That icon will represent the blank disc. You can drag files and folders to that disc until the items you've dragged there would fill up the blank disc that you've inserted. You can then burn the disc in one of two ways:

1. Click the small "burn" icon (it looks a little like the universal sign for radioactivity) that appears next to the disc's icon in the Sidebar of a Finder window.

2. Drag that disc icon to the Trash (the Trash becomes a "burn" icon).

When you choose one of these methods, your Mac will begin the process of "burning" data to that CD or DVD, which can take a little while.

NOTE

You can actually eject the blank disc and still add to its representation on the desktop, if you like, the next time you insert it. Mac OS X will remember the contents you'd wanted previously, but you've got to eject the disc by selecting it and choosing File, Eject.

There are other options, including a new feature in Mac OS X 10.4 called the *burnable folder*, which you can use to set up a disc before you actually insert a blank. We'll cover more of the options and take a closer look at burning data discs and others in Chapter 5.

Trashy Issues

I've mentioned the Trash a few times in this chapter and, if you've used any sort of graphical interface such as an older Macintosh or a Microsoft Windows computer, you're probably familiar with the concept. The general idea is this—moving something to the Trash on your Mac marks it for deletion, but doesn't immediately do away with the file. That gives you a chance to "rescue" it from the Trash if you decide after a while that it doesn't need to be deleted after all. But, once you "empty" the trash, the files is gone for good. (In some cases you can retrieve such files using special disk utilities, but for practical purposes the file is gone.)

To move items to the Trash, you can drag and drop them on the Trash icon, or you can highlight them in the Finder and press ⌘+Delete. That moves them from their current location to the Trash. To see the items that you've placed in the Trash, simply click its icon on the Dock. A folder appears showing you the files and folders that you've marked for deletion.

NOTE

Remember that the contents of a folder—including all subfolders and the contents of those subfolders—are deleted when you drag that folder to the Trash and then empty the Trash. Unlike some Microsoft Windows versions, the folders that you place in the Trash remain intact, and you can drag them back out and return them to their previous location if you feel like it. Also, right after moving something to the Trash, you can press ⌘+Z to "undo" that command and return the item or items if you realize you made a mistake.

Once you have files in the Trash and you're certain that you want them deleted, you have two options—you can empty the Trash or you can *securely* empty the Trash. When the Finder "empties" the Trash, what it actually does is simply tell the underlying file system that it no longer needs to keep track of the files that have been deleted and emptied. That doesn't necessarily mean that those files are overwritten or removed from your disk—it just means that, at some point in the near future, the files may be overwritten by new files that you copy to your Mac or create in your applications. (That's why disk utilities can sometimes recover the files.)

To empty the Trash, simply choose Finder, Empty Trash. In the dialog box that appears, click OK if you're sure that you want to permanently delete those files; if you aren't sure, click Cancel. If you click OK, you may see a small alert appear to show you the progress of the deletion, depending on how many files you have to get rid of.

If you opt to securely empty the Trash, the Mac OS will specifically overwrite those deleted files with zeros, making them impossible to retrieve. To do that, choose File, Secure Empty Trash. Again you'll see a dialog box; click OK if you're sure you want to delete the files. Now you'll see a small alert dialog box showing you the progress— this always takes more time than a simple Empty Trash command and, if you have a lot of files in the Trash, it can take *quite* a while to finish the secure deletion process.

> **TIP**
>
> Don't need to see the confirmation dialog every time you empty something from the Trash? You can open Finder Preferences (Finder, Preferences) and click the Advanced button. There, turn off the option Show Warning Before Emptying the Trash. Close the Finder Preference and, now, the Trash will be emptied immediately after you choose the command in the Finder.

The True Finder: Spotlight

Before we get out of this chapter, we need to explore a brand-new feature in Mac OS X 10.4 called Spotlight. Spotlight makes mincemeat of the notion that the Finder is actually designed to "find" something. At best, the Finder is really a Browser, which, interestingly enough, is what the analogous application was called on OpenStep-based computers back before Apple bought NeXT and turned its technology into Mac OS X. Of course, changing the name of the Finder to the Browser would not only confuse diehard Mac users, but it would step on what we all call a "browser" these days—web browsers like Safari and Internet Explorer. But, it's easy to see the similarities between the Finder and a web browser.

Spotlight, on the other hand, is a true *finder* in that it's designed specifically to help you find things. Apple has been working for years to create advanced search technologies that enable you to use *keywords* to locate not just files by their filenames or icons, but by their actual contents. With Spotlight, Apple makes that possible for all sorts of files, and somewhat blurs the lines between traditional documents—such as Word documents or text files—and new items such as songs, movies, and email messages. Spotlight can search through tons of different types of files and return a report of everything that's stored on your Mac's hard disk, external drives, inserted discs, and even network volumes.

This is particularly handy because—if you're like me—you may not always remember what you named a file. In fact, you may not even remember what type of a file you were creating. It might have been a Microsoft Word document or an Apple Pages document, or even a spreadsheet or a presentation. But if you can remember at least a keyword or two, then you should be able to narrow things down and get at the file.

Using Spotlight

As it happens, using Spotlight is pretty simple. The Spotlight icon is always on the menu bar; simply click it and a small entry box appears so that you can enter a keyword. Type your keyword and, after a moment, items that match that keyword will begin to appear in the Spotlight drop-down menu (see Figure 2.14).

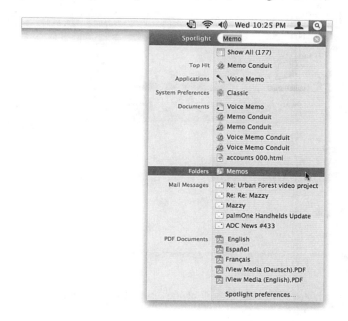

FIGURE 2.14

The Spotlight menu appears with some relevant results to your keyword query.

If you see the document that you're looking for, you can click that item to select it in the Spotlight window, which will cause that item to launch and appear on your Mac. Of course, that's not always what you want to do—if, instead, you want to locate that item's icon in the Finder, you can hold down the ⌘ key and click it; that will "reveal" the item in the Finder.

The Spotlight Window

In many cases you'll be viewing not *every* match, but those that Spotlight feels are most relevant based on certain criteria. If you'd like to see everything that Spotlight seems to think is a match, click the Show All option at the top of the Spotlight area. That will open the special Spotlight window (see Figure 2.15), which you can use to drill down and see if the exact item you're looking for can be found.

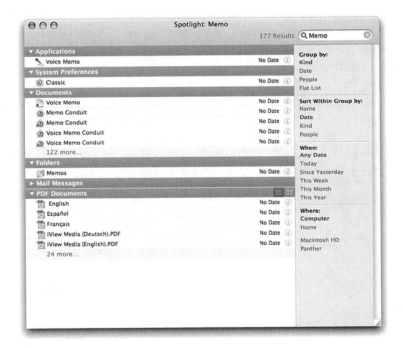

FIGURE 2.15
The Spotlight window enables you to dig into all of the results that Spotlight comes up with.

The Spotlight window is really a pretty sophisticated interface for searching. On the left you'll see the top results, as well as links below those results that enable you to dig deeper—click the 2 More or 11 More entries to see more documents or images or whatever is shown in that section of the window.

You can also view the items in different ways. Click an item in the listing, for instance, and you may see some small icons appear in the title bar for that section. Click the four small boxes and you'll be able to view items as icons instead of as list items.

When you find an item that interests you, you can click the small "i" icon on the right side of the item's listing (in List view only) in order to see more information about that file.

Finally, you can double-click an item to launch it and view it in its associated application, or you can hold down the ⌘ key and click the item to reveal it in the Finder.

On the right side of the window you'll see additional options that sort and parse your results. At the top of the right column you can choose methods for grouping results—by default you'll see items grouped by Kind, but you can change that to grouping them by Date or People or into just a plain, flat list. On that column you can also sort results or show results that only fall within a certain timeframe.

Of particular note are the bottom options, which enable you to choose *where* you want the results to come from. If you're fairly sure that the file you're looking for is on a particular disk or volume or removable disc, then you can select that item at the bottom-right in the window.

Want to change your search slightly? At the top of the window, you can change the keyword to see a different set of results. Or, if you're done with your search, click the close button at the top of the window.

Other Search Tools

Sometimes Spotlight is a little overkill for what you need, particularly if you *do* know the name of the file that you're looking for. In that case, the Finder window is good enough for the search. At the top of any Finder window is a search entry box; enter a partial filename to search for matches. As you type, results appear in the Finder window (see Figure 2.16).

By default the Finder window shows you the broadest set of results, but you can narrow them in a few different ways. First, you can click the folder or folders that you'd like to search from the top of the window. If Computer is selected then all attached disks and discs are searched; if you choose Home, then only your home folder is searched, and if other folders show up, they represent the folder that was selected before you began your search. (Selecting a folder is a great way to narrow the search before entering a keyword or partial filename.)

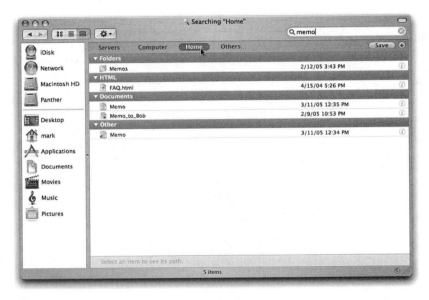

FIGURE 2.16
The Finder windows enables some basic searching.

The other way to narrow the search is the click the small plus sign ("+") icon in the Finder window. That brings up a special *criterion line*, which you can use to narrow the search further. Choose some aspect of the file that you want to search for (when it was last opened or last modified, or its size) and then use the menus and entry boxes to decide what you want that aspect compared against.

Make your selections and the Finder window's results will change to show any matches. If you'd like to add more criteria, click the plus icon again; otherwise, click the minus icon to remove a criterion line or click the "X" icon in the search box at the top of the Finder window to return it to regular operation.

TIP

Choosing File, Find from the Finder menu automatically brings up a Finder window with two criteria lines revealed, enabling you to begin a quick search.

Chapter 3

Applications and the Dock

Well, this is the reason you got your Mac—you want to get
something done in an application of some sort. Makes sense.
Hopefully in your Mac career you'll find reasons to use all sorts
of applications—anything from word processing to video editing
or even programming and database creation—although, as with
anything, there's a first step. And the first step with applications
is to get them launched and working for you.

In this chapter I'd like to take a look at how you get started with
applications, some of the basic commands that you'll find in
nearly any Macintosh application, and one of the methods you'll
use for managing those applications—the Dock.

The Applications Folder

As I've mentioned in previous chapters, Mac OS X can be a bit
of a stickler about where and how files and folders are stored in
the hierarchy of folders. Well, that extends to applications, as
well, which have their own folder within the hierarchy. In a typical Mac OS X installation, the Applications folder is found on
the main level of the startup hard disk. You'll find it nestled there
among the Users folder, the Library folder, the System folder,
and so on (see Figure 3.1).

FIGURE 3.1
The Applications folder is a root-level folder on your Mac's startup disk.

Applications don't *have* to be stored in the Applications folder, but they generally are. Apple puts all its own applications in that folder, or in a subfolder, such as the Utilities folder that is inside the Applications folder. And most third-party installers will also put their application's icons (and sometimes subfolders full of support files for those applications) in the Applications folder.

> **NOTE**
> Where else can an application be installed? You can install applications within your own home folder if desired, ideally by creating a folder inside your home folder called Applications (or Games, for instance, if you do a lot of gaming) and installing them there. That has the added effect of making the application inaccessible to others on your computer—assuming that's something you want to do.

Many Mac OS X application icons actually represent a special kind of folder called a *package*, which you treat like any other icon—drag it around, rename it, double-click it to "launch" it. Interestingly, a package isn't simply a single file, but rather a special folder that can hold a lot of the ancillary bits and pieces that a typical application needs to get up and running. That's why when you look into the Applications folder (by double-clicking its icon in an icon view or list view, or selecting it in a Columns view), you'll see mostly individual icons for each application. (Some applications will have subfolders, but not many of them.) Figure 3.2 shows applications in the Applications folder.

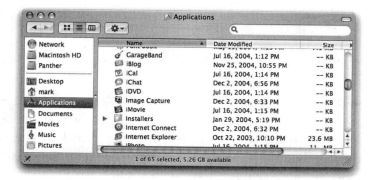

FIGURE 3.2
Here's a typical Applications folder, including some non-Apple stuff I've installed since getting the machine.

NOTE
Applications are installed in one of three ways—Apple's installers put them in the Application folder, a third-party installer program puts the application there, or an administrative-level user drags the application to the Applications folder.

Launching an Application

Okay, so you know what an application is. That part is easy enough. How do you get started with one?

The most obvious way is something you're probably already familiar with—you can double-click the application's icon in the Finder (see Chapter 2, "The Finder and Your Files"). Just as with documents and folders, double-clicking an icon *launches* it, which, in this case, means activating the application and its menu items so that you can use it to accomplish something. Generally you'll see a *splash screen* of some kind, which might tell you the name of the application and a little about it while it's loading. (It's loading information from your Mac's hard disk into its random access memory—RAM—so that you can begin working with the application's tools.)

Once loaded, you'll see the application's menu bar across the top of the display. This bar includes the application menu in the top left corner—the menu named for that particular application. You may also see a new document window, if that's the sort of application you're working with. In the case of an email program, you might see the email viewer; in a Web browser, you'll see a browser window. In other words, things will get started up.

Double-clicking an application isn't the only way to launch it. Some other options include

- Click the application's icon in the Dock. If you have an icon for that application already on the Dock (which is true of many of Apple's built-in applications, although you can also add your own) then you simply click it once to launch it. You'll see the icon bounce up and down (unless you've turned off that preference) and, once the application is started up, a small arrow will appear underneath the icon.

- Choose the application in the Recent Items menu, which is accessed via the Apple menu. If the application is one of the most recent that you've launched, it should be accessible there in the Recent Items menu. That's handy when you think about it, since many of us use the same applications over and over again.

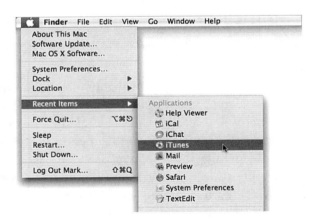

- And, for the sake of completeness, it's worth saying that you can launch an application by highlighting it in the Finder (by clicking it once or by pressing the arrow keys on your keyboard while the Finder or a Finder window is active) and either pressing ⌘+O, Control+clicking the application icon and choosing Open from the contextual menu, or selecting File, Open in the Finder.

Once you're done working with an application, you can *quit* it, which frees up RAM for other programs while forcing you to save changes to any documents that you've been working on. To quit an application, open its application menu (the one named Word or Safari or whatever the name of the application is) and choose Quit from that menu. In most applications, you can also press ⌘+Q. If you have open windows in that application, you may be asked to save your documents. Otherwise the application's commands should disappear from the toolbar and there will no longer be a triangle under that application's icon in the Dock. (In fact, if the application's icon wasn't in the Dock in the first place, it may disappear again altogether.)

Opening, Saving, and Closing Documents

Having covered launching applications pretty thoroughly, now let's get into the method that you'll probably use even more often, at least with certain types of applications—launching *documents*.

Launching Documents

With most documents, the Mac OS has an idea of what application created the document (if it was created on your Mac) or there's a default application that's designed to open it. In the latter case, you can usually double-click the application's icon in the Finder and the document will launch in the application with which it is associated.

If you don't want the document to launch in the application with which it's associated—for instance, you'd prefer an RTF document to launch in Microsoft Word instead of TextEdit—then you can launch it by dragging that document to the application's icon or tile in the Dock. If the icon becomes highlighted when you hover over the application's icon, that means it can accept the document and attempt to launch it. Drop the document icon on the application icon and it'll do just that.

Another way to launch a document is to Control+click the documents icon in the Finder. In the contextual menu that appears, you can then choose either the Open command or the Open With command, which, in turn, opens a submenu. In that submenu you can choose the application that you'd like to use to open the document—Mac OS X will start you off with some helpful options.

If you don't see the application you want to use, you can choose Other in the contextual menu. That brings up a special dialog box that can be used to locate the application that you want to use to open this particular document; choose it in the Choose Application window and then click Open to attempt to open the document with the selected application.

TIP

You can change a document's association in the Finder. Select the document icon and use the Get Info command (File, Get Info) to open the document's info window. In the Open With section of the Info window, you can choose an application that you'd like to use to open this document from now on. In that same section you'll see a Change All button that can be used to change the all documents like this one so that they're associated with the application that you're choosing.

Saving Documents

Once you've gotten an application launched and you've made some changes, the next step is to save that document frequently. (This is also true if you've recently created a new document.)

As with most any modern operating system, the Mac has standardized the way you save a document—you'll do it by choosing File, Save from the application's menu bar or by pressing ⌘+S. If this document already has a name, then invoking the Save command will save any changes that you've made to that document.

If the document doesn't already have a name then you'll be asked to give it one and to choose a location for it. You'll do that via the Save dialog box (or dialog sheet) that appears when you invoke the Save command.

In the Save dialog, you can enter a name for the file. Then, in the Where menu, you can choose a location on your hard disk (or connected volumes) where you'd like the file to be stored. If a suitable location doesn't appear in the menu, you can click the triangle icon to reveal the rest of the Save dialog, which includes an interface that's a little like the Finder's Columns view, in that it lets you maneuver to any folder on your hard disk (see Figure 3.3).

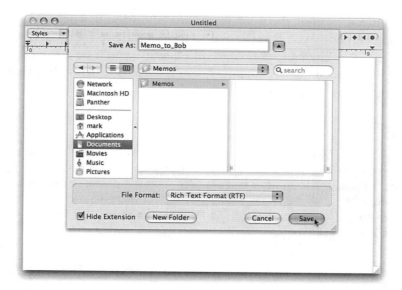

FIGURE 3.3
The full Save dialog sheet includes a Columns-like interface.

With the location chosen, you can choose the file format (in some cases) or make other application-specific choices toward the bottom of the dialog box. Finally, click the Save button to save the document, or the Cancel button if you've decided to change your mind.

Most applications have another Save command, called Save As, which is used to take an existing document and save it (and any changes you've made to it) using another name. So, you could open the file Sales_Report_Draft, make some changes and save it as Sales_Report_Final, for instance. To do that, just choose the File, Save As command. The Save dialog box will appear and you can choose a new name and location for the document that you'll be saving.

Closing Documents

When you're done with a document, you may want to close it to get it out of the way or simply for safekeeping. That's easily done. With the mouse pointer, you can click the Close button on a document window to close its window. If all goes well, it'll disappear.

The Close button is cool, because it visually shows you when there are unsaved changes in a document—you'll see a small black dot if there are unsaved changes. Even if there are unsaved changes, you can still click it—you'll be prompted to save the changes and, if the document is unnamed, you'll see a Save dialog box that enables you to name it and choose a location.

> **TIP**
>
> You can close windows by selecting them and pressing ⌘+W. You can also close more than one open window at a time in a given application by holding down the Option key while clicking the close button or while pressing ⌘+W. That will close *all* open windows in the current application, whether it's the Finder, a word processor, or whatever. (Note that closing a window doesn't necessarily quit an application—you may still need to choose Quit from the Application menu or press ⌘+Q to quit the application.)

The Dock

Down at the bottom of the Mac's screen is something that—believe it or not—is a little controversial for die-hard Mac users. While most of us have gotten used to the Dock (see Figure 3.4) since it was introduced with the first version of Mac OS X, that doesn't mean everyone who has gotten used to it likes it, which is at least one of the reasons why there are a number of add-ons and hacks for the Mac that add the old application-switcher menu back to the interface. (If you don't know what I'm talking about, don't worry about it. It's a Mac-from-ye-olden-days type thing.)

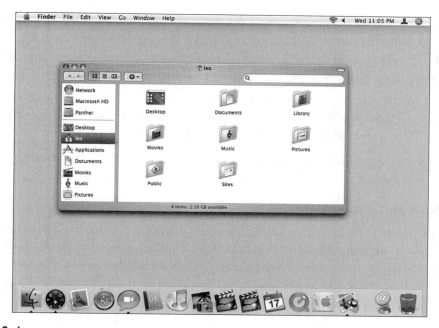

FIGURE 3.4

The Dock is the strip of icons that appears at the bottom on your screen.

One of the reasons that some people dislike the Dock (and others swear by it) is that the Dock is sort of a Dock of All Trades. It has a number of tasks that it performs that were previously handled by different Mac interface elements. Here's a look:

- It's an application launcher—As you've already read, you can click an icon on the Dock to launch the application it's associated with.

- It's an application switcher—Any running application, whether its icon is usually in the Dock or not, will pop up in the Dock while its application is running. That makes it easy to click a running application's icon and switch to it.

- It's a drag-and-drop target—The Dock puts both running applications and your favorite non-running application icons right there at the bottom of your display, making it easy to drag and drop documents onto those icons, thus launching a document in a particular application.

- It manages minimized windows—Remember that Minimize button that appears as one of the control buttons at the top of a Mac window? When you click it, that window leaves the screen and appears as an icon on the Dock. It's there so that you can return to it quickly if necessary.

- It enables you to manage shortcut documents—Along with applications, you can drag documents to the Dock so that you can launch them quickly with a single click. This is especially handy with certain types of documents, such as links to Internet sites, but it'll work with any sort of document.

- It can turn a folder of items into a quick-access menu—Drag a folder to the Dock and you can click and hold the mouse button on that folder to reveal its contents in a special menu. You can then select an item to launch it.

First and foremost, though, the Dock is about launching applications, noting which are running, and switching between them, as we'll see in the next section.

Placing Apps on the Dock

One main idea of the Dock is it makes it easy to launch the applications that you use frequently. By default, Apple puts a bunch of their stuff on the Dock, because, you know, it's theirs. But you don't have to leave it that way. Whenever you come across an application that you'd like quick access to, you can put it on the Dock. That way, the application is both a quick click away for launching and a drag-and-drop target for documents. You can easily drag an application icon to the Dock to add it.

He that giveth to the Dock can taketh away from it. Grab an application icon on the Dock, click and hold on the icon, and then drag the icon off the Dock. Once you're a safe distance away from the Dock, release the mouse button and your application icon will disappear in a puff of smoke.

No need to be alarmed, though—only the Dock icon is destroyed in this operation—your original application is safe.

For the record, icons on the Dock can also be moved around according to your whim. Simply click and drag an icon from one place on the Dock to the other and you'll see a space open up whenever you hover for a few moments. Release the mouse button to place the icon there.

Actually, you might find that a space doesn't open up if you drag an application icon from the left side of the Dock *across the dividing line* to the right side. That's because the right side of the Dock is for documents and minimized windows only—you can't put applications over there.

NOTE

Notice how the application icon is just, well, an *icon* when you put it on the Dock? If you haven't yet memorized all your application icons (which we can sarcastically blame on your poor time-management skills), you can point the mouse at a particular icon to see its name pop up over the icon. In fact, you can sweep your mouse pointer along the Dock and you'll see the names of icons pop up rather quickly.

Launching and Switching Between Applications

Once you've got application icons on the Dock, what do you do with them? Well, if you want to launch the associated application, just click its icon in the Dock. You'll see the icon bounce up and down a few times and then a small triangle will appear beneath it. That tells you that application is currently active.

As mentioned, you can also drag and drop a document onto a Dock icon if you'd like to use a particular application to open the document that you're dragging. That's really convenient with documents such as graphics files or text documents that you'd like to open in a particular program. For instance, if you have a JPEG file and you'd like to open it in Photoshop, but the JPEG is associated with a different application, such as Preview, then you can drag the JPEG to the Photoshop icon on the Dock to open it in Photoshop.

Once an application is running, you can click its icon in the Dock to switch to it—this is one of the ways that the Mac enables you to multitask by moving from application to application. You can have many different applications running at once and they should all have icons on the Dock, so that you can switch between them quickly.

> **TIP**
>
> Another interesting thing happens when you click the icon of a running application on the Dock—if you switch to that application and it doesn't have a document window open, often a new blank document window will open automatically. This even includes the Finder, which will open a new Finder window if one isn't already open. I've gotten to the point with this where even if I'm *in* the Finder already but there isn't a Finder window open, I'll click the Finder icon in the Dock to open a new window. Somehow it seems faster than opening the File menu.

There's another way to switch between running applications, and while it isn't strictly about the Dock, there's at least a tangential relationship. While you're working in the Mac OS, at any time you can press the ⌘ and Tab keys to bring up an overlay graphic of the icons of running applications. You can then continue to press ⌘+Tab to rotate through them; when you've highlighted the application you want to switch to, you can release the keys. (You can also press ⌘+Shift+Tab to rotate through them in the opposite direction.)

One thing that's neat about the way this works is that you can use it to quickly toggle between two different applications. Say you're working in a word processing application and you want to switch to Mail. Well, do that, either by clicking Mail in the Dock or using the ⌘+Tab trick to select it. Now, after you're done in Mail, say you want to switch right back to the word processor. Just press ⌘+Tab once and release. You'll switch immediately back to the word processor if that was your most recent application.

And the coolest thing about this trick is you can keep at it. Work in the word processor then press ⌘+Tab and release, and, *razzmatazz!*, you're back in Mail. You can go back and forth like that, which you'll find handy often when you're doing research or having a boring time with a report and switching to your Mail constantly to see if you have a message from your sweetheart.

Docs and Folders and Windows on the Dock

On the right side of the famous Dock dividing line is where you'll find three things of importance—it's where you can place document icons and folder for frequent access; it's where you'll access minimized windows; and it's where you'll find the Trash. Let's look at all three.

First of all, adding documents that you'd like quick access to is just as easy as adding applications—you just drag and drop the document from the Finder into the right side of the Dock. The result of this is a small document icon that you can click to launch that document at a moment's notice.

Probably the most annoying thing about adding documents to the Dock is the fact that they end up with a less than meaningful icon—I mean, they may look like a Word document or a QuickTime file, but that's only so helpful. (As with application icons, you can point the mouse pointer at a document icon to see the filename.) The other annoying thing is that if you add more than, say, three documents to your Dock, you're going to start filling it up and making the icons tiny on your screen.

TIP

You can actually change the icon of a document or even a folder by cutting a new image and pasting it into the item's icon box found at the top of the Get Info window.

One solution to that is to use folders on the Dock instead of individual documents. Drag, for instance, your Documents or Movies or any similar folder to the Dock (on the right side) and release the mouse button. When you do, a folder will appear on the Dock. So far, so cool. You can then Control+click that folder (or right-click it if you happen to have a two-button mouse) and up will pop the contents of that folder in a contextual menu. You can even click and hold the mouse button on the item in the Dock and, after a moment, the menu will spring to life.

Select an item in that menu and click (or, if you were holding the mouse button down the whole time since opening the menu, you can highlight the item and *release* the mouse button) and you'll launch it immediately. Notice also that this menu will change dynamically based on what you put in the folder using the Finder, and it doesn't have to have just documents—it can have application icons (or even aliases to application icons) in it as well. In fact, it can have subfolders inside the main folder, which will turn into *submenus* in this Dock icon menu.

> **NOTE**
> Because this is a folder icon and not an application, it needs to be placed on the right side of the Dock. The folder can, however, contain application icons and absolutely nothing bad happens to the menu, the application, or the space-time continuum as a result.

Finally, you add windows to the Dock by clicking the Minimize button in an active window. That causes the window to shrink down to Dock size and appear on the right side along with any documents and, of course, the Trash.

Minimizing a window is just a handy way to keep it open for later access but out of the way. The Dock helps you identify windows by making the minimized version look like the window that it represents—so much so that you can even continue to see QuickTime movies play in minimized windows.

> **NOTE**
> As with applications, you can drag minimized windows and documents around on the Dock to reposition them, as long as you stay on the right side of the dividing line. In fact, the only items you can't drag around are the Finder icon and the Trash icon.

Icon Menu on the Dock

Aside from the menu of folder items that you can bring up using a Control+click or a right click, you can also use the same Control+click on application icons in the Dock, which gives you a contextual menu for that particular application.

What you see in this menu depends on whether the application is currently running. If it's not, then you'll generally see the options to open the application, to remove it from the Dock, or to reveal its icon in the Finder. You should also see an option that enables you to set this application to launch whenever you log in to your user account. (If that option is already checked then you can select it again to remove the check mark and stop it from launching when you log in.)

If the application is running already, you'll probably see more commands and sometimes a variety of them. In the menu, you can choose from that application's open windows in most cases, and in certain applications you can choose to open a blank document or new window. You'll also see a number of other commands, including the ability to add the icon to the Dock (meaning it will stay in the Dock for quick launching after it's quit), choose to open this application when you log in, hide the application, show its icon in the Finder, and quit the application. When the application isn't responding to user input, you can also use this menu to force the application to quit (more on that in Chapter 13, "Common Problems and Solutions").

> **NOTE**
>
> The Hide command can generally be accessed via a Dock item's menu the same way it can be found in the application menu for that program. Hide causes the windows and menu bar of an application to disappear, but without minimizing the windows to the right side of the Dock. The only indication that the application is still running is the small triangle beneath its icon in the Dock and the fact that the application's icon will appear in the ⌘+Tab switcher menu.

Dock Preferences

You've got one more contextual menu on the Dock that's interesting to work with. Hold down the Control key and click the dividing line between to the two sides of the Dock (or right-click with a multi-button mouse) and you'll see a menu that enables you to make different choices about the appearance and behavior of the Dock. These options are also accessible via the Apple menu at Apple, Dock (as well as via the Dock pane in the System Preferences application). They are

- Turn Hiding On—This option causes the Dock to disappear "below" the visible screen when you're not using it, which gives you the entire screen to work with. You can then mouse all the way to the edge of the screen (by default that's the bottom edge, although you can change the position of the Dock) and the Dock pops back up.

- Turn Magnification On—When this is turned on, the Dock is magnified as you mouse over it. It's a fun effect and it may make it a little easier for you get a sense of what's on your Dock.

- Position on Screen—This option enables you to decide whether you want the Dock to appear at the bottom of the screen or if you prefer the left or right side of your display.

- Minimize Using—This command enables you to choose between two different visual effects when you minimize windows to the Dock. By default, the Genie effect is used, which is a very visual, animated approach where the window bends down to its place on the Dock like an animated genie returning to its bottle. With the Scale effect, the window simply shrinks down to the Dock.

TIP

You can hold down the Shift key while minimizing a window (that is, while clicking its minimize button) to see the minimize effect happen in slow motion.

Finally, both the menu in the Dock and the Dock submenu of the Apple menu have a Dock Preferences command that opens the Dock preferences pane in the System Preferences application. That gives you access to two additional options—the Dock Size slider and the Animated Opening Applications option. The Dock Size slider can be used to change the size of the Dock—the smaller it is, the less intrusive but the tougher it is to see items. (Of course, you can turn on magnification to get past that problem.)

And if you're sick of icons jumping up and down in the Dock, you can turn off the Animate Opening Applications option. (The animation can also affect the performance of older Macs.) When you're done, close the System Preferences application.

TIP

The dividing line in the middle of the Dock can be used to resize the Dock. Click and hold while pointing at the dividing line, then drag the mouse up the screen to make the Dock larger (it will only grow until its edges touch the side of the display) or drag it down to make the Dock smaller.

Getting Help

Mac OS X offers application developers a special help system, called Apple Help, that the application developer can use to offer onscreen guidance to users. Apple uses the system in nearly all of their applications, as do many third-party developers. Apple Help is a fairly straightforward approach to online documentation, based on the same tools and metaphors as a web browser, with which many people are familiar.

NOTE

The command to launch the Apple Help system isn't always the only command on the Help menu. You'll often find a link to the application developer's website, a link to their registration tools, and other commands that you can access there, as well.

Nearly all Mac applications have a Help menu, where you'll find the Help command. In the Help menu for the Safari application you'll find the command Safari Help— select that and you'll see a window that looks like Figure 3.5.

As I mentioned, the Help Browser isn't unlike a web browser. In the main part of the window, you'll see hyperlinks—blue text—that you can click to move to a new help page. For instance, in Safari Help there's a link to the Index page, which can then be used to find different help articles directly. Or, for a more circuitous route, I might start with the link to "Internet browsing at its best," which leads to a discussion of some of Safari's unique features along with links to more articles that discuss those features in depth.

FIGURE 3.5
Here's a sample Help interface.

Another way that the Apple Help browser is similar to a web browser is that it has Forward and Back buttons at the top of the interface that can be used to move back and forth between articles. If you're reading something and think "this isn't what I need; I'd prefer to return to the previous page" then click the Back button and that's what will happen. If you then subsequently decide "actually, I do need to read that article that I just came back from" then you can click the Forward button to return to it.

TIP
The Go menu can also be used to return to earlier articles.

The Help Browser also has a Home button (again, like a web browser) that you can use to return to the main page for the current help system—if I've dug deep into the Safari help articles and want to find my way back to its main page, I can just click the Home button.

It turns out that the Home button is actually a menu, too. Click and hold the Home button for a moment and you'll see a menu appear that includes a number of different help systems that have been installed on your Mac—these are help systems for other applications. Select one of those help systems and you'll be taken to *its* home page, where you can learn more about that new application. (You can also use the Library menu to switch between the different applications' help systems.)

NOTE

The granddaddy of all the help systems is Mac Help, which is used for the Finder, System Preferences, Dock, and tons of other interface elements. So, if you ever get confused and wonder where to find something, try Mac Help, which is accessible from the Help menu in the Finder or from the Home button menu in the Help Browser.

The last interface that makes the Help Browser like a web browser (particularly the latest round of web browsers) is that it includes a search box right at the top of the window. There you can enter keywords or a full question about something that you need help on and, when you press Return, the results appear in the Help Browser window (see Figure 3.6).

FIGURE 3.6

You can search the help system by keyword to learn more about a particular topic.

As you can see in Figure 3.6, the list of results includes a relevance ranking, which may help you get a sense of whether or not the resulting article will answer your question or appears to be on topic. When you find one that looks promising, you can either double-click it or highlight it and select the Show button. You can then read the article. If it doesn't answer your question, click the Back button at the top of the window and try a different article.

TIP

The small "x" icon can be used to clear the search box if you'd like to search again. And, if you need to, you can use the Back button to back out of the search results and return to previous articles.

The Help Browser offers you the option of searching the current help system by default (the Safari Help system, for instance) or you can search *all* help systems at once. To do that, click the smaller magnifying glass in the search entry box and choose to Search All Help.

It's worth nothing that the Help System will also search online articles at Apple's support website, but you can turn this off if you find that the attempts to access the Internet are slowing your Mac down. Choose Help Viewer, Include Product Support Searches to remove the check mark, thus deselecting it and keeping Help from accessing the Internet.

Part **II**

TAKE IT TO THE NEXT LEVEL

Chapter 4

Conquering the Mac OS X Interface

If you read the first few chapters then you've seen a discussion of some of the Mac OS X interface basics, including a look at the "metaphor" involved in working with Mac OS X. In this chapter, I'd like to dig a little more deeply into some of the unique features that make working with a Mac a little different from working with other PCs, as well as some fundamentals that aren't just exclusive to the Finder, but used throughout Macintosh applications to make things go a bit more smoothly and efficiently—or, failing that, stuff that's just plain cool.

Cut, Copy, and Paste

The first technique I want to cover quickly is something you're probably familiar with if you've used other graphical operating systems—the cut, copy, and paste commands. In fact, you saw one use of them in Chapter 2, "The Finder and Your Files"—copying and pasting icons from one folder to another in the Finder.

The Skinny on Cut, Copy, and Paste

Cut, copy, and paste started out more exclusively as commands that you would find in applications such as word processing or desktop layout programs. That Cut command enables you to remove a portion of a document (whether it's a few words or entire pages of paragraphs), and later place it elsewhere in that document—or in a different document—using the Paste command. Similarly, the Copy command can be used to duplicate a portion of a document so that it can be pasted elsewhere.

In Mac OS X, when you choose an item and copy or cut it, it's placed in a bit of memory called the Clipboard. The Clipboard is interesting because it can handle only certain data formats and only one copy or cut document segment at a time; when you copy or cut again, the previous text and/or images are removed from the Clipboard and the new text and/or images are placed there, even if the previous items hadn't been pasted anywhere. (So, you've got to watch out for that.)

Most of the time, copying and pasting maintains a great deal of rich text formatting, particularly within the same application; though when you move text from one application to another, you may lose some formatting along the way. Also, the Clipboard in Mac OS X uses the PDF format for graphical items, so you may sometimes find that pasting an image from one application to another doesn't have the exact desired effect; if you're dealing with high-resolution images or if the file format of the image is important, it's better to save or export the image from the first application and then open or import it into the second application.

Put Cut, Copy, and Paste into Action

So that's the lowdown. To put these commands into action, you've got simple steps to take:

1. Highlight or select the item(s) you want to cut or copy from a document window.

2. From the Edit menu, choose Copy if you'd like to place a copy of the selection on the Clipboard but leave the original in its place. Choose Cut if you'd like to place the selection on the Clipboard and remove it from its current location.

TIP

We'll get deeper into keyboard shortcuts in a moment, but it's worth knowing that you can press ⌘+c to copy a selection and ⌘+x to cut a selection.

3. Place your cursor elsewhere in the document or in another document where you'd like to paste your selection.

4. Choose Edit, Paste (or press ⌘+v) to paste the contents of the Clipboard into the document.

It's actually pretty straightforward. Once you've finished the operation, it's worth knowing that you could paste again, if desired; the items you'd copied or cut onto the Clipboard are still there until you copy or cut something again. (It's also cleared out when you restart your Mac or when you switch to another user account on this same Mac.)

TIP

One popular add-on is a utility that gives you more than one clipboard, so that you can cut or copy multiple items to different locations and then paste them as needed. CopyPaste (http://www.scriptsoftware.com/copypaste/) offers not only multiple clipboards (you access them by holding down number keys while copying and pasting), but also has features to let you record your most recent Copy and Cut operations and even edit items on your clipboard.

Taking Drag and Drop Seriously

Perhaps more so than Microsoft Windows, the Mac has always been about using a mouse extensively. Therefore, you'll find that there are lots of opportunities to drag and drop items from one place to another in both the Finder and in applications. If you don't already think "maybe I could drag that x onto that y" when you're trying to figure out how to accomplish something, maybe you should try to put it foremost in your mind.

One issue I come across a lot with novice—and even intermediate—Mac users is opening a document in an application with which the document is not associated. Say you've got an RTF (Rich Text Format) document that is associated with TextEdit, but which you'd prefer to open in Microsoft Word. All the double-clicking in the world won't overcome that—the document will keep opening in TextEdit. Instead, you can simply drag the file's icon to the Word icon in the Finder or on the Dock, then drop it on the Word icon. That should open the document in Word.

Beyond the Finder, you can often drag and drop within applications. For instance, one approach to a cut-and-paste situation is dragging text from one location to another in a document—many Mac applications will allow you to do this. Begin by highlighting text, and then click and drag that text to move it around in the document. When you get to a part of the document where you want that text to be, release the mouse button (see Figure 4.1).

FIGURE 4.1
Moving text around in a document can be as easy as drag and drop.

Here's a fun one—in most Mac OS X applications, once the document has been saved, a small icon appears next to its name in the document window. That icon is, in most cases, drag-and-drop aware. I use this all the time for attaching documents to email messages or sending them to someone else via iChat—just click and hold the mouse button on that document icon, and then drag it away to the desktop, a Finder window, or something like an email message window that will accept the document as an attachment. (Note that you may only be able to grab the icon if the document has had all of its recent changes saved.)

Hidden Powers of the Keyboard

I've hinted at this already, but the Mac OS and applications have tons of keyboard commands (sometimes called keyboard shortcuts) that you should get to know. Using a Mac without the occasional keyboard command is a little like driving a car only in first gear—you might get where you're going, but no where near as efficiently as you might using the whole gearbox. (By the way, this might actually be my first car-to-computer metaphor, which has to be some sort of record. I got all the way to Chapter 4 before slipping one in!)

Keyboard Shortcuts

You've already seen a few keyboard commands—some of the most common are the sequences for copying (⌘+c), cutting (⌘+x), and pasting (⌘+v). To use a keyboard command, you hold down the modifier key or keys (⌘, Option, Control, or Shift) and then press the other keys as close to simultaneously as possible. Then, release them and OS X should invoke the command.

A number of keyboard commands are extremely common throughout typical Macintosh applications. Some of those include:

Keyboard command	What it does...
⌘+s	Save the document
⌘+o	Open a new document
⌘+w	Close the current document or window
⌘+p	Print the document
⌘+z	Undo last command
Shift+z or ⌘+y	Redo most recently undone command
⌘+a	Select all
⌘+h	Hide the current application
⌘+q	Quit the current application

In many text-oriented applications, you can press ⌘+b to begin typing in bold and then, when you're done, press it again to turn off bold. The same works for ⌘+i for italics and ⌘+u for underlined text.

Aside from some of those basics, most applications will build upon them with more complex keystrokes that are used for application-specific tasks. In many graphical and page layout applications, for instance, ⌘+0 will zoom out so that an entire document fits in the window, while ⌘++ and ⌘+- can be used to change the zoom factor.

From there, keyboard commands are often built by application developers using a series of keystrokes, and they're not always uniform from application to application. For instance, Shift+⌘+p brings up the Page Setup dialog box in Adobe Acrobat, but it brings up the Project Gallery in Microsoft Word. (By the way, as a general rule, you can count on Microsoft applications to a be a little off from the others; that's just how they are up in Redmond.)

Since we can't possibly cover all the conceivable keyboard commands in this chapter, you're better off looking them up yourself. Fortunately, that's easy—nearly any Mac application will tell you its keyboard commands right there in its menus. Pull down a typical application menu and you'll see a legend of sorts to its various keyboard commands.

The command key symbol means to press that key along with the characters shown; the up arrow symbol represents the Shift key; the odd-looking slanted "T" is the symbol for the Option key. Using those symbols, you can figure out the keyboard shortcut associated with a particular command in the application.

> **TIP**
>
> Via the Keyboard & Mouse pane in System Preferences, you can access a list of keyboard commands that are built in to Mac OS X by selecting the Keyboard Shortcuts tab and scrolling the list. (You can also turn them on and off, if desired.)

Move by Keystroke

You're probably already familiar with the Page Up and Page Down keys, which can be handy for moving quickly though long documents in applications such as Word, Safari, or Preview. Less used are the Home and End keys, which will generally take you to the beginning or end of a document, respectively.

You may also find that it's worth experimenting with various combinations of the arrow keys and the modifier keys. In Microsoft Word, for instance, holding down the Control key and pressing the up or down arrow will move you to the beginning of a line. In Acrobat Reader, pressing Control and the left or right arrows move you back and forth to different pages. In iCal, holding Control and pressing the left or right arrow keys moves you to different days of the week (or weeks or months, depending on the calendar view).

Another useful keyboard combo is holding down the Shift key while pressing the arrow keys—this is generally how you can select or highlight text in a word processor document or objects in other applications, so that you can then perform commands on that selection. Using Shift and the arrow keys, for instance, you could highlight a paragraph of text that you then cut using ⌘+x—all without ever handling the mouse.

Switching Applications

One powerful keyboard combination is ⌘+Tab, which can be used to switch between applications without requiring you to grab the mouse and head down to the Dock. When you press ⌘+Tab and hold it down, you'll see a floating window that shows the icons for all applications that are currently running (see Figure 4.2). Press the Tab key again to highlight an application's icon, or keep pressing Tab until you reach the application to which you want to switch.

TIP

If you go flying past the icon you wanted to select, you can press ⌘+Shift+Tab to move backward in the list. You can also use the mouse to select an item, if you have your mousing hand free.

FIGURE 4.2
You can switch applications quickly using the ⌘ and Tab keys.

Release the keys and you'll switch to that application.

One of the cool things about the way this trick works is that Mac OS X remembers the application that you most recently switched from, as well as the application you switched to. This can be handy for things like Internet research. If you're in Word, for instance, and you switch to Safari to look something up, you can quickly press and release ⌘+Tab to return to Word when you're done in Safari. If you want to switch back to Safari, quickly press ⌘+Tab again. That works for whatever the last two applications you switch between are, until you switch again to some other app.

Using Exposé and Dashboard

Exposé was added to Mac OS X in version 10.3, giving a new, visual way for you to switch not only between applications, but among all open windows in applications. In a word, it's a way to deal with window *clutter*. Plus, it's a cool-looking effect—hey, we're talking Macintosh here.

And now, in Mac OS X 10.4, Apple has added Dashboard, which uses Exposé-like technology to give you access to small applications, most of which access bits of information from the Internet such as flight times, weather, and an online dictionary.

Using Exposé

Exposé is actually three different tricks in one—using keystrokes or special mouse movements, you can focus on all of the windows that are open on your Mac, view all the windows for the current application, or move all your windows out of the way and access the desktop. Figure 4.3 shows Exposé in action—shown are four open windows in Safari.

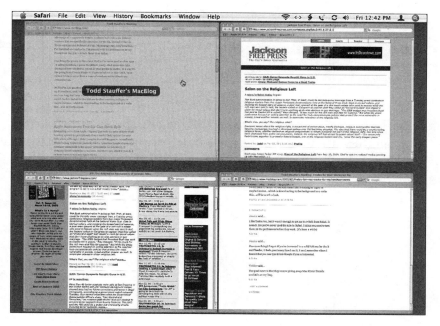

FIGURE 4.3
Exposé enables you to visually switch between an application's open windows.

In the first two scenarios, invoking the Exposé command causes the windows on the screen to get small enough that they all fit on the screen; you can then use the mouse pointer to select a different window. It's handy for quickly looking at your active windows if you need to see if something has changed or for quickly switching between open windows in applications.

In the third scenario, the windows all slide off the screen so that you can access the desktop and Finder commands—all of your windows snap back into place when you invoke the command again or if you switch to another application.

The easiest way to work with Exposé is to use the default function keys:

- Press the F9 key once to "zoom back" to show all open windows on your Mac. This is a serious clutter management tool—once you have a number of applications open on your Mac at once, no doubt you have many different windows layered on top of one another. You can quickly get at a particular window by clicking it with the mouse, or press F9 to jump back to your previous window.

TIP

While you're in the "Exposé effect," you can use the arrow keys to move from window to window, and then select a window with the Return key to turn off the effect and work with that selected window.

- Press the F10 key to see only the windows that are open in your current application. You can then use the mouse to select one of the windows, or use the arrow keys to move around and the Return key to select the window you want to view. When you do, that window comes back front and center and the Exposé effect is turned off.

TIP

You can press the Tab key while you're in "F10 mode" to move from application to application and, in each case, you'll see all of the open windows for the application that you switch to.

- Press the F11 key and you'll see all of your open windows crowd off to the side of your display. Now, you have access to your Mac's desktop and the Finder; you can, if you like, double-click a folder, open a new Finder window, or even delete something, and then press F11 again to move back to the window where you were working (Figure 4.4 shows this last Exposé effect in action.)

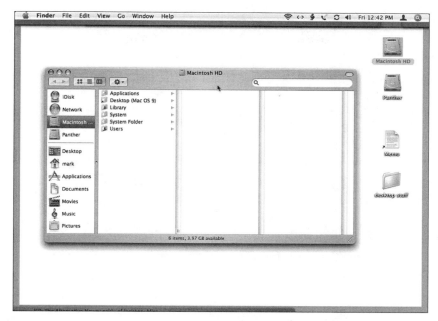

FIGURE 4.4
The F11 Exposé effect gives you quick access to the desktop and Finder.

One reason for switching quickly to the Finder is a cool one—you can press F11, click and drag a file or folder, and then press F11 again and use that icon in your document window or otherwise drop it into your application. It's a quick way to add an image to some document windows, for instance, or to insert a file into an application window (say, for an email attachment, or to view an HTML document in a Safari window—that sort of thing).

If you're not keen on using the F9–F11 keys for Exposé, you can opt to use "hot corners" instead. Launch System Preferences and open the Dashboard & Exposé pane. Toward the top of the window you'll see the Active Screen Corners menus; from those menus you can choose actions that take place when you move your mouse point right up into a particular corner—see Figure 4.5. (An "active screen corner" is also sometimes called a *hotspot*.) Note that this interface also enables you to change the keys that you use for Exposé and Dashboard (covered next), *and* you can set hot corners for turning on your screen saver or making sure the screen saver *doesn't* turn on.

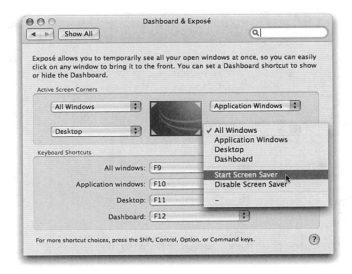

FIGURE 4.5

You can choose your "hot corners" on the screen to activate Exposé (or Dashboard, or. a screen saver).

Using Dashboard

New to Mac OS X 10.4 is Dashboard, a fun little add-on that builds on the Exposé technology to give you a little something different. Dashboard features a number of *widgets* that act as small applications, many of which retrieve information from the Internet, and all of which have a handy little function or two. What's most unique is that this "dashboard" of widgets is available by pressing the F12 key, by default—when you do, the background is dimmed, as with Exposé, and the widgets appear onscreen, as shown in Figure 4.6.

TIP

On iBooks and PowerBooks, you have to hold down the Fn key while pressing F12; otherwise, you'll eject the disc from your CD/DVD drive. Or, in the Keyboard and Mouse pane of System Preferences, you can select the Keyboard tab and turn on the option Use the F1–F12 Keys to Control Software Features. Now, pressing F12 invokes Dashboard and pressing Fn-F12 is required for the Eject command.

The first thing you'll probably want to do is explore and add widgets. At the bottom of the Dashboard screen is a small plus sign icon. Click it, and you'll see other widgets appear. Click and drag one of the widgets from the listing out to the dashboard to see it expand, or click the arrow icons to see what other widgets you have available.

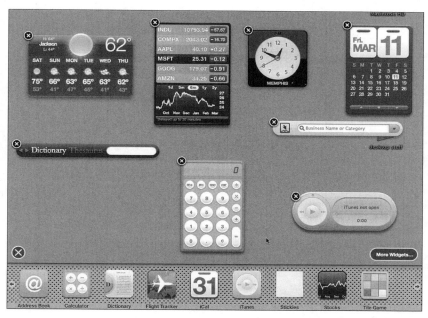

FIGURE 4.6
Press F12 and your Dashboard appears, complete with handy little "widgets."

While you're in this "adding mode," you'll see small "X" icons next to the widgets that are already on your Dashboard; click one of those to remove the widget from the Dashboard. You can always drag it back in if desired.

And, you can use Dashboard to locate and download addition widgets from Apple's website—just click the More Widgets button that appears on the screen and your web browser will launch and take your to Apple's special widget website. Download widgets and they'll install automatically.

When you're done adding widgets, click the large "X" icon at the bottom left of the screen and it will "roll" back into its former "+" icon while closing the small row of icons. Isn't that just darling?

Once you've got a widget on the screen, you may wonder what to do with it. If you need to set some options for the widgets—like your time zone for the clock or your local address for the weather widget—then mouse over the widget until you see the small "*i*" icon appear. Most widgets that have options have that little "info" icon. That should cause the widget to "flip" around, so that you can see its settings. Make changes, then click the OK button.

Automator: Making Magic Happen

Have you ever thought to yourself, "These things are called computers—shouldn't they be more *automatic*?" That seems to be what Apple was thinking when the company's software engineers rolled Automator into Mac OS X 10.4. Automator is a cool new application that enables you to get your *other* Mac applications to do certain things automatically. It works particularly well with Apple's applications (including all the iLife applications and programs such as iCal and Mail) but it also works with a number of other applications, particularly those that were designed to work specifically with Automator.

To get started, locate Automator in your Applications folder and launch it. When you do, you should see a window that looks like Figure 4.7—it's not totally unlike iTunes or iPhoto. On the left side, you'll see a Library column, where you can choose from Automator-compatible applications. The next column lists the actions you can accomplish with a given application. At the bottom is an information pane, and on the right side is the main Workflow pane.

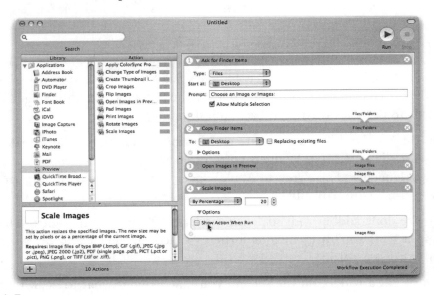

FIGURE 4.7
The Automator interface allows you to build "workflows" that make certain tasks automatic.

What Automator allows you to do is take a repetitive task—something you seem to be doing all of the time using the same set of actions or motions—and try to help you make that happen more automatically. You do that using the predefined actions to create a workflow.

The best way to show off Automator is with an example. Let's say that as part of your work, you often have to scale digital photos to a smaller size, and that you're sick of first opening up Preview, then scaling the image to 480 pixels tall, and so on. Well, instead of all those steps, you can build a workflow that does that for you. Here's how this example would work:

1. In Automator, begin by selecting the Finder in the Library column.

2. In the action column, locate the action "Ask for Finder Items," and then drag it into the Workflow pane. You'll see that it appears as the #1 item. Note it has options—you can click the disclosure triangle to see them. In this case you can choose a location where the Choose Files dialog box will open up to, the prompt, and you can decide whether you're going to allow multiple files to be selected.

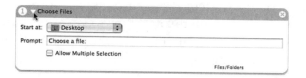

3. Now locate the action Copy Finder Items and drag that into the workflow. In the To menu, choose Desktop. This way you're working with a copy of the image file that is opened, not the original.

4. Next, select Preview in the Library pane, locate the action Scale Images, and drag it to the workflow. Click its disclosure triangle and choose your settings.

That's all it takes! If you'd like to test your workflow, click the Run button at the top-right of the window and Automator will step through the actions that you've specified.

When it looks like you've got a good workflow going, choose File, Save. In the Save dialog sheet, name the file and then select from two options in the File Format menu—Workflow or Application. Save the file as a Workflow if you want to be able to open it up and edit it again—if you're simply not done with it yet. (You can also opt to save it as a Workflow if you don't mind opening Automator and clicking Run each time you want to invoke the workflow.)

If your workflow is set properly and you're ready to run with it, choose Application in the File Format menu. Click Save and a new application icon will be created that represents your workflow.

> **TIP**
>
> You'll probably find that it's handy to turn on the Show Action When Run option on many of your steps, particularly if you end up saving your workflow as an application—otherwise the workflow can seem to be doing very little when it doesn't interact much with the user.

Workflows in Automator can be quite a bit more complicated; in the Library pane is a folder of Example Workflows that you might want to look through and study a bit to figure out how they work. Otherwise, it just takes a task that needs to be automated and some creative thought as to how to go about doing that!

The System Preferences Basics

We've touched briefly on the System Preferences application, but it's a place that you may spend some time in, so it's good to know how to get around and make things happen. System Preferences is the one application where you'll do almost 90% of your configuring and option-choosing for Mac OS X. Aside from some special little utility applications, the System Preferences is one-stop-shopping for settings that range from configuring your Internet connection to determining the general appearance of your Mac's interface. You can also dig into some serious stuff in here, such as file security and encryption settings, creating new user accounts and configuring your Mac's accessibility (Apple calls them "universal access") technologies that may help you work with your Mac if you have certain physical challenges.

In this section I'd like to take a general look at how to work with System Preferences and then dig into some of the settings that we probably won't be covering much in other chapters.

Meet System Preferences

You've got a few different ways to launch System Preferences. If you see its big Apple-with-a-lightswitch icon on the Dock, you can click that, or you can go find it in the Applications folder. The easiest way, though, is to choose System Preferences from the Apple menu. Doing so launches the System Preferences application and shows you the icons for each of the available *preference panes* (see Figure 4.8).

NOTE

You'll sometimes get to System Preferences by selecting the Preferences command for a particular item, such as Control+clicking the Dock and choosing Dock Preferences, or Control+clicking on the desktop and choosing Change Desktop Background, which launches the Desktop & Screensaver pane of System Preferences.

FIGURE 4.8

System Preferences is a special application that gives you access to preference panes where you set options for your Mac.

Each pane has its own set of options—most of them make sense, and some of them can get downright complex. To select one, simply click its icon once and the window will reconfigure to display that pane's items and options. To return to the full list, you can click the Show All button at the top of the window; the window also has Back and Forward buttons that can be used to trace your steps through the panes.

By default the preference panes are arranged by categories, but you can change that. To do so, choose View, Organize Alphabetically and you'll see an alphabetical list of the preference panes without the category headings.

The System Preferences window also has a search box, which can be used to help locate the correct pane for a given option you need to set. Simply begin typing in the search box and it will help you to narrow down the item you're looking for, as shown in Figure 4.9.

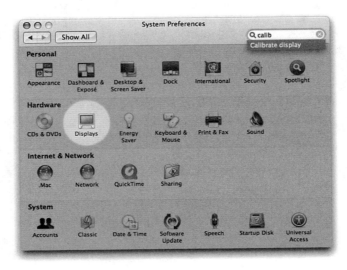

FIGURE 4.9
You can search System Preferences to figure out what preference pane to use.

When you're done with System Preferences, you can click the close button in the window to quit the application, or choose System Preferences, Quit System Preferences from the menu.

In some preference panes, you need an administrator's account and password in order to make changes. This is done to keep an unauthorized user from making changes that affect the entire Mac OS system—even items such as changing the clock's settings or the date for the internal calendar are protected.

You'll know when an item is protected when you see the padlock icon in the preference pane's window. If the padlock is closed, it means certain items in the preference pane are locked and can't be altered without entering an administrator's name and password.

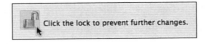

If you *are* an administrator, and you're logged in as such, most of those padlocks will be unlocked unless you specifically lock them. You're free to do that; click an open lock and that preference pane will require an administrator's username and password before they'll be editable again.

If a padlock is locked, click it and a dialog will appear. Enter the username and password for an administrator and click the OK button. If they're accepted, the padlock will swing to the "unlocked" position and you'll be free to make edits in the preference pane.

Exploring the Panes

Many of the preference panes will be covered elsewhere in this book, since many offer involved settings and options that we need to discuss. So, in this section I'd like to quickly touch on all of them, so that we mention some of the panes that we won't be talking about elsewhere, too. Here's a look:

- .Mac—The .Mac pane is where you can enter your .Mac account information so that the Finder and other applications can access your iDisk and other .Mac tools automatically. .Mac also houses some other options for how your iDisk is managed and how applications such as Address Book and iCal synchronize data via your .Mac account. More on .Mac in Chapters 6, 8, and 9.

- Accounts—We'll cover this one in the next section; the Accounts pane is where you head to set up your own or other users accounts, passwords, and personalized stuff for your Mac.

- Appearance—The Appearance pane is used to allow you to make some basic decisions about your Mac's windows, scrollbars, and color scheme. You can also choose how many items appear in the "Recent" menus and some other minor interface tweaks.

- CDs & DVDs—Use this pane to decide what happens by default when a CD or DVD in inserted in your Mac. You can set different actions for blank discs, data discs, video discs, and so on.

- Classic—The Classic pane is used to manage the Classic environment, which is necessary if you want to launch and work with an application that was written for a Mac OS version written prior to Mac OS X. See Appendix A, "Classic and Classic Applications," for more.

- Dashboard & Exposé—As discussed earlier in this chapter, this pane lets you choose hot corners and keyboard shortcuts for these features.

- Date & Time—Use this pane to set the clock and calendar that are internal to your Mac, or set them to use an Apple time server to get "Internet time" settings automatically. On the Time Zone tab, you can select your current time zone, and on the Clock tab, you can make choices about the clock that appears on your Mac's menu bar (or, if you choose, in a window.)

- Desktop & Screensaver—On this pane, you can choose an image for your Mac's desktop or switch to the Screen Saver tab and choose a screen saver from the list. You can also choose hot corners from this pane.

- Displays—On the Displays tab, you can choose settings for your Mac display and you can configure multiple displays, if you have them. You can also calibrate your Mac's color; more on this in Chapter 5, "Work Those Peripherals."

- Dock—As discussed in Chapter 3, "Applications and the Dock," the Dock pane is used to set your preferences for the Dock.

- Energy Saver—These options allow you to decide when your Mac goes into sleep mode, which is a low-power mode that doesn't totally shut your Mac down, so that you can get back to work almost instantly. You can also determine when your Mac's display "sleeps" and takes other power saving measures. Dig further into the options and you can decide if and when your Mac will automatically turn itself on and off, using the Schedule button on the Options tab. (If you have a portable, you'll find a number of settings in here for making that portable run on battery power more efficiently.)

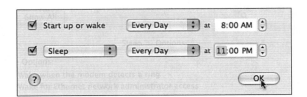

- International—On this tab, you can choose the primary language for your Mac, and you can select different currency and date formats and even choose a different keyboard layout. Note that when you choose more than one keyboard layout (via the Input Menu tab), a menu can be made to appear on the menu bar that enables you to switch between the different keyboard languages or layouts.

- Keyboard & Mouse—In this pane, you can set the reaction speeds and other options for your keyboard and mouse. (You might experiment with the Tracking Speed on the Mouse tab if you feel like your mouse is too slow or too fast.) On the Keyboard Shortcuts tab, you can turn on and off a number of universal keyboard commands that are built in to Mac OS X—you can also *learn* about a lot of them, which is handy.

- Network—The Network pane is used to configure your network and Internet connections; it's discussed in detail in Chapters 8 and 11.

- Print & Fax—This pane is used to configure printers and your modem for faxing; we'll cover it in Chapter 5.

- QuickTime—The QuickTime pane is used to set preferences for viewing QuickTime movies and accessing them over the Internet. You'll also use the pane to enter registration information if you upgrade to QuickTime Pro. (See http://www.quicktime.com/ for details.)

- Security—The Security pane is used to set a variety of options that are designed to keep your data from prying eyes. Chapter 14, "Securing Your Mac," will dig pretty deeply into this pane.

- Sharing—The Sharing pane is used to turn on networking and Internet servers so that remote Macs can access files on your Mac. It's discussed in Chapter 11, "Build a Home Office Network."

- Software Update—This pane is used to connect to Apple's update servers and check for any downloadable additions or updates to your system software. Chapter 13, "Common Problems and Solutions," covers it in detail.

- Sound—On the Sound pane, you can change the alert sound that plays when your Mac needs your attention, and you can set the alert and main Output volume levels. You can also choose the output devices (speakers or headphones) and input devices (internal or external microphones or other sources) that you want to use for playback and recording.

- Speech—The Speech pane can be used to turn on and configure two different technologies on your Mac. The first, Speech Recognition, is a technology that allows you to speak commands to your Mac and, hopefully, get it to understand you. You do that by turning on Speakable Items on the Speech Recognition tab, and then calibrating the microphone and testing things out. On the smaller Commands tab, you can choose the set of commands that you want to try and use for Speakable items. On the Text to Speech tab, you can choose a speaking voice for your Mac and turn on various items that can be spoken aloud through your Mac's speakers by the computer voice.

- Spotlight—On the Spotlight pane, you can choose which categories of found files and documents will be displayed, and you can change the order of them. On the Privacy tab, you can add any folders that shouldn't be searched by Spotlight. (Spotlight was covered in Chapter 2.)

- Startup Disk—On this pane, you can choose the volume that you would like to use to start up your Mac—it can be your Mac's main hard disk, or it can be an external disk, an inserted optical disc, or even a network volume. You can also use this pane to put your Mac into Target Disk Mode, which enables it to act as an external FireWire hard disk for another Mac.

- Universal Access—On the Universal Access pane, you can set various options that can be helpful if you're sight or hearing impaired or if you have certain challenges to your motor skills. The Mac has built into it a number of utilities that can useful for overcoming challenges.

User Accounts and Fast User Switching

By default, your Mac has one user account—the one you created when you started up the Mac for the first time and ran through the Setup Assistant. That account is an administrator account and you probably don't log in to your account at startup—instead, your Mac probably logs in to it automatically, and goes straight to your desktop when you power up your Mac after it's been shut down or restarted.

But, things can be very different from that. First, you can have multiple users on your Mac—the advantage is that each user can have his or her own desktop, home folder, special document folders, and a little private space away from others on your Mac. Second, those users needn't all have administrative capabilities; you can have users who are "Standard" users who can do anything but access system files and settings, or you can create "Managed" users who don't even have access to every application and utility on the system.

Once you've created those users, you can use Fast User Switching to switch between them without logging out first—that's handy for making the use of multiple accounts more practical and a little less time consuming.

Creating User Accounts

If you have some users to whom you want to give individual user accounts, it's easy enough to do. Start by launching System Preferences and selecting the Accounts icon. In the Accounts pane, you'll see a list of your current accounts on the left, complete with plus ("+") and minus ("–") icons at the bottom of it. To add a new account, click the plus icon. A dialog sheet appears, in which you can enter information about your new account, including full user name, a short user name, a password, password verification, and a password hint. You can also choose to make this user an administrator. (Figure 4.10 shows adding a new user in the Accounts pane.) Click Create Account to add that account to your list.

TIP

Next to the Password entry box is a small key icon, which you can click to get expert help from your Mac on choosing a secure password.

Once an account is created, you can edit the account by selecting it in the list and changing the entry boxes that are highlighted for change. (The exception is usually the Short Name entry box, since the Short Name can't be changed for a user account.) Click the Change Password button to change the password for this account; note that you can turn the Allow User to Administer This Computer option on and off. If this option is on, the user is an administrator; if the option is off, the user is a "regular" user.

On the Picture tab, you can choose or change the picture that will be used to identify this user account in the Login window as well as other places, such as in the Address Book and in iChat windows. You can select one of the images that appears on the right side of the window or click the Edit button to launch the Images window. There you can click Choose to open an image from your hard disk, you can drag an image from the Finder into the window, or you can click the Camera icon to take a snapshot of yourself using a digital camcorder or an iSight camera and the snapshot is used as your user picture.

FIGURE 4.10
When you add a user, a dialog sheet appears asking for his vitals.

TIP

The image in the Images window can be clicked and dragged around in the window to position it, and the slider at the bottom of the screen can be used to zoom in on it. In that way you can "crop" the image so that only the parts you want to use appear as the user image.

If you're looking at your own account, you'll see the Login Items tab, which is used to specify applications that should automatically launch when this user account logs in. Some of these may be placed here automatically by applications or utilities—for instance, Virex, the virus application that Apple makes available with a .Mac subscription, likes to set itself to launch automatically every time you log in, so that it can automatically check for viruses. You may or may not want it to do that.

To add an application that will launch automatically, either drag its icon into this list or click the plus ("+") icon and choose the application in the Open dialog that appears. To remove an item from the list, highlight it and click the minus ("–") icon. Notice also that you can click the check box next to the item to "hide" it—that causes it to launch, but in the background without opening a window on your screen. The hidden application can still be seen in the Dock and switched to when you're ready to use it.

On the Parental Controls tab, you'll see options *if* you're viewing an account that is not an administrator's account. In that case, you can make it a *managed* account—one that has limited access to various applications and utilities. Figure 4.11 shows the parental controls screen.

FIGURE 4.11

For a Standard user, you can turn on parental controls, making them a Managed user.

To limit a user's access to a particular part of the Mac experience, click the check box next to the item you want to manage. That turns on the parental control; next, click the Configure button and you'll see the options associated with that particular control. (In some cases, the dialog sheet may appear without your clicking Configure.) Here's a quick look at each:

- Mail—With this control, you can specify the email addresses with whom this user is allowed to communicate. (In the dialog sheet that appears, click the plus icon to add a person's email address.) Other people must get permission, first, via a permission email that is sent to the address you specify.

- Finder & System—Turn this option on and click the Configure button if you'd like to limit this user's access to certain applications, folders, and Finder capabilities. It can get a little complicated, but it starts with the decision of whether you want to give the user Some Limits or show them the Simple Finder. With the Simple Finder, the user can only open the applications you specify and save documents created in those applications; they can't modify the Dock, burn data discs, and so on. If you specify the Some Limits option, then you can select from a number of options that limit what this user can and can't do, as shown in Figure 4.12.

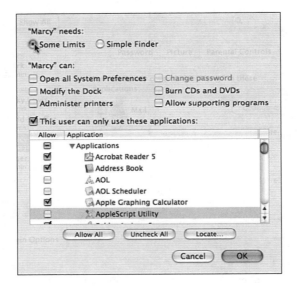

FIGURE 4.12
With Some Limits turned on, you can pick and choose what you want this user to be able to work with.

- iChat—This option allows you to limit the people with whom this person is allowed to chat via iChat; simply turn it on and click Configure. In the dialog sheet that appears, click the plus icon to add a "buddy" from your Address Book, or click New Person to add a new authorized "buddy."
- Safari—Setting bookmarks that a user account can access is a two step process. First, you need to turn on the parental control here in the Accounts pane. Then, log in as that user and open up Safari. There, any website that's already a

bookmark or that you add as a bookmark (using an administrator password) can be viewed by the user without interference. If the user tries to visit a site that isn't currently bookmarked, the user will see a page that says the site is blocked, complete with an Add Website button that allows you to add that site on a case-by-case basis.

NOTE

> This Safari blocking system is handy for young children, but there are some loopholes. Note that if you allow the user to access a web search engine, such as Google or Yahoo, those sites often show results in frames—particularly when you search for photos or multimedia—which Safari will not block. It's possible that some of those results would be objectionable, unless you also dig into the search engine's options and set up passwords and restrictions.

- Dictionary—Turn on this option if you'd like to block the user from looking up certain objectionable words in the Dictionary that's available via the Dashboard.

Login Options and Fast User Switching

Also in the Accounts pane, you'll find the Login Options button (at the bottom of the Accounts list), where you can set some global options for how your Mac deals with the login process. Those include

- Automatically Log In As—This option, when turned on, enables you to choose an account that the Mac will automatically log in to, without stopping first at the Login window. This is more convenient but less secure.

- Display Login Window As—A list of users is easier to select from, but if you show just the name and password entry boxes, the system is more secure, because a hacker would have to guess at the names as well as the passwords.

- Show Restart, Sleep and Shut Down Buttons—This is another security option; if someone confronted with the Login window can't restart or shut down the machine, it makes it a little more difficult for them to attempt to restart the machine with a startup disc, which could then be used to change passwords. (It doesn't make it *much* tougher, though, because that nefarious soul could always recycle the power to your Mac, if he has access to the Power button and/or power cable.)

- Show Input Menu in Login Window—Turn this on if you'd like the user to be able to choose from different keyboard layouts when viewing the Login window; this is handy if you've got users who access the same Mac in different languages or using different keyboard layouts (like Dvorak).

- Use VoiceOver at Login Window—Turn this on to get VoiceOver's spoken cues in the Login window.

- Show Password Hints—It's less secure to show a user's password hints, but can be handy if they forgot their passwords and need some prompting in order to gain access to the Mac.

- Enable Fast User Switching—Turn on this option and your multiple user accounts can be "active" at the same time, so that you can switch between them without logging out. Turning on this option places a menu item on your menubar, so you can use the View As menu to decide if that menu item should be an icon or the name of the current user.

  If you enable Fast User switching, it means you can allow another user on your Mac to quickly jump over to his or her account and do some work without requiring you to log out of your account first. What's coolest about that is that you don't have to close down your open documents and applications—the switch lets the other user do his or her thing, and then you can switch back and keep working.

TIP

It's always a good idea to save changes in your documents before switching to a new user account, as an administrative user has the authority to shut down your account if it's in the background and that admin attempts to restart the Mac.

If you have Fast User Switching activated, putting it to use couldn't be simpler. Just mouse up to the Fast User Switching menu (it's either an icon of a person's silhouette or the name of the current user) and choose the user account to which you want to switch.

Now you'll see a login window; enter the password for this user and click Log In. If it's accepted then that user's workspace will load and he or she will be ready to work.

At any point, you can return to the Fast User Switching menu and choose another user account to log in to, or you can choose an account that's already active. When you choose an active account (it'll have a check mark next to its name), you'll be asked for a password; enter it and click Log In. In an animated rotation effect, you'll see the display switch back to that user account and that user's applications and documents will become active.

At any time, you can log out of one user account and you'll be returned to the Login screen, where other users (whether active or not) can log in and access their accounts. You can also, at any time, choose Login Window from the Fast User Switching menu, which brings up the Login window so that you can access other accounts. And it's a handy way to quickly secure your Mac if you need to get up and leave it unattended, as well as to make it clear to other users that the Mac is available for them to log in to.

Chapter 5

Work Those Peripherals

Eventually you're going to need to (or want to) connect some stuff to your Mac. Whether you're interested in printing, customizing your display, or working with a digital camera or camcorder, you'll find that most of your connections are handled using the variety of ports and slots on the back and side of your Mac. In this chapter, we'll take a look at the technology behind those ports, along with the utility programs and interface elements designed to help you work with and manage your peripherals.

Hardware Ports and Support

The Mac has a number of ports that can be used for upgrades and peripherals. By *ports*, I mean the connectors on the side or back of your Mac that enable you to connect other hardware to your Mac, including printers, broadband modems, mobile phones, personal digital assistants (PDAs), and so on. There's tons of stuff that has some capacity for communicating with your Mac, so the question becomes how to connect them via a port or, in some cases, using a wireless connection.

The key to understanding ports is to know the technology that each port uses and what the strengths of a particular type of port are. (You might also need to know what they look like—Figure 5.1 shows the ports on an iMac G4.)

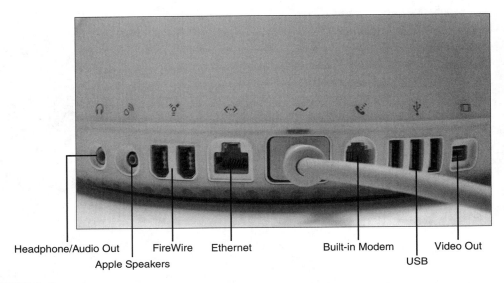

Headphone/Audio Out   FireWire   Ethernet   Built-in Modem   Video Out
Apple Speakers   USB

FIGURE 5.1
Here are the ports on the back of an iMac; they're representative of the array of ports you'll generally see on a modern Mac.

Here's a quick look at the basic ports you'll encounter on a modern Mac:

- USB—Universal Serial Bus (USB) is an industrywide standard for connecting all sorts of peripherals to a Macintosh. And since it's also the standard for Windows PCs, many peripherals work with both Windows computers and Macs these days. USB has both low-speed and high-speed variants, as discussed in the sidebar "Understanding USB Speeds and Standards."

UNDERSTANDING USB SPEEDS AND STANDARDS

You'll encounter two USB standards when you're shopping for devices. USB 1.1 is the older standard, capable of transferring data at speeds up to 12 megabits per second (Mbps), or about 1.5 megabytes per second (MBps). While there are some "pocket" hard disks and other devices that are designed to work with USB 1.1, it's used more often with devices that don't require as much throughput, such as printers and scanners.

The USB 2.0 standard offers speeds up to 480Mbps, or about 60MB per second. That's fast enough for external hard disks and the like, and such devices are very popular because USB 2.0 is the primary high-speed connection standard for Windows-compatible PCs, too. The two types of USB use the same port, so a USB 2.0 device can usually connect to a USB 1.1 port, even though it may run quite a bit slower than intended.

Although your Mac may only have two or three USB ports, each USB bus can actually handle up to 127 USB devices. So if you need to connect more devices, your best bet is a to get a USB hub, which enables you to connect multiple peripherals to a single USB port on your Mac. (Note that the Apple USB keyboard is a USB hub, offering two ports. One is generally used for a mouse, but the other can be used for any USB device that doesn't require power from the USB connection.)

- FireWire—Apple actually invented this technology, which is a high-speed connection that takes up where USB leaves off. Called IEEE-1394 by the "PC" world, FireWire is used most often for connections to digital camcorders, although it's popular for external hard disks, burners, and even RAID arrays (large, redundant storage), and devices such as iPods, particularly on the Mac platform. (Apple also makes an adapter for iPods that offers a USB 2.0 connection designed primarily for Windows-compatible PCs, although you can use it with USB 2.0-equipped Macs.) FireWire comes in two flavors—original FireWire has a connection bandwidth of about 400Mbps, or 50MB per second; FireWire 800 is double that at 800Mbps or a theoretical 100MB per second.

NOTE

Like USB, FireWire can handle many more devices per port than you have available connectors. Unlike USB devices, FireWire devices can be "chained" together, so that you can plug one FireWire device into another, and so on, as long as the chain isn't broken and the first device is plugged into the Mac. That's why many FireWire devices have multiple FireWire ports. If necessary and desired, you can get a FireWire hub that allows you to connect multiple devices at once.

- Ethernet—All modern Macs have an Ethernet port that's designed primarily for wired networking. Ethernet can be 10BaseT (10Mbps), 100BaseT (100Mbps), or Gigabit Ethernet, which offers 1Gbps of throughput, or approximately 150MB per second. Ethernet is used almost exclusively for connecting to a network hub or switch, or to a device such as a DSL or Cable modem for high-speed Internet access.

- Video out—Nearly all modern Macs offer some sort of video out port; what's different is the standard that's supported. For years the basic standard has been VGA (Video Graphics Array), which allows for an analog connection to an external video monitor. The more popular approach these days is the DVI (Digital Video Interface) port, which connects to modern digital flat-panel displays without making a lower-quality digital-to-analog conversion. Apple in the past has had their own version of DVI, called ADC (Apple Digital Connector), which included USB, power, and video in the same cable; Apple has since switched to the more standard DVI port on the Power Macintosh G5 and the Mac mini.

NOTE

PowerBooks, iBooks, eMacs, and iMacs all have video out, as well, which is designed for the most part to enable you to give presentations or display the computer's image on another screen (often called video mirroring). The most recent models of these Macs have a special "mini-VGA" (shown in Figure 5.1) or "mini-DVI" port that requires an adapter to connect to an external display; check your Mac's specs (and the box it came in) for such an adapter. It's also worth knowing that many of these models can use a different adapter to display images on a TV screen or to a similar video device using the Apple Video Adapter, which offers an S-Video or Composite video connector, meaning you can plug it into most TVs or video players.

- Audio out—All Macs have a headphone port of some sort that often doubles as a line-out port for connecting your Mac to a stereo system or similar receiver.
- Speaker out—Many Mac models support special speakers made by Apple (and some made by other manufacturers specifically for Apple).
- Audio in—The latest Power Macintosh G5 models include both digital (S/PDIF) and analog audio in and out; some Power Macintosh G4 models (and many iBooks and PowerBooks) only support USB for audio-in connections.

NOTE

S/PDIF stands for Sony Phillips Digital Interface, and it's common for use with professional audio equipment and with many home theater components.

- Built-in modem—Finally, many Mac models have a port designed to attach to a standard phone line via an RJ-11 connector. That's to give the internal modem access to a phone line for dial-up Internet/AOL connections or to make use of the Mac's faxing capabilities.

So, those are the ports. In the sections that follow, we'll take a closer look at configuring and working with various types of peripherals and devices, after a quick detour through the System Profiler.

Checking Out System Profiler

The System Profiler is a special utility application included with Mac OS X that enables you to quickly get a sense of the devices that are attached to—and installed in—your Mac. If you aren't quite sure of the specifications of your Mac, or anytime you come upon a new model that you'd like to learn about—you can launch System Profiler to get a better sense of your Mac's vital signs (see Figure 5.2).

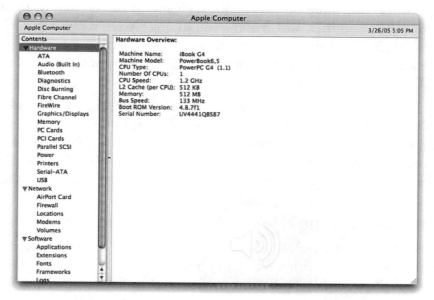

FIGURE 5.2

The System Profiler is useful for learning all sorts of technical details about your Mac.

You can launch System Profiler in one of two ways. First, you can locate its icon in the Utilities folder inside the Applications folder and double-click it there. Or, you can open the About This Mac window (Apple, About This Mac) and then click the More Info button.

To explore a particular set of statistics about your Mac, simply click something in the Contents list. You can select FireWire in the Contents list, for instance, to get a sense of what sort of FireWire support your Mac has. (My iBook G4 says it only supports "Up to 400 Mb/sec" meaning it doesn't have FireWire 800 ports.) When you do, you'll see information about the port that you've selected as well as any devices that have been detected on that port. This can be handy because you might find that System Profiler will detect a device that's connected to your Mac even if it isn't currently "working" in the Finder or elsewhere.

Further down the Contents list, you'll find tons of interesting stuff that you can check about your Mac, including the Network entries, which enable you to quickly check the settings for your network or Internet connections (see Chapter 11, "Build a Home Office Network," for more on networking). Finally, at the bottom of the list are a number of software entries, which allow you to quickly see what's installed on your Mac as well as give you quick access to some important system components such as the logs. (Click the Logs entry under Software in the Contents list to gain access to some of Mac OS X's little techie log files.)

All in all, getting to know System Profiler can be handy when you're dealing with external devices because you can get a little more information about devices that might be giving you a problem. If you ever ask yourself something like, *hey, I plugged this thing into my Mac, why can't I access it?* then you can start in System Profiler to at least get a sense of whether your Mac, on a fundamental level, has recognized the device.

Printing and Faxing

Printing is a big deal to most of us Mac users—fortunately, if you've gotten yourself a Mac-compatible printer, getting set up to print isn't really that difficult. Once you're connected, you'll use the Print dialog box and the Page Setup commands in the Mac OS X to actually send jobs to your printer and manage their output.

That same Print dialog box is the heart of your ability to send a fax from your Mac, and, if you have your Mac connected to an outside phone line, you can receive them as well. We'll cover that in this section along with printing.

Set Up Your Printer

There are two basic types of printers you'll deal with from the perspective of how they connect to your Mac—USB printers and Ethernet or AirPort-based network printers.

Most lower-cost printers that are Mac-compatible connect to your Mac using USB—that includes everything from extremely inexpensive inkjet printers to some relatively low-cost color laser printers. All it takes to work with a printer like this is a USB cable connected from your Mac to the USB port on the printer itself. (Note that this will often be a USB A-to-B cable, since many USB peripherals have the smaller, square "B" USB port instead of the "A" port you find on the side or back of your Mac.)

To connect to an Ethernet network printer, all you have to do is configure your Mac to connect directly to the printer via an Ethernet cable or set your Mac up to connect to the same network that the printer is connected to. That's true even if your Mac gains access to your local network using a wireless AirPort connection—if that AirPort connection allows your Mac access to the Ethernet hub or switch that's connected to the printer, you should be able to access the printer from your Mac.

NOTE

Chapter 11 covers networking in more detail. Note that in some cases you may need a special Ethernet crossover cable in order to connect your Mac directly to an Ethernet printer. (Macs with Gigabit Ethernet ports don't require crossover cables.)

Once you've got your Mac connected to the printer or the printer connected to the network, you're ready to set it up. You do that by launching the Printer Setup Utility, which you can do by double-clicking its icon in the Utilities folder inside the Application folder or by clicking the plus ("+") icon on the Printing tab in the Print & Fax pane of System Preferences.

In the Printer browser window, the first thing you'll see is a list of the printers that your Mac finds automatically for you to access. If you have a single USB printer connected to your Mac, that's likely what you'll see in the list; if you have multiple network printers available, you might see those instead. Figure 5.3 shows the printers that my Mac can see.

NOTE

To see printers that use the AppleTalk language—which means, largely, older Apple and Mac-compatible PostScript laser printers—you need to have AppleTalk turned on for the port that you use for networking. In the example shown in Figure 5.3, you're looking at my iBook, which connects to my local network wirelessly using AirPort. So, I selected my AirPort card in the Network pane of System Preferences and, on the AppleTalk tab, turned on AppleTalk. AppleTalk can only be on for one network port at a time, but when it's on, you'll be able to detect AppleTalk printers on your network.

FIGURE 5.3

The Printer Browser, part of the Printer Setup Utility, is where you'll locate the printers that your Mac can communicate with so that you can set them up.

To configure your Mac to connect to one of those printers, select the printer in the list and give it a name in the Name entry box (if you'd like to change what's shown there). In the Print Using menu, choose a driver or description for the printer—you'll find that you can select the printer manufacturer first, then scroll through a list of drivers or descriptions. Ideally, you'll find a driver's name that's similar or exactly the same as your printer model, although you may have reason to choose a different driver.

TIP

You can choose Other if you'd like to access an Open dialog box and manually locate a printer driver or description that's on your hard disk. That's probably only recommended if your printer manufacturer's documentation tells you to do that; most printer drivers and descriptions are either installed by the Mac OS X installer or installed by an application given to you by the printer manufacturer when you buy the printer. Often those installers can also be downloaded from the manufacturer's website.

When you've made the printer driver choice, you can click the Add button to add the printer to your Mac's list of available printers. You'll be returned to the Print & Fax pane of System Preferences or the Printer Setup Utility (depending on which one you launched from), where you will see that printer in the Printer List. (Figure 5.4 shows the Print & Fax pane with the Printing tab selected.) Once a printer is in this list, it's ready for you to print to it from your Mac's installed applications.

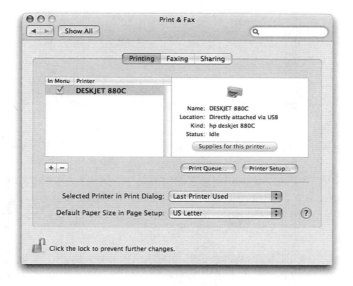

FIGURE 5.4

After adding the printer, it appears in the Print & Fax pane of System Preferences where other features can be accessed.

Page Setup and Printing

With your printer configured, you're ready to set up your applications to print and then send *print jobs* to the printer. You do that using the Page Setup and Print commands.

In an application, choose File, Page Setup to see the Page Setup dialog (see Figure 5.5). You don't have to access this dialog every time you print; instead, you'll dig into it when you need to change something in particular about the way pages are printed, such as the orientation of the printing (is it printing "regular" or "wide" on the page) or the size of paper that you want to use. Click OK when you're done with the dialog.

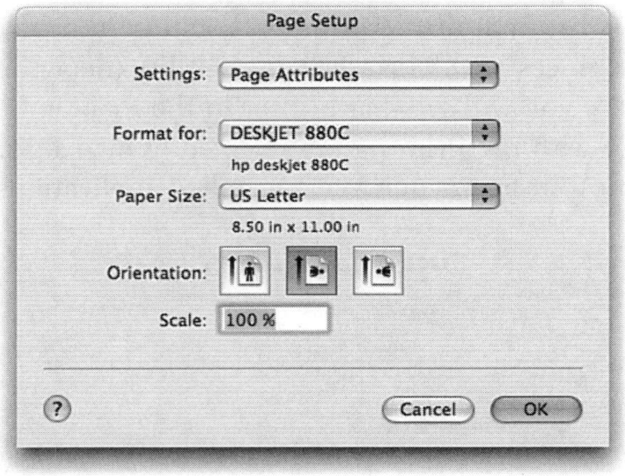

FIGURE 5.5

The Page Setup dialog is used to make some basic choices about how a page will be printed.

With your Page Setup choices made, you're ready to print the document. To open the Print dialog, choose File, Print. Mac OS X has a standard Print dialog that's built in to the operating system, so most applications will make use of it—you can see an example in Figure 5.6.

At the top of the Print dialog box, you'll see the Printer menu, where you can select the printer that you'd like to send this print job to, if you have more than one printer set up for your Mac. From that menu, you can also set up a printer or open the Print & Fax pane of System Preferences. The next menu is the Preset menu; you can use this menu to select from one or more saved sets of settings once you've made some changes and saved them as a set. You do that by making changes and then pulling down the menu and choosing Save As.

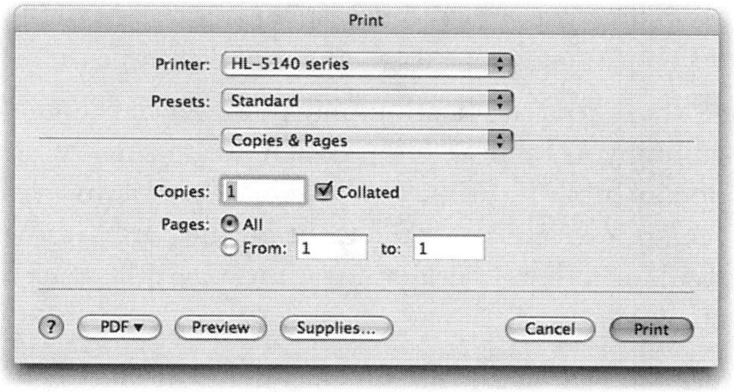

FIGURE 5.6
The Print dialog box is a standard way of sending jobs to your printer.

So what settings can you change? That's what the third menu is for. By default, you'll see Copies & Pages, where you can change the number of copies that will be printed of this document and/or you can select a range of pages that you'd like to print.

From that third menu, you can choose a number of other options as well. Here's a look at some of the items in that menu:

- Layout—On this screen, you can tell the printer to print more than one page per sheet of paper, creating special little booklets. These are great if you can read small type and want to save some paper.

- Scheduler—Using these controls, you can set a print job to print at a certain time.

- Paper Handling—For more sophisticated printers, you can set where the paper should be retrieved from and what order it should be printed in.

- ColorSync—Again, with a more sophisticated color printer, you may have special choices on the Color Conversion menu; you can use the Quartz Filter menu to print color documents with various filters.

- Cover Page—You can send a cover page with your print job, which might be useful for large corporate or institutional settings.

- Paper Type/Quality—On this screen, you can tell your Mac what type of paper you'll be printing to, which may affect the density or other settings in terms of how much ink or toner is used on the page. You can also sometimes set a Quality level for your printer, which may use less ink or toner for "draft" quality documents.

- Printer specific—Some printers add their own settings to the Print dialog box's options so that you can take advantage of special features the printer offers.

- Application specific—Your application may put a special screen of options in this dialog, enabling you to make choices that are specific to how this application's unique documents will print. For instance, in Firefox (a popular web browser), you can opt to shrink a page to fit on the paper it's being printed to, and you can decide whether or not you want to print the background color or image on a web page.

When you're done making choices, you can click the Print button to begin sending the job to your printer.

TIP

If you've made a set of choices that you think you may want to use for future print jobs, don't forget to select Save As from the Presets menu and give this set of options a name so you can access them again in the future via the Presets menu.

Other than immediately clicking Print, you have two other interesting options. The Preview button will create a PDF version of your print job and immediately display that PDF in the Preview application, so that you can see what your printed page will look like. That can be handy if you're testing different settings and don't want to waste paper. If you like what you see, you can choose File, Print in the Preview application to continue the printing process.

NOTE

PDF stands for Portable Document Format, and it's a file type that was developed by Adobe Corporation, a company that focuses on high-end desktop and web publishing applications. PDF is a format that can be used to accurately display entire documents on multiple computer systems; for instance, I can save a document from Microsoft Word as a PDF and send it to you via email; when you open it in Preview or Adobe Reader, you'll see the same fonts, images, and formatting that I used originally in Word—even though you might not have Word. PDF is popular for online brochures, technical manuals, and even electronic novels and other publications. Mac OS X works natively in PDF, meaning it's integrated in the Print dialog box of nearly any application.

The other option is to select the PDF button menu. There you'll see a number of choices, including the option to save the print job as a PDF or turn it into a PDF and then fax that PDF using your internal modem. You'll see some more sophisticated options there as well.

The basic choices will often suffice—choose Save As PDF if you'd like to turn this print job into an electronic PDF document that you can email to someone or store as a file for printing later. (You can choose Mail PDF if you'd like to have a new email opened in Mail automatically with this PDF as an attachment.) When you choose one of the Save options, you'll see a dialog box appear, enabling you give the file a name.

Manage Print Jobs

Once you've sent a job to the printer, you can watch its progress in the printer queue application that appears on your Dock—it'll be an icon named for the printer to which you send the document. Select that icon and you'll see the printer queue window (see Figure 5.7).

In this window you can select a job and click Hold if you'd like it to hold off on printing; if you have more than one active job then holding one allows the other to go ahead of it. You can highlight a held job and click Resume to get it going again. You can also select a job and click Delete to remove it from the queue.

The Stop Jobs button can be used to stop all jobs that are queued from your Mac to that printer; once stopped, click Start Jobs to get them going again. The queue window offers some other interesting options, such as the Utility button, which can launch a utility application associated with your printer (if you have one installed), and the Supply Levels button, which can be used with some printers to find out if you need more ink, toner, or such supplies.

FIGURE 5.7

The printer queue window is used for managing the jobs that you send to that printer.

> **TIP**
>
> You can use the Printer Setup Utility to create a desktop printer, which is simply an icon on your desktop that's used to launch the printer's queue window. In the Printer List, highlight the printer and choose Printers, Create Desktop Printer. Give the printer a name in the dialog sheet and click Save to save the icon; now you can double-click that icon to see your print jobs, including the completed jobs that you can access by clicking the Completed tab in the queue window.

Faxing Documents

If you read the previous section on printing, you may have seen how a fax can be sent from any Print dialog box; from the PDF button menu, simply choose Fax PDF. When you do, the Print dialog reconfigures to enable you to enter information about the person to whom you plan to send the fax (see Figure 5.8).

In the To section, you can either enter a phone number or enter the name of a person or company that is found in your Address Book; you can also click the small person icon to open up Address Book and select someone. In the Dialing Prefix section, enter anything you need to dial before dialing the fax number, such as a 9 to dial out or a long distance code. (Note that you can add a comma—or multiple commas—after a number to insert a pause.)

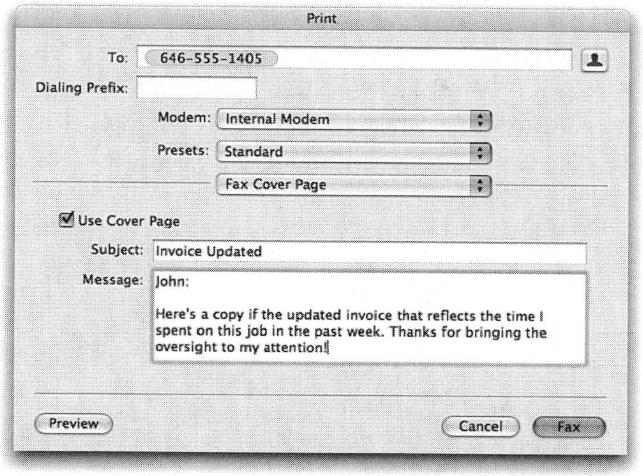

FIGURE 5.8
Choose to send a fax and you'll see a slightly different Print dialog box.

If you'd like to use a cover page with your fax, turn on the Use Cover Page option, and then type in a subject and a message for the cover page. When you're done, click the Fax button to send the fax on its way. When you do, you'll see a new addition on your Dock—the Internal Modem queue. Click it to see the Internal Modem window, which shows you the progress that's being made sending your fax.

You'll notice that this is very similar to the printer queue window used to manage print jobs—you can hold faxes, resume them, stop all jobs, and so forth.

What about receiving faxes? You can control whether or not your Mac will receive faxes via its modem by opening the Print & Fax pane of System Preferences and selecting the Faxing tab (see Figure 5.9).

NOTE

If you're working with your Mac's internal modem then there shouldn't be any setup necessary for faxing, as the Mac OS has a pretty good idea how to work with an internal modem. If you're having trouble or if you have a third-party modem for your Mac, click the Set Up Fax Modem button in the Faxing tab of the Print & Fax tab in order to make changes.

To receive faxes, make sure your Mac's modem is attached to a phone outlet, and then turn on the option Receive Faxes on This Computer. In the My Fax Number entry box, enter your fax number. You can then make a number of other choices about how many rings to wait before the fax picks up and what to do with a received fax—it can be saved to a local folder, emailed, or automatically printed.

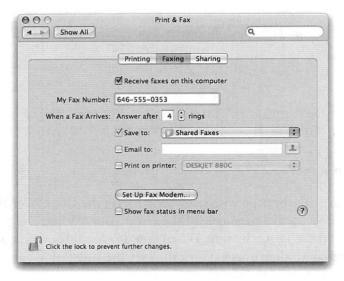

FIGURE 5.9
On the Faxing tab of the Print & Fax pane, you can set up your Mac to receive faxes.

Print (and Fax) Sharing

Mac OS X offers a cool little feature called Printer Sharing, which can be used if you have a printer that's connected directly to your Mac that you'd like to share with others who have a network connection to your Mac. For instance, if you have a USB printer that doesn't offer an Ethernet-based network connection, but you have a network of Macs, you can connect that printer to your Mac via USB and, as long as your Mac is on, it can share that printer with the rest of the network.

Once you have that printer configured, all you have to do is open the Print & Fax pane of System Preferences and click the Sharing tab. Now, turn on the Share These Printers with Other Computers option and, once the printers light up as active, click the check box to turn off any that you *don't* want to share (assuming you have more than one connected).

Your printer will then show up in the Printer List of the Printer Setup Utility for anyone else who has a network connection that can see your Mac. (It uses Bonjour technology, the Mac's "automatic discovery" technology discussed in more depth in Chapter 11.) Other users can simply select the printer and add it to their list of printers in Mac OS X, giving them the option of printing to it when appropriate.

Aside from printer sharing, the Sharing tab of the Print & Fax pane offers another option that you can check to turn on, Let Others Send Faxes Through This Computer. Turn that on and other users can use your Mac's modem connection to send faxes, by selecting Shared Faxes from the Modem menu that appears in the Print dialog box.

TIP

If you're going to share your modem for faxing, it's a good idea to rename it, so that others can find it more easily. You can rename your modem by clicking Set Up Fax Modem in the Print & Fax pane of System Preferences. Then, in the Printer Setup Utility, select your modem and click Show Info. On the Name & Location screen of the Info window, you can rename the modem to something more meaningful (like "Leo's Modem") and click Apply Changes.

Customizing Your Display

You probably spend enough time looking at your Mac's display that you've occasionally come up with something about it that you'd like to adjust. Those adjustments are made via the Displays pane of System Preferences, as shown in Figure 5.9. What you see in the Displays pane will depend somewhat on your Mac—in Figure 5.10, you see the pane for my iBook, which offers a limited number of resolution choices and has an internal brightness control.

The resolution setting means the number of pixels that are used on your display to represent images and text; the smaller the resolution, the larger things will appear on the screen, but the less you can see at once. With most LCD displays (like those built into PowerBooks, iBooks, and the latest iMac models) there's a "native" resolution where the LCD looks its best; so, you likely won't change the resolution on your display often if you have an LCD screen.

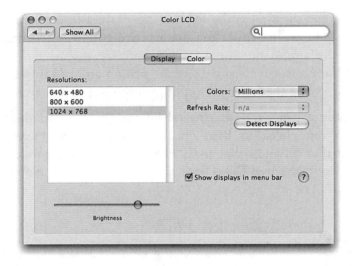

FIGURE 5.10

The Displays pane of System Preferences enables me to change the resolution, brightness, and color settings on my iBook.

NOTE

One common reason for changing screen resolution is to play computer games, which may run at a different resolution than your default setting. Most games that need to change resolution will do so automatically, but you may sometimes have to change resolutions *back* manually, particularly if the game crashes or unexpectedly quits.

The Colors option enables you to choose Millions, Thousands, or, in some cases, 256 colors. These days there aren't many reasons not to run with Millions of colors, especially since Mac OS X's interface looks best that way. You may occasionally have a reason, such as an older application or game.

If your Mac shows sliders for Brightness (and sometimes Contrast), that means you can set those options from the operating system—if you don't see the sliders, you'll need to use the physical controls on your display to make changes.

One of the more interesting uses of the Display control panel is to manage multiple displays. Most Macs that have their own displays (both desktops and portables) also have an external display port (refer to Figure 5.1). Depending on the Mac model, that port may be used for mirroring the Mac's internal display to the external display (for presentations, for instance) or you can use the two screens together for an expanded workspace. (Most Power Macintosh models that have two video ports also offer multi-monitor support, and you can install cards in the Power Macs for even more displays.)

When you plug in a second monitor, often your Mac will detect it and react accordingly; if it doesn't, click the Detect Displays button in the control pane. Once the second display has been detected, you'll see two windows, one for each display, as shown in Figure 5.11. You can make changes to each separately, including different resolutions, color depths, and brightness and contrast settings.

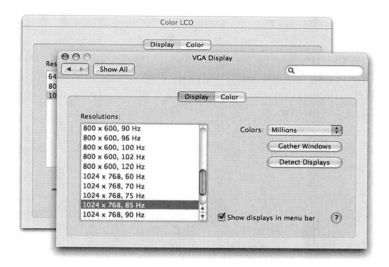

FIGURE 5.11
Two windows appear when you've attached a second display to a Mac that supports multiple displays.

If you see an Arrangement tab in your Displays window, that means you're able to use them for increasing the amount of workspace you have available by "spanning" across the displays. You can arrange the images that represent the displays so that one is on the "left" and one is on the "right"—when you move the mouse pointer off the screen in one direction, it'll appear on the other display if they're arranged correctly.

Getting Pictures Off Your Digital Camera

Most digital cameras connect to your Mac using a special USB cable that connects from the camera to an available USB port on your Mac. Often the mere act of connecting the camera to your Mac will automatically cause something to happen; usually that "something" is the launching of iPhoto if you have a recent version of iPhoto installed. iPhoto is Apple's iLife application dedicated to helping you upload and manage digital images using your Mac. You might see a message pop up when you first connect the camera or when you first launch iPhoto.

iPhoto isn't the only option—your Mac also includes an application called Image Capture, which you will find in your main Applications folder. Image Capture can be used to quickly download images from your camera to folders on your hard disk without using iPhoto as a go-between. Figure 5.12 shows Image Capture's main window. Simply click Download Now to download the images to the selected folder, or click Download Some to see a window that enables you to choose the individual photos you want to download.

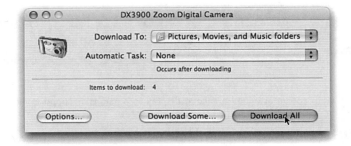

FIGURE 5.12
You can use the Image Capture application to quickly get photos from your USB-connected digital camera.

If you opt to use iPhoto, you'll be downloading the images into iPhoto's database, where you can then store, rename, manipulate, and then export the images as image files, to the Web and a variety of other possibilities. (You can even print them in books.)

We're worried about getting them off your camera first, though. To do that is simple—with your camera connected and iPhoto either automatically or manually launched, you'll see the import window (see Figure 5.13). Give the "roll" a name—each time you import into iPhoto, it creates a new "roll," which is akin to getting a roll of film developed at the drug store. You can also type a description for this import session. With those things accomplished, you can check the Delete Items from Camera After Importing option if that's what you want to do, and then click Import.

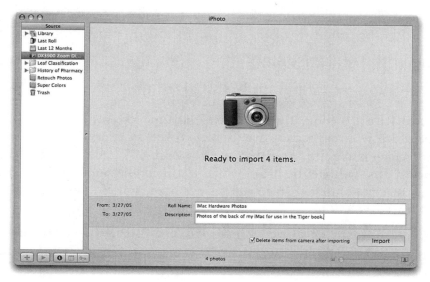

FIGURE 5.13

iPhoto makes importing images easy—and each session is saved as a "roll" that can be named and described.

In iPhoto, you'll watch as the images are imported; you can click the Stop Import button if desired. When you're done importing, you can unplug the camera's USB connection and start working with the images in iPhoto.

NOTE

External "card readers" are popular peripherals for folks who take a lot of digital photos or who have older cameras that lack USB connectivity. A card reader is an external device that usually connects via USB. (Many of the latest models use USB 2.0 for a faster connection.) Then, instead of plugging your camera into a USB port on your Mac, you release the storage card from your camera and plug it into the reader. You can copy the images directly from the card, which will appear on your desktop or in a Finder window. iPhoto also recognizes many card readers.

Using FireWire Devices

Partly because Apple invented FireWire and partly because it was an early high-speed standard, FireWire is a big part of the Mac experience. Many Mac models don't offer much in the way of internal expansion, but, via the FireWire port, you're able to add external hard disks, disc burners, and other high speed devices such as digital camcorders. In this section, I'd like to take a look at those different technologies.

Working with DV Camcorders

Digital Video (DV) camcorders require high-speed connections because digital video data takes up a lot of storage space—about 1 gigabyte for every five minutes of video. Over a USB 1.1 connection, it would take a long time to transfer even a short amount of video, which was one reason that Apple worked to create FireWire technology. (USB 2.0, which is slightly faster than the FireWire 400 standard, didn't come along until much later.) With the combination of DV camcorders and FireWire connections, however, a new era of digital video editing was born, and Macs have been front-and-center for that revolution.

Getting footage from your DV camcorder into your Mac generally requires that you use a digital editing application, such as iMovie or Apple's Final Cut. With the camera attached to your Mac via a FireWire cable, you can then use the Import function of the editing software to bring footage in for editing—because the camera has stored the images on tape (as opposed to on something such as a CD or external hard disk), you can't simply "copy" a file from the camera to your Mac via drag-and-drop. That's essentially what you're doing—copying a computer file from the camera to the Mac—it just takes a little longer.

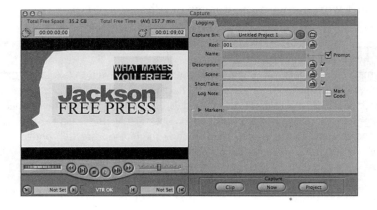

Once you have your footage imported into the editing software, you can save it, edit it, and even export it as an edited and/or compression digital video file, such as a QuickTime movie. You'll also find that your editing software gives you the ability to export the video back to your camcorder (or to another DV recording device) via the FireWire connection. (Or, if your Mac has a built-in DVD-R drive, your software may allow you to create DVDs using that video.)

That FireWire connection isn't only good for importing and exporting video; a camcorder that's connected via FireWire can be used for "live" feeds of video as well, including for use with applications such as iChat AV, which enables you to video conference over the Internet. Figure 5.14 shows a DV camcorder connected for use with iChat AV.

FIGURE 5.14
You can use your digital video camcorder with iChat AV to do a little video conferencing on the Internet.

Storing Files on External Hard Disks

Using either FireWire or USB 2.0 (with some disks; you can also use USB 1.1, though much more slowly), you can attach an external hard disk to your Mac that performs nearly or completely as well as an internal hard disk does. The advantage is that the external hard disk can be used to considerably expand your Mac's capability, and it can be used with other Macs, or transported offsite easily when needed.

Connecting an external hard disk is simple—just run a FireWire cable between the disk's FireWire port and your Mac's FireWire port, and then power up the disk. After it spins up, it should be recognized by your Mac and placed on the desktop and/or in the Sidebar of your Finder windows. You should then be able to access the drive as you normally would an internal disk or an optical disc that you've inserted into your Mac.

Like CDs and DVDs, an external hard disk should also be ejected, particularly before you shut off power to the hard disk. To eject an external hard disk, either drag its icon from the desktop to the Trash can or click the small eject icon that appears next to the disk in the Finder window's Sidebar.

Creating CDs and DVDs

In Chapter 2, "The Finder and Your Files," we covered the basics of burning data CDs and DVDs, but I'd like to go a little more in-depth in this section. Aside from the basic Finder method of inserting a disc, dragging files to it, and burning those files, we have two other approaches worth looking at: Burn Folder and Disk Utility.

> **NOTE**
>
> You'll find all sorts of writeable discs out there to work with, and it's important to know that the "+" and "-" symbols in the names are important distinctions. Macs have traditionally been compatible with CD-R, CD-RW, DVD-R, and DVD-RW media. Later models also work with CD+R, CD+RW, DVD+R, and DVD+RW formats. When in doubt, opt for the -R and -RW versions.

Burn Folder

Burn Folder is an approach that's new to Mac OS X 10.4. A Burn Folder essentially enables you to gather together aliases to files that you'd like to burn in a special folder *without* first requiring that you insert a blank disc. To create a Burn Folder, choose File, New Burn Folder, and one will appear in the current Finder window. You can rename it like you would any folder, then start dragging items to it.

When you're ready to burn the folder to a disc, click the Burn button in the top right corner of the Burn Folder's open window. (Alternatively, you can Control+click the Burn Folder and choose Burn Disc from the contextual menu.) You'll see a dialog box appear, telling you to insert a disc and alerting you to the amount of space you'll need on that disc for storage (see Figure 5.15). (If it's over a recordable CD's limit of about 700 megabytes then you'll need to burn a DVD, if your Mac has the capability. If not, you may need to cancel and remove some items.)

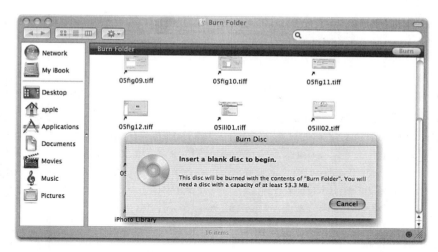

FIGURE 5.15

After clicking Burn Disc, you'll be told how much free space will be required on that disc.

Once the inserted disc spins up, you'll see another window appear, asking you if you'd like to enter a different name for the disc and enabling you to choose a burn speed. (If you ever have trouble with your burner set at a higher speed, you can choose a lower speed to see if that improves things.) Make those choices and click Burn. A small window appears to update you on the progress.

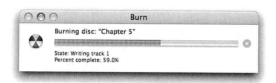

When the disc is done, you can eject it, give it a label, and store it in a safe place.

Use Disk Utility

There are actually two different reasons to use Disk Utility, which is Apple's application designed for managing both hard disks and optical discs. First, Disk Utility is how you can erase a rewriteable CD or DVD so that you can use it again. Here's how that works:

1. Insert the CD-RW or DVD-RW that you'd like to erase.

2. Launch Disk Utility, which is found in the Utilities folder inside your Applications folder.

3. In Disk Utility, select the disc's icon on the left side of the window.

4. Click the Erase tab.

5. On the Erase screen, click the Erase button.

That begins the process of erasing the disc so that you can use it again for burning data.

Disk Utility can also be used to burn data to discs, and it's particularly good at burning *disk images* to disc. A disk image is a special file that, when double-clicked, is "mounted" on your Mac's desktop and/or in the Sidebar of a Finder window, just as if it were a removable disk. If you've ever downloaded a software update from Apple's website, then you've likely experienced a disk image, and many third-party application developers use them, as well.

To burn a disk image using Disk Utility, you should first mount that disk image in the Finder. Then, switch to Disk Utility and that disk image will appear in the list of volumes on the left side of the window. Select that disk image's icon, and then click the Burn icon in the Disk Utility toolbar. A dialog sheet will appear that prompts you to insert a blank disc; do so, then click the Burn button. That begins the process of burning that disk image to the inserted disc. When it's done, the finished disc will be mounted on your desktop and/or in a Finder window's Sidebar, where you can open it, work with it, or eject it for transport or safekeeping.

Chapter 6

Manage Your Contacts and Schedule

In each successive version of Mac OS X, Apple has been working to make contact and schedule management a bit more of an operating system-level task, instead of something you'd get a third-party application to handle. That's why Address Book and iCal are included in a Mac OS X installation and it's why Apple continues to make them integrate well with other Apple products and services such as the iPod or .Mac online service. With Address Book and iCal, you have applications that can handle your meetings and appointments, keep track of your friends or clients, and work together with those external tools and devices to manage your life.

In this chapter I want to start with the basics of the Address Book and show you how you can not only track contacts, but try to make it as painless as possible. We'll then look into iCal, a program that does amazing things with calendars, computers and the Web.

Work with Address Book

The Address Book is an unassuming little application that can be really handy to have around. (You know it's unassuming in the Apple pantheon because it isn't named iAddies or iContacts or something). At its most basic, you can use it to enter and keep track of the people you know and work with—get a little more advanced and you can swap virtual business cards and synchronize your contacts with a variety of devices.

To get started with the Address Book, launch it from the Dock or the Applications folder on your Mac. When it appears, you'll see the simple interface shown in Figure 6.1.

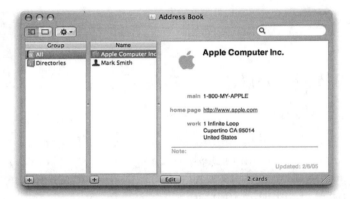

FIGURE 6.1
The Address Book interface is a real charmer.

The default look for the Address Book interface is three panes—almost like columns in the Finder. The leftmost column represents groups of addresses that you can create, the middle column lists the names of contacts in that group, and the right-side column is the business-card–like presentation of a contact's information, which is you can edit directly.

TIP

By default, you, personally, already have a card in Address Book, which you should go ahead and fill in with accurate information. When you do, that information can be exchanged electronically with others, and it's used automatically by applications such as Safari for "autofill" features in HTML forms and elsewhere.

Create Contacts

You can start by not worrying about groups and just dig in and add some contacts. With All selected in the group column, click the small plus ("+") icon at the bottom of the Name column. That creates a new contact card and immediately tosses you into the editing mode for the person you're adding, as shown in Figure 6.2. You can get started quickly by typing a first name for your contact, then pressing Tab to move to the last name entry area and type that. Press Tab again to move to the different parts of the card.

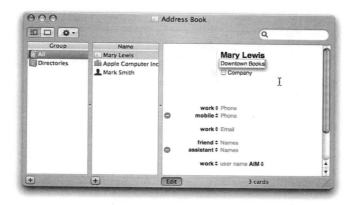

FIGURE 6.2
Here's what it looks like when you're editing a contact.

As you're editing, there are a few things to look out for. First, as you're entering a full name and company name for your contact, you might notice the company check box; selecting that check box turns this into a company card, with the person's name secondary. This can be handy if the name of the company is more important to see at a glance than the name of the contact person.

NOTE

As the sample entry for Apple shows, you don't have to have a personal contact in order to create a company-based card; just leave the First and Last name fields blank if you simply want a card that has the name, phone number, and address for a company. There's also the command Card, Swap First/Last Name, which can be used if you'd prefer to enter last names first.

If you want to add more than one of a particular contact field—multiple phone numbers, for instance—you'll see small plus and minus sign icons. To add another phone number entry, click the plus sign next to the current phone entry. If you end up not needing a certain entry field, you can click its minus ("–") icon.

Second, each of the phone, email, and address lines has a small menu that can be used to tailor it to the actual item you're entering—if you're entering a contact's mobile phone number, you can select that from the menu, or if it's their work email address you can choose that, too.

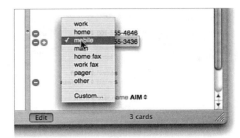

If you don't see the field that you want to add, or if you simply want to take another approach, you can choose Card, Add Field and then choose a new field from the menu.

You can add an image for your contact while you're editing his or her information, which can be handy not just for remembering what he looks like, but also because the image gets used automatically by other applications such as iChat and Mail. To add an image, you can simply drag a photo to the image box next to the person's name while you're in edit mode. For finer control, double-click that image (or the blank box) and you'll get the image interface shown in Figure 6.3. You can also choose Card, Choose Custom Image.

If you haven't yet added an image via drag-and-drop, you can do so now by dragging an image into the Image window. Or, if you need to locate an image, click the Choose button to reveal an Open dialog box that you can use to hunt down an image file.

TIP

You've got another option—if you have a video camera attached to your Mac (such as the Apple iSight), you can click the small camera icon to take a still shot of yourself on that camera. Add this (or some other) image to your own card in the Address Book and it'll appear automatically in iChat and elsewhere as your personal picture.

With an image in the window, you can use the slider to zoom in and out on the image, and then you can drag the image around in order to line it up with the small box that represents how the image will be cropped. Click the Set button and you'll see the image in the Address Book.

FIGURE 6.3
You can use the Image window to add an image to your Address Book card.

When you're done adding photos and editing the rest of the info about your contact, click the Edit button again and you'll be taken out of the editing mode. At this point, you can see the finished card in all its glory. The final card doesn't show fields that you didn't use (in this example, I didn't use the Friend/Family field), which keeps things nice and neat in the window.

If you need to edit the card again, just click the Edit button underneath it and you're off to the races.

TIP

You can edit the basic template for your contacts if you get sick of adding and deleting fields that you rarely or never use. Choose Address Book, Preferences and click the Template button; now you can add and remove fields to set up your defaults. Close the dialog box when you're done and the new template is set.

Viewing and Sorting Cards

The columns-style view is very useful, but the Address Book interface has a button that you can use to change from the Columns view to a more simple Card Only view when desired. Click that button to change things around.

The Address Book Preferences give you an opportunity to change how cards are sorted; choose Address Book, Preferences and select the General icon. On the General preferences tab you'll see the Display Order option, which enables you to change the order in which first and last names are displayed in the Name column of the Address Book window. You can also choose whether the sort the list by first or last name from the Sort By menu.

When you've made your choices, click the Close button to close the preferences window and make those changes stick.

Deleting a Contact

If you need to delete a contact from Address Book, you can select it in the Name list and press the Delete key. You'll see a dialog sheet asking you to confirm your decision; click OK and the card is deleted.

You can also highlight (or simply view) a card and choose Edit, Delete Card. The card is deleted instantly in that case, apparently on the assumption that you're not likely to select that command accidentally.

If you do, you can immediately choose Edit, Undo to return the contact card to Address Book.

Do Stuff with Your Contacts

The Address Book features a special Action menu that enables you to do some fun things with your contact, depending, in part, on what sort of information you've input for each contact. Select a contact in the Name column and then click the Action menu to see what you can do.

Here's a quick look at some of those commands:

- Spotlight—This enables you to toss the current contact into a Spotlight search, as described in Chapter 2, "The Finder and Your Files." You'll see any emails, documents, and other items that relate to this person.

- Send Email—If you have a valid email address entered for a contact, you can choose this to launch your email application (most likely it's Apple Mail) and send this person a message.

- iChat—If you have an iChat-compatible messaging address entered for this contact, then you can choose this command to attempt to begin an iChat discussion with her.

- Map This Address—This is a cool one—it tosses your contact's address into Mapquest via a web browser. If you're connected to the Internet, you can get a map of the address or even driving directions.

- Visit Homepage—If you've entered a URL for this contact's web home, you can choose the Visit Homepage command to launch Safari (or your default web browser if you've changed it) and see his or her page.

- Print—The Print command can be used to print the information on the card in a variety of ways, including as a label, as an envelope, and in other configurations. We'll look at printing a bit more closely in a later section.

- Merge Cards—If you have two cards that are for the same person but they have different information, you can select them both and choose Merge Cards to turn them into one card with all of the relevant information.

Aside from these commands it's worth knowing that the Note command on a contact can be used at any given time to enter something about that person—for instance, when you last talked to the him on the phone or what you need to remember to buy her for her birthday.

You can also search through the cards when you need to find someone quickly and you've got a ton of cards, or if you need to find people in your Address Book that fit a certain criterion, such as they live in a certain place or their name starts with "Log." You can enter a keyword (or portion of a word) in the Search box at the top right of the Address Book window and press the Return key to begin a search.

Creating Groups

So far we've been sticking with editing individual contact entries. One of the strengths of Address Book is the fact that you can gather your contacts into different groups and use them for a variety of reasons. And there are even a few different ways to create those groups.

The most straightforward way is to simply click the plus icon under the Group column in the Address Book window. When you do that, you'll see a new Group Name entry appear, highlighted and ready to be edited—just begin typing to give the group a name, and then press Return. That's a new group.

Now, to populate the new group with people, you can simply drag and drop from the Name column (you may have to switch back to the All group first) to the name of your new group in the Group list. Here I'm dragging three different people to the group:

You can also create groups automatically using a feature called Smart Groups. A smart group is based on searching your contacts and coming up with those who have similar characteristics. To create a new smart group choose File, Smart Group from the menu. You'll see a dialog sheet appear from the top of the Address Book window (see Figure 6.4).

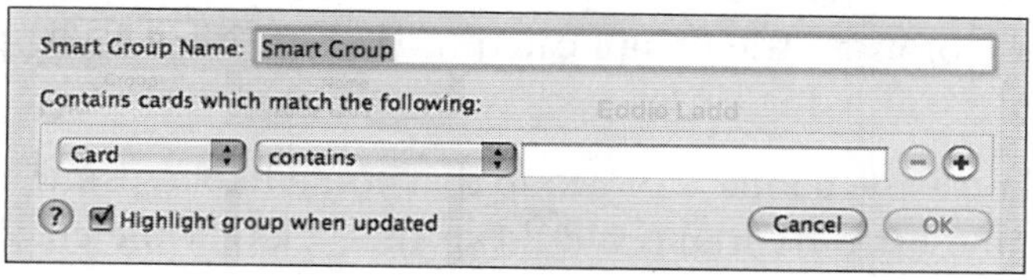

FIGURE 6.4

To create a smart group, you'll use criterion lines to automatically filter your address cards and create the group of people with similar characteristics.

Begin by giving the new group a name in the Smart Group Name entry box. Next, use the Criterion line to build a search sentence. The first menu can be opened to reveal different fields (Card is used to search the entire card), and the second menu is used to decide *how* you're going to search that first field ("contains," "does not contain," "is," and so on). The third section—either a menu or an entry box—is used to complete the search sentence.

What does all this mean? An example would be a smart group that uses the search sentence "company contains Apple," which would come up with anyone in our Address Book who works for a company that has Apple in its name. Other smart groups could be "State is TX" to get all your contacts in Texas into one group. At this point, you can probably see how this could be handy.

If you need to add another search sentence line, you can do that by clicking the plus icon at the end of the first line. A smart group can be a result of multiple criteria.

When you're done setting the rules for the group, click OK. The group will be created and will appear on the Group list with a slightly different icon; you can select it to see whether it found any relevant contacts.

TIP

Groups are particularly handy for sending out emails to multiple recipients at once; see Chapter 9, "Mail and Chat Basics," for more details on sending to groups.

Printing Your Contacts and Groups

Address Book's ability to print out contacts is pretty extensive—depending on what you select and your printer's features, you can use Address Book to print envelopes, labels, and even a pocket address book that you can and carry around with you. And while the Print dialog is a little complicated to look at, it's actually pretty easy to get some decent results.

To get started, choose the contacts or group that you'd like to print. You can click individuals in the Name list if desired (hold down the ⌘ key while clicking names to add them to your selection) or simply choose one or more groups. With that selection made, choose File, Print. The Print dialog box appears, as shown in Figure 6.5.

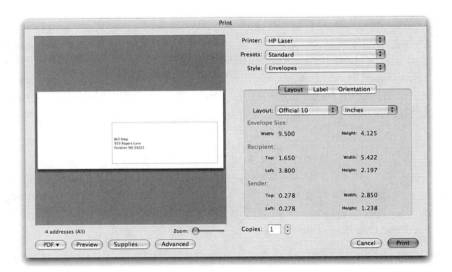

FIGURE 6.5
The Print dialog box in Address Book enables you to print lists, labels, envelopes and more using data from your contact cards.

The key to the Print dialog box is the Style menu, where you can choose from the different types of printouts that are possible, such as Mailing Labels, Envelopes, Lists, and Pocket Address Book. What you choose in that menu affects most of the other options that you'll see.

If you choose Mailing Labels, for instance, you'll see options on the Layout tab that allow you to choose from standard types of laser or inkjet labels. (Most of them are compatible with one of the Avery model numbers, so look for that if you're buying labels in an office supply warehouse or similar store.) On the Label tab, you can choose which addresses should be used, what order should be used, and even what font you prefer.

If you choose Envelopes, you'll see options for the different types and sizes of envelopes on the Layout tab, how you want the text to appear on the Label tab, and what direction the envelope is going to be fed through the printer on the Orientation tab. (You almost always have to experiment with printers and the orientation setting to get it right, but you can change it here if necessary.)

The Lists options are simpler—you choose the size of paper you're going to be printing to, the fields (Attributes) that you want to see, and the size of the font that should be used.

Finally, the Pocket Address Book options include choosing the paper size, orientation, fields to display, and the Flip Style. You can choose the font and size (click the Set button) and then you're ready to print.

When you like your settings, you can click Print to get started with the print job or choose Preview to see what the output is going to look like. As with most Mac applications, you can choose to save the output as a PDF or a PostScript file, if you'd prefer an electronic "printout" instead of sending the job to a printer immediately.

Import, Export, and vCard

Address Book is very adept at working with the vCard standard, which is a universal format for personal information documents that can be shared among different applications and platforms. You can use vCard files to export and import contact information from Address Book and a wide variety of similar applications. In fact, with Address Book, importing a vCard document is as easy as dragging and dropping it onto the Address Book window, as shown in Figure 6.6.

You can also use the File, Import, vCards command to import vCard files. Address Book can also read LDIF files and plain text files that are comma- or tab-delimited (meaning they have commas or tabs separating the values). These plain text files are a very common way to get database information from one application to another, so you'll find that you can, for instance, export a tab-delimited file from Palm Desktop and import it into Address Book fairly easily.

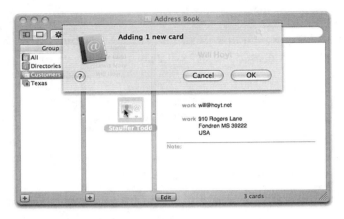

FIGURE 6.6
Drag and drop a vCard document onto the Address Book window to add it to your collection of contacts.

NOTE
LDIF stands for LDAP Interchange Format, which is a way to create a file that's exported from an LDAP server and imported into an application such as Address Book. So what's an LDAP server, you ask? The Lightweight Directory Access Protocol is a method used over a network connection to access addresses and contact information in a standardized way. Address Book can enable you to look up addresses on such a server if you specify an LDAP server in Address Book's Preferences (choose the LDAP button) and then click the Directories item in the group list. LDAP servers are popular with colleges, corporations, and other organizations that want to offer centralized contact information.

If you do opt to import a text file of addresses, there's generally an additional step—you need to match up the fields in the text file with the fields in Address Book. As you can see in Figure 6.7, the fields will match up fairly well, but you may have to opt not to import a field that doesn't have an equivalent in Address Book, or you may end up needing to help the program understand that Job Title and Title are the same field—that sort of thing.

You can export from Address Book in one format—vCard. The easiest way to do that is to drag a name out of the Name list and drop it on the desktop or in a Finder window; the result is a vCard file for that person. You can also drag multiple names or a group's name out of Address Book at once to create a multi-contact vCard—such files are great for moving contacts from one person to another. If drag and drop isn't your thing, you can select one contact, multiple contacts, or a group and choose File, Export vCard.

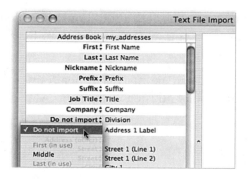

FIGURE 6.7
If you import addresses from another program using a text file, you may need to match up the fields.

If you haven't yet figured it out, I think vCard is pretty cool. If you're the sort of person who needs a lot of people to have your contact information, you might even consider making a vCard available on your web page or as an attachment to the email messages that you send out to clients or colleagues. A vCard makes it easy for others—whether or not they use Address Book—to drop your contact information into their contact management software.

Share Contacts

So how great is this? In Address Book, starting in Mac OS X 10.4, you can share your contacts with other Mac users who have .Mac accounts. (.Mac is a subscription service offered by Apple that has various online tools and capabilities and is covered fully in Chapter 8,, "Get on the Internet.") That means they can access your contacts and, if you so desire, they can even make changes to your Address Book.

If you have a .Mac account and it's been configured on the .Mac pane of System Preferences, you can share your Address Book. Here's how:

1. Choose Address Book, Preferences and click the Sharing icon.
2. Click the check mark to turn on Share Your Address Book. After a moment, sharing is turned on.

3. When you're ready to invite people to access your Address Book, you can do that by clicking the Send Invite button or by clicking the plus ("+") icon at the bottom of the dialog box and choosing someone in your Address Book who has a valid .Mac account.

4. When you find somebody, click OK. (You'll only be able to click OK if that person is a valid .Mac user.) If you want that person to have editing access, click the check box for Allow Editing.

Now, the person you've added can go into his or her copy of Address Book and choose File, Subscribe to Address Book and then enter your .Mac email address in the dialog sheet that appears.

Explore iCal

If you read the previous section about Address Book then you know that the vCard standard is a handy way that applications can swap contact information, and Apple gets kudos for building Address Book around it. In a similar way, iCal uses ".ics" files in a way that makes your calendar accessible to others and easy to publish on the Internet or share among users. That and the fact that iCal is a great piece of software for managing your appointments and tasks and reminders means it's also quite a bit of fun to explore and talk about.

> **NOTE**
>
> Interestingly, there's a vCal standard (a standard file format for appointment calendars) that iCal *doesn't* use. The .ics approach is popular, but not as open of a standard as vCal. iCal can *import* a vCal calendar via the File, Import command if you ever need to open one on your Mac.

When you first launch iCal, you'll see the main iCal interface showing you the calendars that are automatically created—Home and Work—and a blank weekly view of the current week (see Figure 6.8). So, if you like, you can jump right into creating an event.

As you'll see, iCal can track both Events and To Dos, so its probably important to differentiate between the two. In most cases, Events are something that begin at a certain time or, at the very least, on a certain day. To Dos may have a deadline that's important, but when they start isn't as important. They're just something that needs to get done.

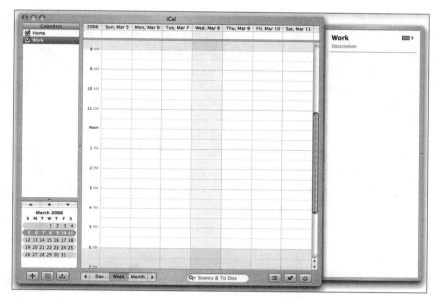

FIGURE 6.8
The blank iCal interface is mission control for your appointments and To Do items.

Most events that I keep track of in my calendar are meetings I need to attend or phone calls that I need to make. Events can also be used to note when a day is a holiday or the stretch of time that you plan to be at a conference or on vacation.

Add Events

To create an event that starts and ends on the same day, first select the calendar in which you would like this event to appear. By default you have two calendars, Home and Work, available in the Calendars list. Functionally they aren't any different—they simply allow you to categorize your events. Select one of them to highlight it. Now, in the weekly calendar view, click and hold down the mouse button on the day and time when you'd like to begin your event. Now drag down the selection to set it for 15 or 30 minutes or even an hour or more.

The words New Event should be highlighted in the small box that you've created; you can begin typing to the give the event a name. If the Info window is open, you'll see the name change there, as well, as you type.

> **TIP**
> You can open the Info window by clicking the small "i" icon at the bottom right of the calendar window; by choosing View, Show Info; or by double-clicking the top bar of an event box in the calendar. (Each event has a small bar at the top of its box that's slightly darker in color.) By default, the Info window appears as an attached "drawer" on the side of the iCal window.

If the time and name of the event are good enough for you, then that's all you have to do. But if you'd like the tweak a bit more, you can do that in the Info window (see Figure 6.9). In fact, it's via the Info window that you can create all-day and multi-day events.

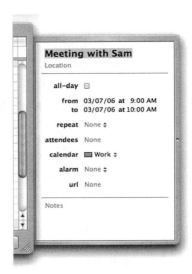

FIGURE 6.9
The Info window for an event.

Here are some of the things you can change about the event you just created:

- All-Day—If you'd like the event to be an all-day event—meaning it doesn't have a start or end time (like a holiday or anniversary) then click the All-day check box. That places the event at the very top of the weekly view, prior to the portion of the calendar that shows times.

- From and To—On these lines you can be very exact about when you want an event to begin, including the date and time. Click the month, for instance, and you can type a new month, or you can also change it by pressing the up and down arrows. The same goes for the day and year. More than likely, though, you're going to tweak the times—you can make an event one minute or ten minutes or five hours long, as necessary.

TIP

You can make an event more than one day long using the From and To lines. If you have an event start at 12:00 p.m. on 03/07/06 and last until 03/10/06, it will display as spanning all that time in your iCal.

- Repeat—If this is an event that happens on a regular basis, you can cause it to appear in the calendar at regular intervals. Just click the word None next to Repeat to reveal a menu; you can then choose to have the event repeat itself once a day, once a week, or once a month, or choose the Custom entry to pick the days when it should be scheduled. (You can get creative with the custom window, choosing every three weeks on a Thursday, for instance.)

- Attendees—Here you can add names to the list for a meeting that you're scheduling; the trick is that those names have to come from the Address Book. Click the word Attendees and hold down the mouse button, then choose Open Address Book. Now, drag people from the Address Book to the attendees list. When you drop them, their names appear in the list and a message appears at the bottom of the Info window. If you would like to automatically send invitations to your list of attendees, click the Send button.

- Calendar—If you need to, you can change the calendar that this event is associated with by selecting a different calendar in this menu.

- Alarm—This is something I use all the time. If you'd like to be reminded of the event, then choose a method of reminder from the Alarm menu. You can choose a message (dialog box), a message with sound, an email, or you can have iCal automatically open a file or run a script. In many cases you'll have iCal pop up a message or play a sound as a reminder, and these other options are pretty cool, too. Once you've made your choice, you'll see another menu that asks you how soon before the meeting you want your reminder; make a choice from the options (minutes before, days before, and so on) and then type in a number if you don't like the default of 15 (anything from 1 to 32,767 is acceptable).

NOTE

I like the idea of having iCal send me email reminders, so that's one option I choose a lot. As you'll see if you try it, iCal requires that your *own* entry in the Address Book have an email address in order for iCal to send you reminders. And don't forget to consider the implications of the option to open a file or run a script as an "alarm"—that's a capability that makes iCal pretty handy for all sorts of Mac tasks from maintenance to backup to launching your email program, or doing something even more automatic with a script you write with AppleScript or Automator (see Chapter 4, "Conquer the Mac OS X Interface").

- URL—This final entry allows you to enter a URL that has some relevance for the meeting or event; you can click the word URL and select Go to Location to visit that site in a web browser (or appropriate Internet application if it's not a Web URL).

Edit and Delete Events

To edit an event, simply click it once in the calendar and its information will appear in the Info window.

To delete an event, select it in the calendar and press the Delete key or choose Edit, Delete. The event disappears immediately; if you made a mistake and need it back, immediately choose Edit, Undo.

Create To Dos

A To Do is a bit simpler than an event, with fewer options, but still pretty powerful. I like to use these for things that have a deadline that I can't let slip much, such as "pay the insurance bill" or "get office supplies."

Again, start by selecting the calendar that you want to associate with this To Do. Now, choose File, New To Do or press ⌘+K. That will both open the To Do pane and create a new To Do item. The name is highlighted, so start typing to give it a meaningful title (see Figure 6.10).

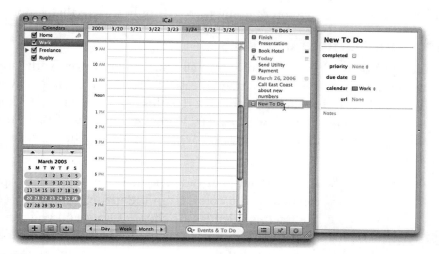

FIGURE 6.10
I've added a number of ToDo items to my calendar, including some with due dates and some with alarms.

When you're done naming it, press Return. Now, in the Info window, you have some selections you can make:

- Completed—When the task is done, you can click this checkbox. When a To Do task is completed it isn't moved forward to the next day, whereas uncompleted tasks are. (You can also set preferences that cause completed To Do tasks to disappear after a certain amount of time.)

- Priority—You can set a priority for the task if you'd like it to appear more urgent and higher in the list of tasks. The priority appears as small color bars next to the To Do item in the To Dos list. You can change the priority in that list, as well, by clicking the color bars and choosing from the menu that appears.

- Due Date—Place a check mark here and you'll be able to set a date when this item will come due. When checked, another option appears—Alarm. You can set an alarm for an item that has a due date so that you're reminded that the due date is upon you. Set this alarm the same way you set an alarm for an event, as discussed previously in the section "Add Events."

- Calendar—Choose the calendar to associate with this task if the current selection isn't the right one.
- URL—Enter a web address to associate with this task if desired.

That's it. The task is set in iCal and all that remains is for you to actually follow through and do what you say you're going to do. (If only it were that simple!)

Working with Multiple Calendars

The Home and Work calendars are nice, but you may need to work with more calendars as you dig into iCal; fortunately they're easy to create. To create a new calendar you can double-click in the calendar list, click the plus ("+") icon at the bottom of the Calendars list, or choose File, New Calendar. When you do any of these things, the new calendar's title is highlighted and ready for you to type its name. Do so and press Return.

In the Info window, your only choice when it comes to options for a new calendar is the color; from the menu, choose the color that you'd like for this calendar, or choose Other and you can specify a color using the Mac's color-picking tools. You now have a named, colorful calendar that you can use for something other than Home or Work. (Or, something more specific than those things.)

To delete a calendar, select it and press the Delete key or choose Edit, Delete. If you want it back, choose Edit, Undo.

Once you have multiple calendars and a fair bit of information in them, you'll find it handy that you can actually turn on and off the display of your different calendars. If you just want to look at the Rugby calendar, to see when you have practices, games, and team meetings, then you can turn off the check mark next to all other calendars. When a calendar is checked, its events and tasks appear in the calendar window; when a calendar is unchecked, you won't see the items associated with it.

To make it easier to turn multiple calendars on and off, you can create calendar groups. A calendar group is simply a higher-level calendar that can hold multiple regular calendars. You could create a calendar group called Social that has the Dates and Volunteering and Poker Night calendars all underneath that one Social calendar

group. That lets you turn all of them on and off at once so that you quickly decide to view those events and tasks or not.

To create a calendar group, choose File, New Calendar Group. You can then give the calendar group a name and press Return. Now, drag other calendars in the calendar list to this calendar group. With that accomplished, you can turn the group on and off together using the check box for the group.

Publish Your Calendar

Built into iCal is the ability to publish your calendars to the Web so that other people can look up your schedule and see what you're doing; this is most easily done if you have subscribed to a .Mac account from Apple, but you can use iCal to publish calendars to certain types of websites as well.

TIP

Published calendars aren't just for your own events, but they can be handy for any type of event calendar. You could publish a calendar of sales meetings that your sales reps can download into their own copies of iCal. You could also publish the soccer practice schedule for your child's team or the schedule for the yoga class you're going to be teaching at the community center.

Here's how to publish your calendar:

1. Begin by highlighting the calendar that you want to publish in the Calendars list. (You can only publish one calendar at a time.)
2. Choose Calendar, Publish from the iCal menu. A dialog sheet appears.

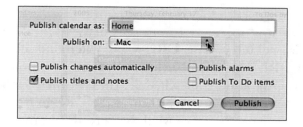

3. At the top of the dialog sheet, type a name of the calendar if you want to name it something other than its name in iCal. (You might opt for something more descriptive.)

4. In the Publish On menu, choose .Mac if you'd like to publish to your .Mac space or choose A Private Server if you have a WebDAV-compatible web server that you'd like to use for the calendar.

If you've chosen .Mac, you can make additional choices from the options at the bottom on the dialog sheet and then click Publish. Those choices include whether you want to publish alarms and To Do items along with titles and notes. If you choose Publish Changes Automatically then any changes to the published calendar will be changed on the Web, as well, whenever your Mac is connected to the Internet.

NOTE

You'll encounter an error in iCal if you don't have your .Mac information set up in the .Mac preference pane in System Preferences. See Chapter 8 for details.

If you've chosen A Private Server, you can make the same option choices as with .Mac, but you also need to enter the URL, login, and password for the WebDAV server to which you are going to publish your calendar. Then, click Publish and wait for confirmation that your page is published.

NOTE

A WebDAV server is a special type of web server that's specifically designed to offer direct access to the server with a user name and password. Typical web servers require you to upload pages via FTP (File Transfer Protocol). You *cannot* publish your calendar to such servers if they don't support WebDAV.

Once published, iCal will tell you the URL where you'll find the calendar online. You can then share that URL with others or link to it from your other web documents so that people know where to find your schedule. (In fact, there's a Send Mail button in the iCal dialog box that encourages you to email the URL to friends and colleagues—click it to launch a new email in Apple Mail that already has the URL in its body.)

If you haven't decided to auto-publish your calendar, you can select the Calendar, Refresh command to update the calendar that you have currently selected in iCal; if you have multiple calendars, you can use the Calendar, Refresh All command to update them all.

If, once the calendar is online, you decide that you'd like to change the location where it's published (from .Mac to a WebDAV server, for instance) then choose Calendar, Change Location. You'll then see the same options you saw when initially publishing the calendar.

If you decide that you no longer want to have a particular calendar on the Web, select it in the Calendars list in iCal and then choose Calendar, Unpublish. You'll be asked to confirm the decision in a dialog box; click Unpublish if you really do want to remove it from the Web.

Subscribe to Calendars

One of the keys to the success of iCal is the fact that calendars created in the program (or those using the .ics format) are incredibly easy to share with others. This is handy for publishing your own calendars, as you just read. But iCal can also subscribe to calendars posted and published by others, which can make for some useful additions to your own iCal experience.

 The easiest way to subscribe to someone else's calendar is to find the Subscribe button *on* that calendar while you're surfing the Web.

Doing so will launch iCal on your Mac and open a dialog sheet, where you'll see the URL for the calendar you just clicked. Choose Subscribe and that calendar will be added to iCal—it will be listed in the Calendars list and its items will appear in your daily, weekly, and monthly views.

Another way to subscribe is to simply choose Calendar, Subscribe from the iCal menu. A dialog sheet appears where you can enter a URL to a calendar—you'll need to use the webcal:// URL type and a full path to the calendar document (which should end with a .ics extension).

Probably the most *fun* way to subscribe to calendars is to select the command Calendar, Find Shared Calendars. That launches a page on Apple's website that lists a number of different publicly published calendars that you can then subscribe to. They include sports calendars, holiday calendars, entertainment calendars, tours by musicians, and so on. When you find a calendar you like, click its Subscribe icon and it will be added to your iCal.

> **TIP**
>
> You can also choose to download calendars using the Download command on most published iCal calendars. That won't subscribe you to any updates that are made to the calendar, but it can be used for more static calendars like those that list sporting event calendars or holidays and moon phases.

In addition to Apple's own web links to these calendars, iCalShare.com is also a very popular spot for calendars to which you can subscribe.

Sync Address Book and iCal

Now that we've covered Address Book and iCal, I want to quickly discuss syncing both with the .Mac service before we close out this chapter. As you'll see in Chapter 7, "iPods, iTunes, and iSync," both Address Book and iCal can be synchronized with your PDA, iPod, or similar device as well, so that you can carry your contact information, meetings, events, and To Do items along with you.

But before we get to synchronizing with external devices, it's worth knowing that you can use your .Mac subscription, if you have one, to synchronize your Address Book and calendars between multiple Macs. This is useful if you have multiple Macs—one in the office and one at home, for instance.

> **NOTE**
>
> Syncing is a little different from sharing your Address Book, which we covered earlier in the chapter or publishing iCal calendars. The Sync feature is specifically designed for *you* to synchronize your calendar and address book on your own Macs, if you have more than one.

To synchronize either Address Book or iCal, you first need to turn on .Mac synchronization. Do that by opening the System Preferences application and choosing the .Mac preference pane. You'll need to have an accurate .Mac account name and password on the .Mac tab, as discussed in Chapter 9.

Now, click the Sync tab (see Figure 6.11). Your Mac will connect with .Mac to ensure that you have a correct account login. If you do, then you can click the check box next to Synchronize with .Mac in order to turn on the feature; from the pull-down menu, choose Manually or Automatically. (If you choose Manually, you'll have to return to this window periodically and click the Sync Now button.)

FIGURE 6.11

The .Mac pane in System Preferences gives you the option of synchronizing many of your applications with other Macs via Apple's .Mac service.

With synchronization turned on, you can now decide what, exactly, you'd like to synchronize—click to place a check mark next to Calendars and Contacts for iCal and Address Book (as you can see, you can synchronize other things as well, which we'll discuss in different sections of the book). Now, click Sync Now to begin the synchronization process.

The final step is to register this (and other) Macs for synchronizing with your Calendars and/or Contacts. Select the Advanced tab. Now, click Register This Computer to add it to the list of computers that can synchronize to this .Mac account. On your other Macs, you'll need to enter the same .Mac account information in the .Mac preference pane and then register those computers as well. Each registered computer is then able to synchronize with the .Mac server and, thus, have access to the same data.

Chapter 7

iPods, iTunes, and iSync

Just a few years back, few would have thought that a device like the iPod would play such a role in reversing Apple's fortunes. Once considered "beleaguered" and "downtrodden" by the media and pundits, Apple is again a rising star of the technology market in large part because of two technologies we're going to discuss in this chapter—iTunes and the iPod. iTunes has changed the way many of us buy and enjoy commercial music, not to mention how we manage our iPods.

The iPod is more than just a music device although, clearly, that's a big part of it. The iPod can also be used for storing data and holding contact and event information, which we'll see later in this chapter. Synchronizing that data involves iSync, Apple's built-in application for dealing with personal information devices—not just the iPod, but Palm OS devices, mobile phones, and other items that can be connected to your Mac and "synched."

The iPod and iTunes Music

While it's the combination of the iPod and iTunes that is making such a big splash and, apparently, changing the way a lot of people buy music, it's iTunes (and, particularly, the iTunes Music Store) that is the more revolutionary of the two items.

While the iPod is quite a piece of hardware, iTunes did something pretty impressive—it took some of the energy of the file-swapping "wild west" days of Napster-style music file exchange and came up with a way to turn it into a commercial enterprise, thus introducing the $0.99 song. By making a song relatively inexpensive to download at high-quality—while giving the user the satisfaction of knowing that the transaction is legal—Apple has used the iTunes Music Store to shake things up quite nicely in the music industry.

The iPod, on the other hand is a well-designed piece of hardware, and it's clever partly because of its large capacity and partly because of its simple interface. But compared to the implementation of the iTunes Music Store, the iPod is a bit more evolutionary than revolutionary, since digital music players existed prior to the iPod. The combination of great ideas and great design, however, make the iPod and iTunes combo pretty darned unique.

Get Songs into iTunes

Even if you don't have an iPod, iTunes, in its own right, is a great program. With a central library of music files, iTunes enables you to "rip" music from the CDs that you own, incorporate any other MP3 or digital audio music that you have available, and store them alongside the music files that you buy and download from the iTunes Music Store. You can then create special playlists, play back songs randomly, and even send those songs over a wireless connection to an AirPort Express device and play the songs back through your stereo system. iTunes is a great way to manage a music collection.

NOTE

A few years back, the dominant form of digital music file on the Mac platform was the "MP3" file, short for *MPEG-3*, which in turn, is short for *Motion Picture Expert Group Type 3*. MP3 is a file format that supports high-quality playback but offers heavy compression, such that a good recording only requires about 1MB of storage space per minute of song. The result is a very "downloadable" but nearly CD-quality song file, which is why MP3 became so popular. iTunes can play back (and encode) MP3s, but the dominant form in iTunes is AAC, for *Advanced Audio Codec*, both because it offers higher quality and *digital rights management*—Apple uses the file format via its iTunes Music store to limit what you can do with the file and how you can play it back, as we'll see later in this section.

To begin, you need to launch and configure iTunes. By default, you should see an iTunes icon on your Dock; if not, you'll find the application in your Applications folder. The first time you launch iTunes, you'll see the iTunes Setup Assistant (shown in Figure 7.1), which steps you through the process of adding any digital music files that you may already have on your hard disk. Just use the Next and Previous buttons as you would in any Assistant, answering the questions as they come up. (You may, for instance, *not* want iTunes to automatically connect to the Internet if you have a dial-up modem connection.)

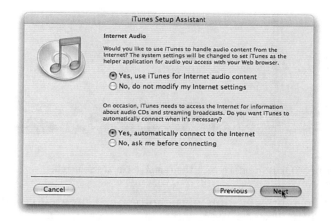

FIGURE 7.1

The iTunes Setup Assistant is used to tell iTunes whether it's allowed to access the Internet and if it should look on your hard disk for music files.

Once iTunes has launched, you'll see the main interface and, depending on your choice in the Assistant, you'll either see the Library or the iTunes Music Store. The Library is your main interface into the music that is stored on your hard disk or on devices such as the iPod. Figure 7.2 shows the main iTunes window with the Library selected in the Source list.

The Source list is one of the key areas in the interface, as it's where you'll switch between the various "sources" you have for listings of songs. On that list, you'll see the Library, of course, where every song that is on your Mac and tracked by iTunes will be listed. But the Source list is also where you'll see your iPod pop up, when connected, and the Source list holds a link to the Music Store and to the built-in Internet radio stations that you can connect to from iTunes.

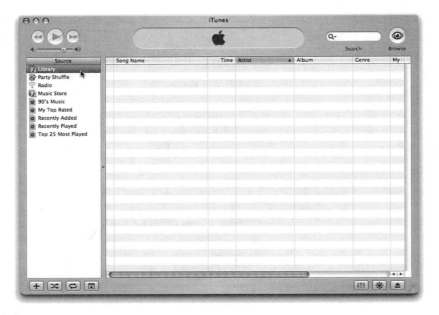

FIGURE 7.2
Here's a somewhat barren iTunes interface with the (empty) Library selected.

First, though, you need to get some music into your Library if you don't already have some. There are three different ways to do that: You can import music from existing music files, you can rip songs from audio CDs, or you can buy music from the iTunes Music Store. Let's start with importing and ripping.

Import Audio Files and CD Audio

If you already have audio files that iTunes would be compatible with—which means MP3s and AAC files (as well as a few other formats such as WAV and AIFF), you can add them to the Library most simply by dragging and dropping the music file from the Finder onto the Library icon or into the Library window. You can also choose File, Import to open an Import dialog box that, like an Open dialog, enables you to locate files that you want to import. (You can even drag audio files onto the iTunes icon in the Dock.) Once imported, the songs will appear in the Library listing.

To add songs or tracks from an audio CD, insert the CD into your Mac. After a moment, you'll see its icon appear in the Source list. Select it, and you'll see a list of the songs on that CD in the main content window (see Figure 7.3).

NOTE

You won't always necessarily see song titles in this listing for a CD. In order for you to see the titles, they must be associated with the audio CD's title in the GraceNote CDDB (www.gracenote.com) database on the Internet. And, for that matter, you've got to have Internet access in order to retrieve the titles if they haven't been retrieved in the past.

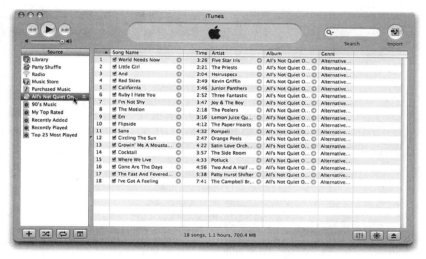

FIGURE 7.3

A list of song titles appears (if you're connected to the Internet), enabling you to access each track on the CD.

Just as an aside here, you may have noticed something already about these CD tracks—you can play them from within iTunes. Simply double-click a song or select it and then click the Play button at the top-left of the window. Whenever you want to play an audio CD, you simply insert it in your Mac's drive and start playing—no need to import first.

If you do want to import all the songs from the CD, though, you can. Simply click the Import button at the top-right of the iTunes window. When you do, you'll see a small icon appear next to the first song on that album and, in the information area at the top of the window you'll see a progress bar. The import process will continue until all the songs are imported, unless you cancel the process for some reason. You can cancel by clicking the Import button again.

iTunes

Importing "World Needs Now"
Time remaining: 0:11 (5.1x)

Search   Import

▲	Song Name		Time	Artist	Album	Genre
1	☑ World Needs Now	⊙	3:26	Five Star Iris	All's Not Quiet O... ⊙	Alternative...
2	☑ Little Girl	⊙	2:21	The Priests	All's Not Quiet O... ⊙	Alternative...

TIP

Want to import just one song? Select it in the content window and drag it to the Library icon in the Source list. That will import just that one song. (You can do the same thing with a selection of multiple songs if you want to limit the import to just that group.)

When you're done with a CD, you can click the small Eject icon that appears next to the CD in the Source list, or you can click the Eject icon that appears in the bottom-right corner of the iTunes window. That clears the CD out of your Mac's drive and gets it ready for the next one.

Eject Disc.

NOTE

You can choose iTunes, Preferences and click the Importing icon to see preferences for how you import audio files, including the file format and the quality setting. iTunes, by default, imports songs as AAC files, but you can use the MP3 Encoder (or even the AIFF or WAV encoders) if you'd like CD tracks in a different format. AIFF offers high-quality playback, but very large file sizes compared to MP3 or AAC; WAV is a similar format that's popular on Microsoft Windows-based PCs.

The iTunes Music Store

The other way to get songs into your library is to buy them. That's what the iTunes Music Store is so good at—enticing you into spending just a *few extra* dollars on some new songs for your library. And, the truth is that it can be fun just to browse.

To launch the iTune Music Store, click its entry on the Source list to visit it. If you're connected to the Internet, the Music Store will appear. The interface is pretty straightforward; if you've spent any time at e-commerce websites, the Music Store will seem pretty familiar. You can jump right in by clicking one of the images of an album cover or an artist, or you can browse the music using the links and lists you'll find on the main page of the Music Store.

There are two items worth noting in the Music Store: One is the Search box, at the top-right corner, which enables you to quickly use keywords or key names to look up songs, artists or albums. The Browse button is handy, because you can use it to quickly rework the iTunes interface, enabling you to drill down and find songs by genre, artist, and album.

The point of moving through the iTunes interface is to come up with lists of songs that you want to listen to and, perhaps, buy. You do that by searching and browsing until you have an album selected; then, in the list, you can double-click a song to hear a 30-second sample. Next to the artist's name and other elements in the list, you'll often see a small arrow icon; click that to see all of the results for that artist or album.

The other important item? In the list, you'll see a Buy Song button, which you can click if you see a song that you need to add to your collection. When you do, you'll be walked through the registration process if you don't already have an Apple ID (or an AOL account) in order to make the purchase.

NOTE

You can also, at least *often*, buy an entire album (or all of the songs that iTunes offers of a particular album) by clicking the Buy Album button that appears near the album cover art at the top of the iTunes Music window. It's also worth noting that albums often cost $9.99, which is a great deal if the album has more than 10 tracks at the regular $0.99 per track.

Once you've bought a song or album, that song appears in the Library on the Mac that you downloaded the songs to, as well as in the Purchased Music playlist that appears on the Source list. You can access them in either place to play the songs back, or you can arrange those songs in playlists and, as we'll discuss, you can burn the songs to CD.

There are some rules for how you can use purchased songs, however. A song that you've purchased from the iTunes Music Store can be burnt to as many CDs as you'd like, but the same playlist that includes bought songs can only be burned seven times before it has to be rearranged. (That's to keep you from burning too many "mix" CDs and handing them out to friends.) A purchased song will only play on Macs and Windows machines in copies of iTunes that are *authorized* to play songs associated with your Apple ID. (This is the practical manifestation of the digital rights management technology that's built in to the AAC format.) Only five machines can be authorized at once, so you can't exactly take the song and e-mail it off to all your friends. Or, rather, you *can*, but only authorized computers can *play* those songs.

NOTE

It's important to deauthorize a computer if you plan to sell it or stop using it, because even a computer that you no longer own can end up keeping you from authorizing new (or other) computers for playback. To deauthorize a computer, choose Advanced, Deauthorize Computer in iTunes.

Managing Songs in iTunes

So, now that you have some songs in the iTunes library, what can you do with them? Aside from browsing through them and playing them back, the key housekeeping functions enable you to create playlists (so you can play songs for different moods or settings) and burn CDs. You can also take advantage of the built-in automation, such as the Party Shuffle feature and the Smart Playlists that can do things with a little less input from you.

You'll start in the Library, where, as you'll find after a while, things can quickly get pretty overwhelming. Even with only 30 or 40 songs in the Library, you'll find that you're doing a lot of scrolling to see what you have; once it gets in the hundreds or thousands of songs, which iTunes is perfectly capable of dealing with, then you'll really find that moving through the list isn't much fun.

To whittle away at that, you can start by using the column headings—Song Name, Time, Artist, Album, and so on—in much the same way that you can use column headings in a Finder list view. Click them. When you click a column heading, the list sorts based on that column—usually the list is alphabetical or, in the case of the length of a song (for instance), the list goes from lowest to highest or highest to lowest. And, as an added bonus, you can click a list again to change its *sort order*.

If sorting is not working for you, iTunes offers a Search box that's also familiar to seasoned Finder window users; start typing in that Search box and you'll see that the list quickly reacts to what you type, showing only songs that have some relationship to the letters that you've put in that box. Note that the keyword can be part of the name of the song, the album, or even a portion of the artist's name and all relevant songs will appear (see Figure 7.4).

FIGURE 7.4

In this example, searching for the keyword love brings up plenty of songs with "love" in the title, as well as all the songs on the De-Lovely soundtrack and one song by a group that has Love as part of their name.

NOTE

Like the iTunes Music Store interface, your Library also has a Browse mode; click the Browse button and the window changes around a bit to enable you to dig through songs by genre, artist, or album. Note that if, for instance, you *don't* want to limit the list by genre, you don't have to—select All at the top of the list first, and then move on to the Artist column. After all, some artists show up in different genres occasionally, right?

The other solution to Library clutter is to start building playlists. A playlist is simply a collection of songs that can be reordered, added to, and subtracted from at your whim; the songs listed in a playlist remain in the Library, so you can have the same song in different playlists, if you like. The classic example of a playlist is a list of songs you like to use for your workout versus the songs you like to listen to for a romantic evening at home; there might be some songs that cross over between the two (for instance, Survivor's "Eye of the Tiger" from the *Rocky* films…I'm kidding) and you can add the same song to two or more playlists easily.

To create a playlist, click the plus ("+") icon that appears at the bottom of the Source list and, when the Untitled Playlist appears, begin typing to give it a title. That creates a playlist icon on the Source list; now, add songs to it by dragging them from the Library window to that icon.

TIP

Here's a fun way to create a playlist: Highlight the songs first, and then choose File, New Playlist from Selection. A new playlist will appear in the Source list, which you can rename; it'll already have all the selected songs in it. You might also want to play with Smart Playlists, which can use keyword searches and other criteria to create playlists automatically.

Once songs are in a playlist, you can re-order them to your desire; you aren't stuck with alphabetical order and such (although you can still use the column headers to switch things around). The whole point is to get them arranged the way you want them for playback—these are your favorites, right?

NOTE

If you point your mouse at a playlist in the Source list, you'll see a small arrow icon appear; you can click that icon to send your playlist to the iTunes Music Store where it becomes an iMix. These iMix collections are a fun way to share titles of your favorite music and artists with others via the store—your iMix can be searched for and it will appear when people search for the artists, albums, on genres that you cover.

The other thing you can do easily with a playlist is burn it to a CD in audio CD format, so that it can be used in a car or home CD player. Here's how:

1. You first want to arrange your songs the way you like them on the playlist. You should also check the bottom of the iTunes window when the playlist is selected to make sure you don't have too much music for an audio CD. (A typical CD can hold a little over 70 minutes of music.)

2. Insert a blank CD-R into your Mac's optical drive. (CD-R is better than CD-RW, as it's more compatible with consumer audio CD players, particularly older ones.) If a dialog box appears, choose Open iTunes.

3. In the iTunes window, click the Burn Disc icon in the top-right corner. It should change so that it looks like a nuclear warning symbol of sorts. (For "burn"—get it?)

4. If you have the correct playlist selected and the Checking Media message is done, you can click the Burn Disc icon to get things started. (Warning: that icon gets a little psychedelic once it starts spinning. Try not to stare—it may affect productivity.)

Once the burning process has begun it's basically a matter of waiting; the info area at the top of the iTunes windows will show you the progress of the burn and let you know how much longer it will take. When it's done, the CD will appear on the Source list as a, well...CD.

> **TIP**
>
> Select iTunes, Preferences, and click the Burning icon to see the options for burning, which include forcing iTunes to burn at a slower speed and setting the gap between songs (you may have better luck with certain audio CD equipment if there's a longer gap). You can also opt to burn other types of CDs, such as MP3 CDs or data CDs, which store the song files as computer files, not as audio CD tracks. That can be handy for backup and for sharing songs with friends; some audio equipment can play back MP3 CDs as if they were audio CDs, except with many more tracks, since you can fit hundreds of MP3s on a single CD.

iTunes and Your iPod

So, if you read some of the preceding sections, it's probably clear that iTunes is its own beast—it's not just about the iPod. Of course, the iPod is a popular little product line, and iTunes the primary iPod-wrangling software, so that's a big part of what it does that shouldn't be ignored. Therefore, I won't ignore it. (If you don't have an iPod, you can learn more about them at www.apple.com/ipod on the Web.)

Using your iPod with iTunes is pretty straightforward. Plug your iPod into your Mac and, by default, iTunes will be launched automatically. When it is, your iPod should appear in the Source list, giving you access to its library (which you get to by selecting the iPod's icon itself).

There are three different ways to manage an iPod using iTunes. (Each of them, incidentally, is accessible by clicking the iPod icon toward the right-bottom of the iTunes window.)

Those methods are

- Automatically Update All Songs and Playlists. If you choose this option, every song and playlist that you have in iTunes will be transferred to your iPod this first time; from then on, any additions in iTunes will be synchronized with the iPod when you plug the iPod in.

- Automatically Update Selected Playlists Only. As capacious as the typical iPod is, you may not always be able to fit every song in your Library on your iPod. (Or, you may not want to.) In that case, you can use the second option to select only certain playlists that are synchronized to your iPod.
- Manually Manage Sounds and Playlists. With this option selected, you can drag and drop songs from your Library and playlists from your Source list onto the iPod in order to "synchronize" with the device.

One thing worth knowing about your iPod is that you can't drag songs *from* it *to* iTunes—it's designed not to allow that. The idea is that Apple doesn't want you to use your iPod to swap songs to others. So, songs can only go in one direction, from iTunes to your iPod, if you want to update it.

TIP

In the interest of full disclosure, there are applications that will let you move songs from your iPod to your Mac; for instance iPodRip (www.thelittleappfactory.com) can let you get files from your iPod—and there's a legitimate reason for doing so, too, if you ever have your Mac crash without a backup of your (rather expensive) AAC collection of downloaded songs.

When you're done with your iPod in iTunes, click the small Eject icon next to the iPod in the Source list; after doing so, you'll see a message on the iPod that says it's okay to disconnect it.

The iPod As a Hard Drive

I mentioned that the iPod is really an evolutionary product, since there are many audio players on the market, and some of them quite good. What was visionary about the iPod and iPod mini, however, was the way that Apple managed to make carrying a hard drive around in your pocket into something trendy and ultra-hip. Think about it—if Apple had tried to sell people a "pocket-sized hard drive you can take with you!" then it certainly wouldn't have altered the computing landscape or cause a stock split for Apple Computer, Inc.

But the truth is, many of us are walking around with hard drives in our pockets or bags, and the result is something that can be handy beyond just music playback and management. You can use your iPod for file storage and transfer, as well as for contact management and for accessing your calendar, if desired. (We'll cover those a bit later in the section on iSync.)

To use your iPod as a hard drive, you may first need to enable that option in iTunes, particularly if your iPod is synched automatically to your Library or to selected playlists. Here's how:

1. Make sure iTunes has recognized your iPod or iPod mini, then click the iPod icon in the Source list.

2. When the iPod button appears at the bottom-right of the iTunes window, click it. That opens iPod Preferences.

3. In the iPod Preferences dialog box, choose the General tab, and then click to turn on the option Enable Disk Use.

4. Click OK to close the dialog box.

Now, you should be able to switch to the Finder and see your iPod appear on the desktop and/or in a Finder window's Sidebar. Figure 7.5 shows a mounted iPod. An iPod works pretty much like any other external disk, allowing you to copy files and folders to it, to delete files and folders from the iPod, to create and rename folders directly on the iPod, and so on. You do not, however, get direct access to the music files stored on the disk and managed by iTunes—at least, not without a third-party utility program.

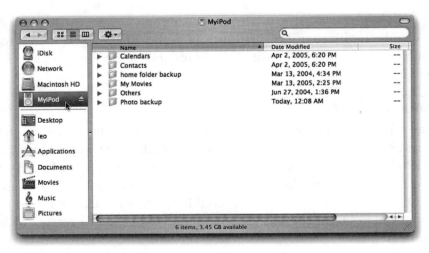

FIGURE 7.5
If you like, you can use your iPod as an external FireWire hard disk, handy for backing up files or transferring them between computers.

What's iSync All About?

Included with Mac OS X is a utility application called iSync, which enables you to synchronize data between various devices—personal digital assistants, mobile phones, iPods—and your Mac's applications such as Address Book and iCal. In past Mac OS X versions, iSync was also used to synchronize data from those applications (as well as bookmarks from Safari and so on) using the .Mac service, but that functionality has been rolled into the .Mac preference pane in the System Preferences application. So, iSync is pretty much about getting stuff from your Mac synchronized with other hardware and devices.

Syncing Your Devices

If you think you have a device that qualifies for compatibility with iSync, you can connect it to your Mac and launch iSync, which is found in your Applications folder. When you do, the iSync window appears.

Now, the next step is to add the connected device. To do that, choose Devices, Add Device. A dialog box appears, showing you that devices are being searched for. When one is found, it appears in that window; double-click it to add it to iSync.

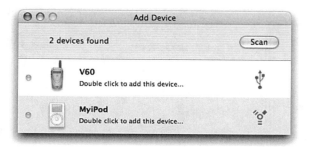

Once added, the device appears at the top of the iSync window. When you select the device, you'll see the iSync window open up, enabling you to decide what and how iSync will synchronize that device with your Mac's data. The fine points on synchronization include whether or not you want to sync both contacts and calendars, which of your contacts and calendars you want to sync, and so on. Figure 7.6 shows the options I have for synchronizing data with my cell phone's internal address book and appointment calendar.

> **NOTE**
> The first time you connect some devices to your Mac via iSync (or if you remove the device and then subsequently add it again) you will see a For First Sync menu, which lets you decide whether you should erase everything on the device and then copy data from your Mac to that device or whether you should simply merge all the data on both the device and your Mac. That menu is also shown in Figure 7.6.

FIGURE 7.6
Here's an example of synchronizing data with a mobile phone that has built-in address book and appointment management.

Any time you have the device connected to your Mac, you can switch to iSync and synchronize data between the Mac and your device, just so that you catch any changes you've made. And, in the iSync Preferences window (select iSync, Preferences from the menu), you'll find an option called Show Status In Menu Bar, which you can turn on if you'd like to be able to quickly initiate a sync from the menu.

To remove a device, simply select it in iSync and choose Devices, Remove Device. You'll be asked if you're sure—click OK to confirm that you want to remove the device from iSync's purview.

Sync Your iPod

Got an iPod? You can use iSync to synchronize the same data—contacts and appointments—to your iPod that you might synchronize to a PDA or mobile phone. The process is the same, too, with the one difference being that you can set iSync to automatically perform a synchronize action whenever the iPod is connected to your Mac.

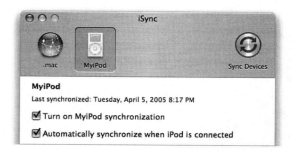

Once synchronized, you can use the Contacts and Calendar features of the iPod's interface (look under Extras on the iPod's screen) to access the data.

Working with Bluetooth Stuff

Bluetooth, the wireless standard for connecting devices, is growing in popularity among the sort of devices we're talking about, such as mobile phones and PDAs. What Bluetooth is, in practice, is sort of a wireless USB. It's designed to handle much less data than, say, an AirPort (or WiFi) networking connection; instead, it's designed for swapping data files between phones or handheld devices or your Mac and other little doodads. That makes Bluetooth devices a great fit for iSync.

> **NOTE**
>
> If you don't have a Mac that supports Bluetooth internally, you can add a USB-to-Bluetooth adapter and driver software that makes support possible. Two companies that manufacture such Mac-compatible devices are Belkin (www.belkin.com) and D-Link (www.d-link.com).

To work with a Bluetooth-enabled device, you first need to *pair* it with your Mac. Here's how:

1. Open the Bluetooth pane of System Preferences, which, by the way, only appears if your Mac supports Bluetooth.

2. On the Settings tab, make sure you have Bluetooth turned on and that the Discoverable option is active so that your Mac can be "found" by other Bluetooth wireless devices.

3. Now, switch to the Devices tab and click the Set Up a New Device button. That brings up the Bluetooth Setup Assistant, which walks you through the process of adding a Bluetooth device.

4. In the Assistant, choose the type of device you want to add. (You'll want to have the device on, with Bluetooth activated, and within a few feet of your Mac.) Click Continue and the device will be searched for.

5. If your Mac finds the device, it will appear in the listing. Select it and click Continue. (If you don't find the device, check the device's settings and make sure it's configured properly, then click Go Back, make sure the correct device is selected, and click Continue again to keep up the search.)

6. With a discovered device, the next step is usually to enter a special passkey (see Figure 7.7). Depending on the device, this may be a code that's built in to the device (check its manual) or it may be something that you enter both on your Mac and on the device. What the passkey does is make sure you're not accidentally pairing with a device that you don't have access to, such as a PDA in your officemate's cubicle next door (or the mobile phone in your competitor's coat pocket) or something similar.

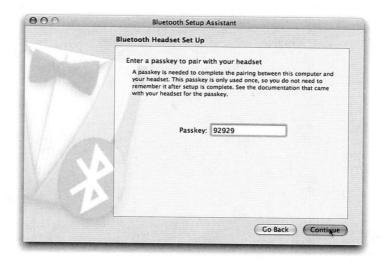

FIGURE 7.7
The passcode is used to ensure that you're pairing your Mac with a device that you're authorized to access.

Once the device is paired with your Mac, it's essentially the same as if it were connected to your Mac using FireWire or USB. So, now you can switch back to iSync and configure the device as you would any other.

TIP

Got a non–Palm OS PDA? A lot of those devices have Bluetooth built in, but not many of them are Mac- and iSync-compatible out of the box. As a workaround, one option is PocketMac Lite (http://www.pocketmac.com/products/pmlite/pmlite.html), which enables you to synchronize that device using Bluetooth and iSync.

Part

Chapter 8

Get on the Internet

The Internet is such a big part of computing these days that it's almost unheard of to have a personal computer that isn't connected to it in some way. After all, the Internet expands the entire universe of computing, enabling you to make purchases, check your banking balance, research just about anything, and, of course, have fascinating (or silly) discussions (or arguments) in chat rooms or on web forums and other such sites.

A Mac running Mac OS X is designed from the ground up to live on the Internet. In fact, as you'll see, the native protocol used for connecting Macs on a local network is the same protocol—TCP/IP—that's used for networking computers around the world into the global network that we call the Internet. Once you're connected, you'll have a gaggle of tools at your disposal for communicating with others and retrieving information from all sorts of sources.

In this chapter, we'll look at the different ways you can get Mac OS X to connect to the Internet and help figure out the best approach for you. Then, we'll discuss Apple's special Internet service—the .Mac service. It requires that you pay a subscription price to use it, but you may find that worthwhile once you've learned a little about it.

How Internet Connections Work

The Internet is a global network of computers that are all running the Transmission Control Protocol/Internet Protocol, or TCP/IP, which governs how packets of data are transmitted from computer to computer along the network so that, eventually, those data packets arrive at their destination. Any computer on the Internet has its own IP address, which is a series of four numbers that give the computer its own unique address on the Internet. (One of the web server computers for the popular Mac magazine *Macworld* has an IP address of 130.94.4.193, for instance.)

To get on the Internet, you need to be connected to it and you need an IP address. Usually you'll accomplish that by connecting to an Internet service provider, or ISP, which acts as the go-between for your Mac and the Internet. Once connected to your ISP, your Mac will be assigned an IP address and you'll be able to connect to other machines on the Internet (the *servers*) where you can retrieve data or pass it along using various applications. For instance, you can connect to a *mail server* to send or receive email messages, a *web server* to access pages on the World Wide Web, or an *FTP server* to upload or download files using the File Transport Protocol.

NOTE

Most services on the Internet—the Web, FTP, email, chat—have their own protocols that work on top of TCP/IP to make that service possible. The Web, for example, uses the Hypertext Transport Protocol (HTTP). A web browser, then, is an application that knows how to retrieve and display documents using the HTTP protocol, and a web server is a computer that knows how to reply to requests and send documents using the HTTP protocol.

So how do you connect to an ISP? There are a number of different ways. In years past, the most common approach for consumers was to use a telephone-based modem to dial in over regular telephone lines. This approach, popularly called *dial-up*, is slower than other types of connections that are generally called *broadband*. Dial-up connections are still handy when you're in a hotel room or a rural location, or when you simply don't want to pay for a broadband connection into your home (or guest house or country house). Generally, all you need is a phone line and service from an ISP that will accept the call from your Mac's modem.

With a broadband connection, things are a little different. The most common types of broadband connection are Digital Subscriber Line (DSL), which uses an upgraded version of the phone line coming into your home or office, and cable, which uses the same connection as cable television service. Other options include wireless broadband (available from some mobile phone service providers) and satellite-based connections that retrieve high-speed access from orbital platforms. (Doesn't *that* sound cool?) And, particularly in a business office, you may have a dedicated connection to the Internet in the form of a T-1 or T-3 line.

For consumers, though, you'll likely call up the phone company, cable company, or a local ISP to get a broadband connection. Then, how you make the connection from your Mac to the Internet via that ISP depends on the technology you're using—we'll cover that in the upcoming sections.

NOTE

The ISP that you've chosen for Internet service should have given you some basic information regarding how you configure the connection. It's a good idea to have that information handy whether you're setting up a dial-up or broadband connection. You'll need to refer to those numbers and settings when you follow my instructions in the following sections.

Regardless of the type of connection you're configuring, you're going to end up spending at least some of your time in the Network pane of System Preferences. That's where you configure any sort of network connection, including Internet connections—even those that take place over a modem. So, for starters, you'll want to launch System Preferences by selecting it from the Apple menu or clicking its icon in the Dock.

NOTE

If you can't seem to edit anything in the Network pane, it's because you need to authenticate as an administrator. Click the padlock icon and enter the username and password of an Admin-level user on your Mac. See Chapter 4, "Conquering the Mac OS X Interface," for details on Admin accounts.

Once launched, select the Network icon by clicking on it once and you should see the Network pane appear. The first screen that you'll generally see when the Network pane is opened is the Network Status window, shown in Figure 8.1.

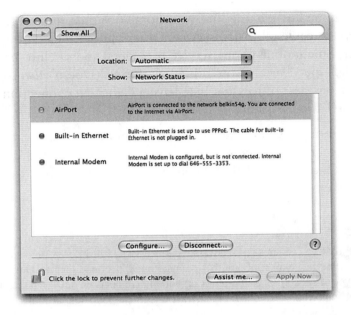

FIGURE 8.1

The Network Status menu is handy for quickly seeing the current state of your Mac's network connections.

The Network Status window gives you a quick snapshot of the state of your network connections, including any modems, wireless (AirPort) connections, and Ethernet (wired) network ports that Mac OS X detects. To configure one of those ports, you can double-click it in that list or you can select it from the Show menu. In either case, the Network Status window is a handy way to quickly get a sense of how your network ports are doing and whether they're currently connected to anything.

NOTE

If you already have an active connection, it may be because you created or configured an Internet connection—either when you set up your new Mac or after you installed a fresh copy of Mac OS X. If that's the case then you can either skip the discussion in this chapter about configuring connections or your can use this discussion to tweak your settings or add new connections if you change Internet providers or add an additional service. And, if you're looking to connect multiple computers to a single Internet connection, you'll find Chapter 11, "Build a Home Office Network," will assist you with that task.

Configure for Dial-Up

Connecting to the Internet for the first time via dial-up is a two-step process. First, you configure your Mac to be prepared for the connection, then you dial out via your modem to make the actual connection.

You'll do the configuration in the Network pane of System Preferences. Since you're looking to configure a dial-up connection, you should either double-click the Internal Modem entry or choose it from the Show menu. That reveals the tabs and settings for your modem, as shown in the next section, in Figure 8.2.

PPP Tab

By default, the first tab you'll see is the PPP tab. On it, you'll find entry boxes that enable you to specify the account name for your dial-up connection, along with the password for that account and the phone number that is supposed to be dialed to connect to the ISP. You can also specify an alternate phone number if your ISP gives you more than one option for dialing in. (Sometimes the first phone number may be busy, for instance.)

Figure 8.2 shows these configuration options.

TIP

If you need to turn off call waiting or enter any codes before you dial out to reach a number (such as a long distance code or *70 to turn off call waiting) you can enter those numbers and then a comma or two (",") to add pauses, as in ***70,,555-3434.**

The PPP tab offers another button, PPP Options, which can be used to access a series of more "advanced" options. Perhaps the most interesting is Connect Automatically When Needed. When you turn on this option, your Mac will attempt to dial up to your ISP whenever you do something that requires Internet access, such as checking your email or entering a web address in Safari. This can be handy, but it can also be irritating, particularly if you end up accidentally dialing the modem frequently when other people in your house are trying to talk on the phone!

Network

Show All

Location: Automatic
Show: Internal Modem

PPP   TCP/IP   Proxies   Modem

Service Provider: Universe ITel   (Optional)
Account Name: macrogerbub
Password: ••••••••••••••••••••••
Telephone Number: 646–555-3353
Alternate Number: 646–555-3354   (Optional)

☑ Save password
Checking this box allows all users of this computer to
access this Internet account without entering a password.

(PPP Options...)   (Dial Now...)

(?)

Click the lock to prevent further changes.   (Assist me...)   (Apply Now)

FIGURE 8.2
Once you've selected your modem, you'll see the PPP tab and its options, as well as some other tabs you'll use to configure the modem for dial-up access.

Another useful set of options in this dialog are the Disconnect options (If Idle, When User Logs Out, and When Switching User Accounts), all of which you can tweak once you get a little more used to the behavior of a modem connection. By default, the connection will disconnect when you change users or log out, but it doesn't have to—if more than one of you are using a modem connection and you switch frequently (so that, say, you can both check your email while you're logged on in a motel room) then you might want to opt to turn off Disconnect When Switching User Accounts, for instance.

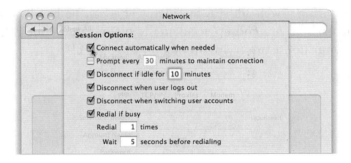

The other options in the PPP Options sheet may come up under special circumstances; if your ISP or company provider requires a terminal window or certain advanced settings, you may need to make those here.

TCP/IP Tab

With most dial-up connections, the TCP/IP tab is relatively similar; you'll set the Configure IPv4 menu to Using PPP and move on to other choices. The Using PPP setting is the default for most dial-up connections, and it means that your Mac will use the ISP's PPP server in order to make the necessary settings, receive its IP address, and determine the addresses for name server computers. (A name server is an Internet server that turns named addresses, such as www.apple.com, into IP addresses, such as 192.168.7.5. Without name servers, we would have to memorize all those numbers in order to reach other servers.)

In some cases, you may need to manually enter a name server address in the DNS Servers entry box; that will generally be an IP address specified by your ISP. In fact, you'll often enter two, so that your Mac has a backup whenever it goes to look up a server name and turn it into an IP address. (When you enter the first IP address, you can press the Return key to enter a second or third one.)

| DNS Servers: | 206.24.35.1
206.24.35.2 | (Optional) |
| Search Domains: | | (Optional) |

You've got two other major options for how your Mac connects to the ISP. In the Configure IPv4 menu, you can select Manually if your ISP allows (or requires) that you specifically enter an IP address for your Mac. This is rare, but it may be necessary if you have a "fixed" IP address from your provider. If that's the case, choose Manually and then enter a valid IP address in the IP Address entry box.

The other option in the Configure IPv4 menu is AOL Dialup, which allows your Mac to use an America Online account for its Internet connection, so that applications other than AOL (such as Mail and Safari) can access the Internet while AOL is active. Choosing AOL Dialup here also enables you to connect to AOL from within the Internet Connect application and the Mac's modem menu on the menu bar, assuming the AOL software is installed and properly configured for a connection.

205

TIP

It's still early and you won't come across many ISPs that support the IPv6 standard, at least not in a consumer setting. But we'll need the extra addresses' space soon on the Internet; IPv6 will gradually replace IPv4 (which is about 20 years old!) as time wears on. And if you work for a company or organization that does support IPv6, you can configure your Mac for that network by clicking the Configure IPv6 button.

Proxies

You probably won't use the Proxies tab unless you're told to. What it does is enable you to enter *proxy server addresses* for a variety of Internet services. What's a proxy server address? It's the address to a server that will be a "proxy" or stand-in (really more of a *go-between*) for the real servers you attempt to access. Instead of accessing the requested server, you access the proxy server, and then the proxy server makes the request of the real server for you.

Proxy servers are often used for parental-control and/or privacy for web surfing. Instead of retrieving a web page directly from the server to your web browser, for instance, the proxy server is accessed first. In the case of a parental-control or other sort of proxy, it may or may not allow the content of the requested page to come through the filter. In the case of a privacy proxy server, it'll probably let the content through, but the distant server won't be able to know it was accessed from your IP address.

If you have a proxy server for some reason, configure it here by selecting a service and placing a check mark next to it in the Select a Proxy Server to Configure box, and then enter an address for that server in the entry box to the right (see Figure 8.3).

If the proxy requires a password, turn on the option Proxy Server Requires Password and then enter the password in the dialog sheet that appears. (If you need to change a password, you can get at it again by clicking the Set Password button.)

In the Bypass Proxy Settings box, you can enter the URL for servers that should bypass your proxy settings and be accessed directly by applications on your Mac.

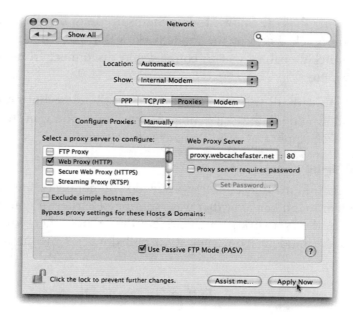

FIGURE 8.3

You can set up proxy servers that intercept requests from your Internet applications and divert them to that proxy.

Modem Tab

The final tab in the Network pane for a dial-up connection is the Modem tab. Here you can choose the type of dial-up modem you're using from the Modem window; this tells the Mac what modem script to use—a lot of modems are slightly different in the way they're configured, so a script is used for those settings. You can also make choices about whether to enable error correction and whether to wait for a dial tone before dialing; generally you'll leave these on unless you're troubleshooting a consistently bad connection or your ISP recommends you turn them off.

One intriguing option on this tab is Notify Me of Oncoming Calls While Connected to the Internet, which does exactly what it says it'll do if you select its check box—you'll see a dialog box appear when the Mac detects an incoming call on a phone line that has call waiting. (Your modem has to support this feature.) If that's the case, you can opt to have your Mac alert you when that happens; just turn on this feature.

Also on the Modem tab is the Show Modem Status in Menu Bar option. When turned on, this gives you quick access to the modem from the Mac's menu bar, including a command that quickly enables you to connect and disconnect from the Internet, as you'll see in a minute.

When you're done with all this configuration, click the close button on the System Preferences window and you'll see a dialog sheet asking if you want to apply configuration changes; click Apply and your changes will be made.

Connect Via Dial-up

So, you're configured for Internet access—how do you connect? The easiest way is to access that modem menu bar icon that was mentioned earlier; if you turned it on via the Modem tab in the Network pane of System Preferences then you should be able to mouse up to the modem icon, click it to pull down its menu, and then choose Connect.

One neat trick in this menu is the ability to select from multiple dial-up numbers if you've entered them via the Network pane. Select one and that number becomes active; you can then choose Connect to dial that number.

Notice that you can also choose Open Internet Connect from the menu in order to gain access to Internet Connect, which is the other way that you can go about making an Internet connection over a modem (see Figure 8.4). Internet Connect is designed to complete the connection that you set up in the Networking pane.

To launch Internet Connect directly (if you don't have the Modem menu bar icon active), you can find its icon in the Applications folder and double-click it.

FIGURE 8.4

The Internet Connect application is used to connect to your ISP.

In Internet Connect, the approach is simply to click the Connect button; if you've already set all this stuff up in the Network pane then you can click Connect and watch the connection status to see if things go well. If it does, you'll see the Connected message and small lights appear at the bottom of the Internet Connect window to report that you are now connected.

The Internet Connect application gives you an interesting option beyond what you can configure in System Preferences; choose Edit Configurations from the Configuration menu and you'll get a new window that you can use to add configurations to Internet Connect (see Figure 8.5). In this case, a configuration is basically a new phone number (and perhaps a different account name and password). When using multiple configurations, remember that each connection has to work with the same basic PPP settings you made in the Network pane of System Preferences.

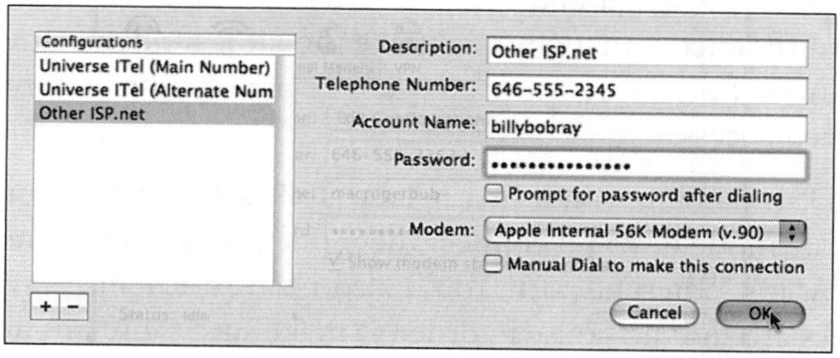

FIGURE 8.5

The Internet Connect application enables you to put together different configurations for your dial-up connections.

To create a configuration, click the plus symbol icon ("+") at the bottom of the list of configurations, and then fill in a description, the phone number, and account name and password. Finally, choose a Modem script from the Modem menu; click OK to add the configuration. This configuration will now be in the Configuration menu in Internet Connect and available in the modem menu bar icon's menu for quick access.

To disconnect, click the Disconnect button in Internet Connect or choose Disconnect from the modem menu bar icon's menu.

> **TIP**
> You can also connect and disconnect your modem connection from the Network Status screen in the Network pane of System Preferences. Just select the modem entry and click Connect.

Configure a DSL Connection

A Digital Subscriber Line (DSL) connection is often similar to a modem connection, at least in the respect that you need to connect and disconnect from your ISP in order to use the connection. A DSL connection requires a special modem device that connects to your Mac and to your phone line—the modem uses special tones outside the range of human hearing to carry the high-speed data. (That means you can continue to use the phone line while surfing high speed, which is one reason DSL is extremely popular.)

DSL often uses a protocol called PPPoE, which stands for *PPP over Ethernet*—again, it's similar to a typical modem connection, except that you connect to the DSL modem from your Mac using Ethernet and then the external modem is connected to a phone jack. The other difference is that you can't take the DSL modem with you on the road; you've got to have special DSL service to your home or office phone line in order to get the high-speed access.

To configure a DSL modem, you'll first need to follow the instructions that came with it for installing the modem; you'll connect the modem to a phone line, then you'll connect it to your Mac's Ethernet port. You'll also need to install special filters on your other phone jacks around the house in order to make sure those phones work correctly.

Configure PPPoE

With everything hooked up, open System Preferences and launch the Network pane. On the Network Status screen, double-click Built-in Ethernet if that's what you used to connect to your DSL modem. You'll see the TCP/IP tab first, but you should immediately switch to the PPPoE tab, as shown in Figure 8.6.

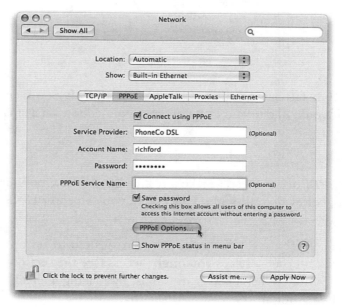

FIGURE 8.6
Configuring for a PPPoE connection.

Turn on the Connect Using PPPoE option to make it possible to enter items in the entry boxes and then begin doing so. You can enter a name for your ISP in the Service Provider box, an account name, password, and the PPPoE service name, if your ISP recommends one.

Go a little further and you can click the PPPoE Options button to set some advanced options; turn on Connect Automatically If Needed if you'd like your Mac to automatically dial the PPPoE connection whenever you access an Internet application. You can also choose from a variety of disconnect behaviors, and you can set some advanced options if your ISP recommends them.

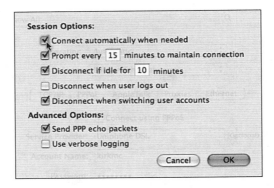

Finally, the PPPoE tab has an option called Show PPPoE Status in Menu Bar; turn this option on if you'd like to keep tabs on your connection via a small menu bar icon and menu.

Other Tabs

Once you select PPPoE, you can't make any changes to the Configure IPv4 menu on the TCP/IP tab; below that, though, if necessary, you can enter DNS Server addresses in the entry box.

As with modem connections, you can use the Proxies tab to set up proxy servers for any of the various Internet services you might access (see the section "Proxies," earlier in this chapter). Simply select a server in the list by placing a check mark next to that server's name, then enter an address for that proxy.

When you're done in the Network pane, click Apply Now to make those changes take effect.

Connect and Disconnect via PPPoE

As I mentioned, a PPPoE connection, like a PPP modem connection, needs to go through a connection phase before you can access the Internet. To do that, you can either click on the PPPoE Status menu bar icon or you can launch Internet Connect by double-clicking it in the Applications folder. When you do that, you'll see Built-in Ethernet selected as your connection type and you should see your ISP's information, your username, and your password all filled in. To connect, just click the Connect button.

Once connected, you should see the Status section light up with the indication that your connection is working. To disconnect, simply click the Disconnect button.

Using the PPPoE Status menu is even easier, if you've turned it on. Simply click the menu bar icon to open the menu, then select Connect.

When you're ready to disconnect, you can head back to that menu and choose Disconnect.

Generally, connecting via a DSL connection will only take a few seconds. If you don't seem to be getting a connection, the problem is most likely something to do with your username or password, or a problem with the way you've configured the connection from your Mac to the DSL modem. Check the modem's documentation for ideas on troubleshooting, or see the section later about troubleshooting connections.

Configure a Cable Modem and Other Connections

For the most part, cable modems are an *always-on* style of Internet connection. Instead of connecting and disconnecting, as long as the cable modem is on, the connection is live; you can then tap into it using your Mac at any time. This is pretty much the same way other connections work, too, such as broadband that's wired into apartment buildings and offices.

With these always-on connections, you'll generally just configure your Mac and forget about it—just head to the Network pane of System Preferences to set things up. You just need to get your Mac talking to the network and, in most cases, receiving its addressing information from a DHCP server.

Most likely you'll configure Built-in Ethernet, which should be connected to your cable modem or to your network (we'll talk about networking your Mac in Chapter 11). To do that, move to the TCP/IP tab and open the Configure IPv4 menu. Based on what you're trying to accomplish, you'll select from one of the following options:

- Using DHCP—This is what you'll use for most cable modems—it retrieves your IP settings from the remote server on the other side of the cable modem connection. In this case, you won't need to fill in other items on the tab.

- Using DHCP with Manual Address—In some cases, you'll use a DHCP server to retrieve settings, but you'll put in your own IP address; this might be because you have *fixed IP* service from your cable company or provider.

NOTE

Broadband is often available as either *dynamic IP* or *fixed IP* service. With a fixed IP address, your Mac's address never changes, making it possible to access it from the Internet as a web server or for remote networking connections. It's also something of a security risk, so dynamic service is available to give you a different IP address whenever a new session begins (or whenever the ISP elects to change your IP address).

- Manually—If you choose manually, you'll need to fill in an IP address, subnet mask, and router address so that your Mac knows how to access your building or ISP router and, hence, gain access to the Internet. You'll need to get these numbers from the ISP or from your network administrator.

Regardless of which of these you choose, you may also want to fill in DNS server addresses so that your Mac can access your ISP's domain name servers. Check your ISP's materials to see if this is done automatically or if you need to enter them.

With an always-on connection, that's *all* you need to do. You can set up proxy servers on the Proxies tab if you like, but otherwise, you should be able to close the System Preferences application and, if everything is configured correctly, begin surfing immediately.

Connecting via AirPort

We'll cover setting up your own AirPort wireless network in more detail in Chapter 11, but it's true that you'll sometimes want to use Airport with your Mac and an existing wireless connection—like in a coffee shop, airport, or your organization or office. If that's the case, you can configure your Mac to take advantage of an existing wireless network easily.

First, it's worth noting that if you have an AirPort card installed in your Mac and you're near an open AirPort or WiFi (IEEE 802.11-compatible) wireless network, your connection will probably "just work." That's because the wireless connection almost always uses a DHCP server connection and that's the default setting for AirPort. To see that, open the Network pane of System Preferences and then open the AirPort settings. On the TCP/IP tab, you should see the Configure IPv4 menu set to Using DHCP.

On the AirPort tab, you can choose whether your Mac automatically connects to any networks it sees, or if it should limit itself to trusted networks. Most of the time, the Automatic setting in the By Default, Join menu is the best setting, but if you live or work where there are a number of networks close by, you might want to choose Preferred to make sure that your Mac only connects to the network that you want it to connect to.

Also, in the Network pane, you'll find the option Show AirPort Status in the Menu Bar; it's almost always a good idea to have this option turned on so that you can quickly select networks and, when necessary, turn on and off your AirPort card.

If your AirPort Base Station or wireless router is connected to an always-on Internet connection then you probably get your Internet access without any additional configuration; once you're connected to the router, you're connected to the Internet. In some cases, though, you may need to configure the base station or router to dial out a PPP or PPPoE connection. If that's the case, you'll see a Connect option in the AirPort menu bar icon menu or in the Internet Connect application on the AirPort tab. Click Connect to get your router to "dial out" and connect to your ISP.

Troubleshooting Connections

Having trouble with your Internet connection? At the bottom of the Network pane is the Assist Me button; click it and you'll see a dialog sheet appear. You can click the Assistant to get help setting up a connection if you're not sure how to go about it, or click the Diagnostics button if you need to see what's going wrong with your current connection.

Clicking Diagnostics brings up the Network Diagnostics application, which will take a look at your current connection and see if it can figure out the problem. Down the side of the window (shown in Figure 8.7) are small lights that show the status according to the Network Diagnostics—green means things are working, yellow is cause for concern, and red means something has gone awry.

TIP

The Network Diagnostics button also comes up in a Safari window when it can't reach a website, which you have to admit is pretty cool.

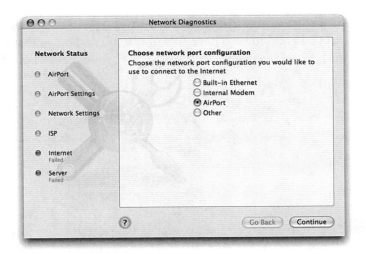

FIGURE 8.7
The Network Diagnostics screen will give you a hint (see the status down the left side for this AirPort connection) as to where your connection is breaking down and try to help you fix it.

Begin by choosing the port you need to analyze and click the Continue button. You can then step through the assistant, making choices as they're presented to you. For instance, with an AirPort connection, you'll select a network (if one can be found) and then the Network Diagnostics application will do its thing, testing for connections, asking about your hardware, and helping you to troubleshoot different items.

As you work through the assistant, use the Continue button to move to new screens or the Go Back button to return to previous choices. At any time you can quit the application and go back to working on your Network settings.

Internet Connections at Multiple Locations

Mac OS X has the ability to work with network connections simultaneously, so that, for instance, you can use AirPort and Ethernet at the same time for different reasons. Mac OS X can also enable you to use different types (AirPort, Ethernet) of network locations under different circumstances, such as when you move your Mac from the office to your home, to your beach house, to your yacht (or wherever). This is most useful for portable Macs (iBooks and PowerBooks) but it's handy to know for any Mac that can use a little redundancy.

Multihoming

The first level of this network flexibility is called *multihoming*. In the Network pane of System Preferences, you can see very clearly on the Network Status screen that you can have multiple *ports* set up for networking. A port is simply a connection to a network; each type of connection—AirPort, modem, Ethernet—is considered an individual "port" in this context.

If those multiple ports are correctly configured for Internet access then you can actually get your Mac to test them in a certain order for a valid connection. For instance, you could enter a URL in your web browser and, as a result, have your Mac check for an AirPort connection, and, failing that, an Ethernet connection. If that fails too, it checks to see if your modem is connected and has a valid PPP connection.

> **NOTE**
> In fact, your Mac could test and fail the AirPort and Ethernet connections, and then automatically dial a PPP connection via your modem if you've turned on Connect Automatically When Needed in the PPP Options window, which you get to by clicking the PPP Options button on the PPP tab when you've selected Internal Modem in the Network pane of System Preferences. (Whew.)

All of that happens automatically, thanks to multihoming. You can alter the order in which items are checked by opening the Network pane and choosing Network Port Configurations from the Show menu. There, you can turn ports on and off if you'd like to control whether or not they can be used and configured (and whether they appear in the Network pane). You can also drag the ports into the order that you would like to have them checked for an active connection. When you're done, click Apply Now.

TIP

Here's something cool: When you turn off ports that you never use, your Mac starts up a little faster.

Locations

What if you have multiple configurations for the same port? For instance, say you want to use PPPoE for your Ethernet connection at home and a manually entered configuration for work? In that case, you need to use Locations.

At the top of the Network pane, choose Locations, New Location. A dialog sheet appears, enabling you to give the location a name—choose something such as Home, Office, or Vacation House. Now, go about setting up your ports the way you want them to be. They'll be saved in that particular configuration under that location name.

Repeat this process for other locations—Work, Denver Office, and so on. Now, with these different configurations saved with named locations, you can switch those locations and instantly have those configurations active. To switch, choose a named location from the Location menu in the Network pane. Or, if you don't currently have System Preferences active, simply choose a new location from the Apple, Location menu. That switches you immediately.

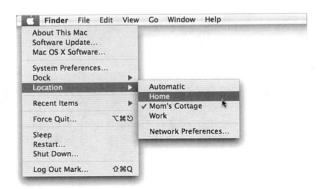

The .Mac Question

Before we get out of this Internet discussion, I want to mention the .Mac service, which Apple offers to Mac users. It's a subscription-only service for most of its features, requiring you to pay (currently) $99 per year in order to use it. In exchange, you get an email address (and access to more), an amount of online storage for that email and for other files (accessible via iDisk), and access to the HomePage service, which you can use to post pages about yourself or make files available to others for downloading.

> **NOTE**
>
> Many of the services that .Mac offers are directly integrated with the Mac OS, so that you're accessing the Internet from within the Mac OS or its application, such as Mail. The HomePage service, by contrast, enables you to build web pages by logging in to www.mac.com with your .Mac user account information. You can use items that you've placed in the Pictures and Movies folders on your iDisk, for instance, but HomePage is mostly an online tool. Log in to check it out.

Along with those services, .Mac can be used for synchronizing your Bookmarks from Safari, your contacts from Address Book, and for sharing calendars from iCal online. And, the .Mac subscription comes with some interesting applications, such as Virex and Apple's Backup, which can be used with the service to keep your files safer.

All in all, the .Mac service is generally worth getting, particularly if you don't already have email and web publishing services elsewhere. If that's the case, you might want to opt for the 60-day trial that Apple offers to see if it's the right approach for you.

Once you have a trial or a subscription to the .Mac service, you should launch System Preferences and choose the .Mac icon; in the .Mac pane, you can enter the username and password for your .Mac account. That gives your Mac automatic access to the .Mac account for a variety of reasons. You'll be able to connect automatically to .Mac services, and various Mac applications—even iPhoto and Safari—will be able to find and connect to your .Mac account easily.

> **NOTE**
>
> In other chapters in the book, I may briefly mention the .Mac service, particularly when an application can be extended somewhat by integration with .Mac.

Accessing Your iDisk

If you do opt for .Mac service, you may find yourself spending a little time with your iDisk. An iDisk is really just designated storage space on Apple's .Mac server computers—a remote Internet accessible location where you can store files. These files can be used for display on the Web—the HomePage service, for instance, can take images or movies you place on your iDisk and display them in web pages—or they can simply be stored for safekeeping. The Backup application, for instance, can be used to back up files to your iDisk so that you have a secure copy of the files on a remote server, just in case something happens to your Mac.

The easiest way to access your iDisk is to enter your information in the .Mac pane of System Preferences and then, with that entered correctly, simply click the iDisk icon in the Places sidebar of a Finder window. When you do that, you'll gain access to the folders on your iDisk (see Figure 8.8).

NOTE

Like your home folder, the iDisk has a number of folders designed for certain types of documents. You should note that items placed in the Music, Photos, and Movies folders are made available for use in the HomePage tool, and these folders can be automatically accessed by some of the iLife applications (such as iPhoto) if you have your account information entered in the .Mac pane of System Preferences.

Now, to access a particular folder, you can work as you would in any Finder window; double-click a folder to open it and drag-and-drop files from one place to another to copy or move them.

Your iDisk isn't always the fastest-responding set of folders and icons, so Apple has another way you can use the iDisk; you can make a *local* copy of the iDisk on your own hard disk, then allow the local copy to synchronize with the actual iDisk on the Internet when the Mac gets a chance to do so. That makes it quicker to work with the iDisk's folders and gives you the extra advantage of being able to access the folders while you're not online. Plus, because updates work in the background while you're connected to the Internet, this also has the advantage of making an iDisk a little easier to deal with over a dial-up connection.

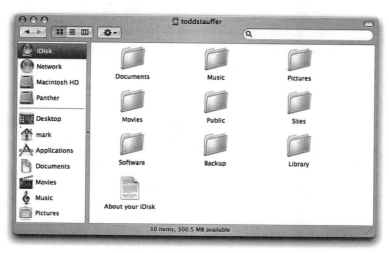

FIGURE 8.8
Accessing your iDisk.

To turn on this feature, choose the iDisk tab in the .Mac pane of System Preferences. There, you can click the Start button under iDisk Synching to create a local copy of your iDisk and allow your Mac to automatically manage the synchronization of items between your local copy and the .Mac stored version on the Internet. The Synchronize option enables you to choose Automatically and Manually; if you choose Manually, you'll need to periodically click the small synchronize button—the two curved arrows—that will appear next to the iDisk icon in your Finder windows, or the network and local versions of your iDisk will not be the same.

Close the .Mac pane and your iDisk will switch to its iDisk Synching mode. It will take a moment for your iDisk to synchronize for the first time. Now, you will be able to access your iDisk on your desktop (if you have desktop icons turned on in Finder Preferences) as well as in the Finder window.

Chapter **9**

Mail and Chat Basics

It takes some people a little while to transition from their favorite third-party email applications to Mail, and it's not always a successful venture. But Mail is a great application for day-to-day email management; it's got its quirks, but it also has some features that make it an all-around good application for your day-to-day email needs. And the integration it offers with other Apple applications and technologies—from iChat, to Address Book, to iCal, to .Mac, and so on—makes it a very attractive option for someone who really wants to dig deep into Mac OS X's built-in tricks and features.

Introducing Mail

To launch Mail, you can click its icon in the Dock—it's there by default—or locate the Mail icon in the Applications folder and double-click it there. When you do, what you see next depends on whether or not you've already set up either a .Mac account or an email account (which you can do when you first set up your Mac via the Mac Setup Assistant). If you have set up an account, you'll go directly to the Mail interface, which we'll talk about in just a moment.

Set Up an Account

If you haven't set up an account yet, you'll see the New Account assistant in Mail that asks you to go ahead and do so, as shown in Figure 9.1. Click Continue to begin the process of adding an email account.

FIGURE 9.1
When you launch Mail without an account set up (or without .Mac information in the System Preferences), you're shown the New Account assistant.

On the General Information screen, you have a few basic choices in the Account Type menu. Those type are

- .Mac. As part of the suite of Internet applications, the .Mac service offers an email account that you can access from Mail. By default, the .Mac mail stays on the .Mac server; meaning you can access it both in Mail here on your Mac and elsewhere via a web browser, if desired. In this way, it's a little like an IMAP account, discussed in a moment.

- POP. A POP (Post Office Protocol) email account is very common with third-party ISPs and many offices. With a POP account, Mail will access the POP server and download any new messages you have; those messages may be left on the server for a while or deleted immediately. But the basic difference is that this is an "offline" account; you download your mail, read it, and then write responses that get uploaded to the email server and sent out.

- **IMAP.** An IMAP (Internet Message Access Protocol) account is one where you use a local application, such as Mail, to access a server-based account. This is very similar to a .Mac account, which can be used in virtually the same way as an IMAP account. With an IMAP account, you even have the option of storing your folders on the server, so that you can access your entire email "desktop" from different client computers.

- **Exchange.** If your company or organization has a Microsoft Exchange email server, you can choose Exchange from the Account Type menu in order to set up Mail to access that Exchange server. This is a nice feature for Mac users on Windows networks.

Which account type you choose dictates exactly what you see in the window. For a .Mac account, you'll enter an account description, along with your full name, your .Mac user name, and your .Mac password. This is all Mail needs to set up your account, so once you've got those entered and you click Continue, you'll see the Mail interface.

> **TIP**
>
> The account description is important because it's how you'll see your account's name in the Mail application. Choose something meaningful ("Leo's .Mac" works fine) or just enter the full email address, as that will probably serve as a good reminder. You can change the account description later, too, if you need to.

The other account types require a bit more. Regardless of which you choose, on the General Information screen, you'll simply enter an account description, your full name, and the email address that you're going to be configuring. Click Continue, and on the next screen, you'll set up the incoming mail server. Enter the address for the server in the Incoming Mail Server entry box, followed by the user name and password for your email account. You'll need to know these things from your ISP or system administrator. Once they're entered, click Continue.

Mail will actually check to make sure it can access the account, and if it can't, you'll be asked if you're sure you've entered things correctly. You probably haven't (even the best of us usually have a typo somewhere), so double-check and click Continue again.

> **NOTE**
>
> While many email accounts only require a one word username (leo) in the User Name space, some will require your full email account (leo@leoville.com). This is often true when your mail server and your email account don't have the same domain. (For instance, if your mail server is mail.yourisp.net and your email address is you@youville.com.)

If Mail is able to connect successfully then it's on to the next step, which is to tell Mail how your account will be *authenticated*. Many accounts use a simple password, but if your ISP offers something more advanced than that, you'll choose the technology here from the Authentication menu. (Note that a mail server that supports SSL will transfer email to and from your Mac in encrypted form, which is pretty cool. Click to turn on the SSL feature if your server supports it.)

The next step is to set up the outgoing mail server or SMTP (Simple Mail Transport Protocol) server. This is sometimes the same account as your incoming mail server, but not always. For security reasons, you are often required to use the SMTP server associated with the ISP that you use to *connect* to the Internet, even if the account you're using is hosted by a different ISP. For instance, you might get your email using the server mail.mycoolsite.com, but send mail out using smtp.mycablecompany.net, because your outgoing mail needs to be routed through the company that provides your Internet connection.

Some SMTP servers support (or require) that you enter your account name and password in order to send out email. If your account is one of those, click to turn on the option Use Authentication and enter your username and password. Click Continue.

On the last page, you'll see a summary of your new account. Click Continue and your account setup is finished. You can click Import Mailboxes if you have another email program on this Mac from which you'd import email and folders, or you can click Create Another Account if you want to go back through the assistant. If neither of those is appealing, click Done. You're ready to begin working with Mail.

> **NOTE**
>
> In Mail, you can choose Mail, Preferences to open the Preferences dialog box. Click the Accounts icon and you'll see the Accounts tab, where you can edit and add email accounts (you can also delete accounts from this tab). Select an account and click the Advanced tab to see

some important choices you can make about your mail account, including whether items are left on the server (for POP accounts) and for how long. I encourage you to consider these settings; it's nice to leave messages on the server for a few days just in case you need to retrieve them again or view them via your web browser, but if you use a POP account and download your email to your Mac, you probably want messages deleted from the server fairly often, if only to cut down on the amount of storage space your email account consumes.

Reading Messages in Mail

If you've worked with a graphical email application in the past then Mail shouldn't look too different at the outset. By default, Mail displays a window with three "panes": a message list, a preview area, and a list of folders or, in Mail parlance, *mailboxes*. Figure 9.2 shows the interface.

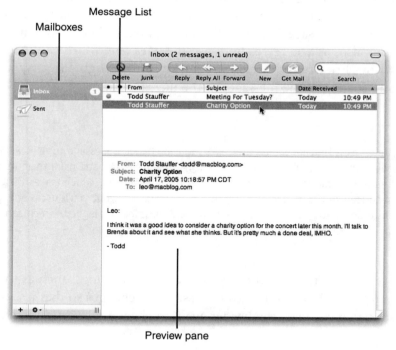

FIGURE 9.2

The main Mail interface offers a "paned" window approach to managing your email.

When a new message comes into your inbox, you'll see it in the message list if your inbox is selected. You can then click the message to view its contents in the preview pane.

> **NOTE**
>
> If you don't see any messages and you think you should have some, click the Get Mail button in the Mail window's toolbar or choose Mailbox, Get New Mail. If you're connected to the Internet, your Mac will check for new messages on the associated mail server. In Mail, Preferences you can click the General tab to set the Check For New Mail option so that it checks for new mail every so often.

Once you've selected a message, it is no longer bold in the message list and the small dot in the left-most column of the message list disappears; the message now has a status of "read." You can change that to a status of "unread" if you like by highlighting the message in the message list and choosing Message, Mark, As Unread from the menu. You can also, as you're reading, use the Message, Mark command to mark a message As Low Priority, As Medium Priority, or As High Priority, which can be handy for later sorting of the messages in the message list.

> **NOTE**
>
> Along with As Unread, there's also an option to change a message to As Read without actually reading it. In fact, you can select multiple messages and mark them As Read if desired; there's less reason to do that than marking them As Unread (which makes them bold and adds the unread icon to the message's entry on the message list), but you'll occasionally come up with a reason to do it. You can also mark an important message As Flagged, which can be handy for searching and other automated tasks we'll discuss later in the chapter.

To sort the message list, click on one of the column headings, such as the Subject or Date Received lines. When you do, the message list changes so that it's sorted by that column header; you can click the header again to change the sort direction.

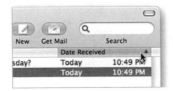

You don't have to read your messages in the preview pane; instead, you can double-click a message to see it in its own window. When you're done reading the message, you can click the Close button in that window to close the message and leave it in your inbox, or you can use another of the buttons—Delete, Junk, Reply, and so on—if you want to do something different with the message.

TIP

You can Control+click a message in the message list to get a number of contextual commands, including the ability to mark it as unread and so on. You can also use View, Customize Toolbar to add buttons to the toolbar for your favorite commands.

Replying To and Forwarding Messages

With messages in your message list (or with a message open in its own window) one of the first things you'll likely want to do is reply to a message. Doing so is easy; in the message list, highlight a message and click the Reply button in the toolbar or choose Message, Reply. (In a message window, you also simply click the Reply button in the toolbar.) The result is a composition window that will automatically show the email address of the recipient as well as the text of the message that you received in "quoted" format (see Figure 9.3).

TIP

You can determine what text, exactly, is quoted from the original in your message by highlighting that text before clicking the Reply button.

Now, type your response to the original message as shown in Figure 9.3. By default, you enter your reply above the original quoted text. You are free to go in and edit the quoted text or place your response after the quotation, too, if that's your choice—experiment with clicking your mouse to place the text insertion point in different parts of the message if you'd like to try different approaches to replying. The most important part, of course, is to enter some interesting text to continue the conversation.

Speaking of conversations, if the email to which you are replying has more than one recipient (you and others) then you can click the Reply All button to reply to all of the recipients at once. You can also click the Reply All button even after you've begun editing your response and the other recipients will be added to your reply.

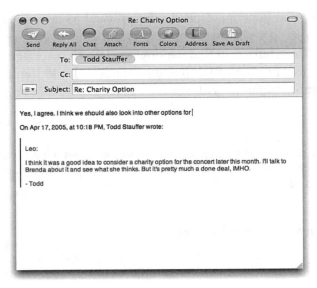

FIGURE 9.3
Replying to a message brings up the composition window.

As you're typing any email message, whether it's an original composition or a reply to something you've received, you have two basic options for sending or saving that message. You can click the Send button if you're ready for the message to be seen by its recipient. Your Mac will attempt to connect to your designated outgoing email server and send the message to it, thus (hopefully) getting it out over the Internet.

You can also choose the Save As Draft option, which saves your changes to the message and places the most recently saved copy in the Drafts mailbox, which you'll find in the Mailboxes pane of the main Mail interface window. You can then close the composition window; your typing is saved in the draft message format until you select the Drafts folder and view the message again. (You'll need to double-click it to edit it once more.) From there, you can make edits at a later date and then, eventually, send the message on.

A message that you want to forward is a bit different. In this case, you're taking an email sent to you by one recipient and forwarding it, or sending it on, to another recipient. You can do that by selecting the message in the message list and clicking the Forward button in the toolbar or by choosing Message, Forward. The result is a message window with a blank To: entry box and a message window that includes the text of the message that you had received (see Figure 9.4). You can now enter the email address for the person to whom you want to forward this message, along with your own message, if desired.

> **TIP**
> You can highlight only a portion of the email message and then click Forward if you'd like to forward only part of a message that you've received. And you can edit the forwarded text before sending, if desired.

FIGURE 9.4
Forwarded messages include the text of the message that you receive and blanks for the To: and other address boxes.

New Messages and Sending Attachments

Sending a new message isn't totally different from sending a reply. You begin by clicking the New button on the toolbar or by selecting File, New Message. When you do, the New Message window appears; aside from the lack of a Reply All button, it should look very similar to the composition window that you use to create replies.

Begin in the To: entry box by typing the email address of the person to whom you would like to send this message. If that person is in your Address Book, you can begin typing their name, instead. Mail uses auto-complete to add in the rest of an address once you've typed a few letters; if it guesses right, you can press the Return key to accept that entry. Otherwise, just keep typing.

The Cc: line is for sending a "courtesy copy" of the email to someone else; you're basically saying, "Hey, Jill, I'd like you to see this as well" but you're doing it without directly addressing the message to Jill. You, of course, don't have to enter anything on this line; as long as you've got at least one recipient on the To: line, you're in good shape.

NOTE

See the small menu button that appears to the left of the Subject entry box? You can use that menu to add two other types of address entry boxes. A BCC address is someone to whom you want to send a copy of this message, but without other recipients knowing you did it. BCC stands for *blind courtesy copy*. The Reply-To field can be used if you would like the email message to have a different "reply" address than the one you're sending from; when the recipient invokes the Reply command in their own email program, your custom Reply-To field will be used.

Now, in the Subject entry box, enter a meaningful subject for your email. Again, you don't have to, but I certainly recommend it—having a meaningful subject line gives your recipient a better idea as to whether or not they need to read the message and how quickly. Something like "Hi" or "Hey there" is not a meaningful subject line in most cases, or at least not as meaningful as "Remember That Lotto Ticket I Bought?" or something a bit more striking like that.

Finally, that vast, uncharted area toward the bottom of the window is where you can type your email. Remember that this works pretty much like a word processor; you don't have to hit the Return key until you get to the end of a paragraph (see Figure 9.5).

NOTE

By default, Mail checks your spelling as you type. If you see a red dotted line under a word, you can Control+click it to get recommendations for spelling changes. You can change this behavior in Mail, Preferences on the Composing tab.

FIGURE 9.5

A new message is similar to a reply or a forward except that you'll need to enter the addresses for your recipients manually.

By default, you are editing this message in Rich Text mode, which means you can use the Font and Colors commands if you'd like to customize the message further; you can also change text to bold or italic using commands in the Format, Style menu. (You'll find that keyboard commands such as ⌘+I and ⌘+B are handy for that, too.) And, you can turn text into a hyperlink by highlighting the text and choosing Edit, Insert Hyperlink. In the dialog sheet that appears, enter a URL; when you do, the highlighted text becomes clickable both to you and to your recipient if he or she can accept a Rich Text email message.

TIP

Rich Text messages are fun to send and great when you're dealing with other Mac users, but not everyone can read them. If you encounter trouble or just want to go the trouble-free route, choose Format, Make Plain Text for that message. If you'd like to change the default, choose Mail, Preferences, then click the Composing button and choose Plain Text from the Message Format menu.

When you're done with your typing, you've got the option of attaching a file to the message if you'd like to send something to the recipient other than the email. When you attach a file, that file is *encoded* into text characters, sent along with the message, and then, on the other side, your recipient's email program has to piece it back together again. Mail uses a highly compatible approach (Base64), which works with most other Macs, Windows PCs, and even most computers running Unix.

You can attach files in a variety of ways; my favorite is to simply drag the file's icon from the Finder to your message window. When you drop it, an icon should appear for that file in the message window, unless it's an image file or a similar type of document that Mail recognizes, in which case you'll see the image itself.

> **TIP**
>
> The Finder has the built-in ability to turn a file (or even a folder of files) into a *compressed archive* in the popular Zip format. Simply Control+click on the file or folder in question (in the Finder) and choose Create Archive Of. That will compress the file or folder into a single file with a name that ends in .zip. You can now attach that archive file to your email.

Another way to add a file is to click the Attach button in the composition window or choose File, Attach File. That's the boring way. A dialog sheet appears, enabling you to locate the file that you want to send. That dialog sheet also offers you the option Send Windows Friendly Attachments, which is almost always a good idea to leave checked; it strips the Macintosh "resource file" information from a file, which the typical Microsoft Windows user doesn't need.

> **TIP**
>
> It's always a good idea to send files with filename extensions—three-letter add-ons such as .doc or .rtf. Sometimes the Finder hides these extensions, but you'll see them in the filename when a file is attached to an email, or you can choose the file and choose File, Get Info in the Finder to check out its full name.

You can often get away with sending more than one attachment to an email at a time, although I generally try to avoid that, as it sometimes doesn't work. Instead, use the archive mentioned in the tip and send a folder full of files if necessary.

Need to remove an attached file? Visually, you should be able to simply highlight its icon in the message window and press the Delete key; it won't be deleted from your hard disk because the icon in your message window is simply a representation, like an alias or an icon in a Finder window Sidebar.

Got your message arranged the way you want it? Click the Send button and, if your Mac is connected to the Internet, the message will be sent along its way. If you're *not* connected to the Internet then your Mac may attempt to do so; if it can't get itself connected, you'll see a dialog sheet telling you that the message will be placed in your Outbox until you are able to connect.

NOTE

As with an email reply, you can click Save As Draft if you'd like to hold on to save the contents of the message but you're not ready to send it yet.

Add Your Signature

As you're composing and replying to a message, you may find it useful to have a signature (or multiple signatures) with which you can end your messages. Signatures are fairly common today in email, particularly for professional or academic correspondences. Generally, a signature is four or five lines about you; your email address, any websites you manage, and, in many cases, other types of contact information such as phone numbers or physical addresses.

Mail has the ability not only to store your signature and use it automatically, but, to store multiple email signatures and choose from them on-the-fly. This can be handy when you use your email for a variety of reasons. You may not always want to send a signature with your office P.O. Box address and your main customer service line; when you'd prefer to send the one that has a quote from your cat, you can select it.

To customize your signatures, choose Mail, Preferences and click the Signatures button. In the dialog box, note that you can choose to create a signature that is for all of your accounts, or you can create signatures for specific email accounts. Select All Signatures or an icon that represents a particular email account, and then click the plus ("+") icon to create a new signature (see Figure 9.6).

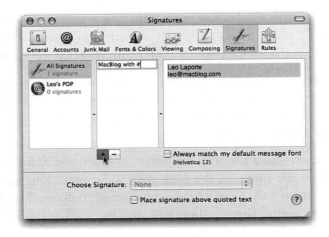

FIGURE 9.6

In the Signatures section of Preferences, you can create and manage multiple email signatures and easily assign them to different accounts.

In the second column, you can name the signature; in the third column, you can edit the signature. Include your email address, a quote, a website, an address—whatever is appropriate for this entry. When you're done, you can choose the Always Match My Default Message Font option if desired; when you're done, simply click in another part of the window.

You can create as many signatures as you like; you can also assign a signature to a particular email account at any point by dragging its name from the second column to the account's icon in the first column.

Once you have multiple signatures defined, you can use the Choose Signature menu to decide which signature should appear by default (if any), or you can choose to randomize signatures. It's not necessary to make a selection in the Choose Signature menu if you'd prefer to choose a signature when you're working in the composition window. (Note, also, the option to Place Signature Above Quoted Text, which is handy if you'd like your signature to appear above any text that you're quoting in a reply or forward situation.)

With your signatures created, you can close the Preferences dialog window and return to the main Mail interface. When you're ready to send something, you'll find a new menu in the composition window, the Signature menu. You can use it to select the signature that you'd like to send along with this email; if you don't want to use one of them, choose None from that menu.

Mail and the Address Book

As you might have read earlier in the chapter, Mail can auto-complete some email addresses for you as you're typing them into a composition window. This is true because Mail keeps track of email addresses from which you've received email in the past; you can turn off auto-complete in Mail Preferences, on the Composing tab, by turning off the Automatically Complete Addresses option.

Mail and Address Book have a tight relationship, as that auto-complete information can come from Address Book, and you can send new addresses to Address Book when you feel like it. As you're working in a composition window, you can also add addresses by clicking the Address button in the window's toolbar. That pops up a miniature interface to Address Book, enabling you to drag over addresses or even groups of addresses that you've defined in Address Book.

Things can work in the opposite direction, too. When you're viewing a message from someone who isn't in your Address Book, highlight the message and choose Message, Add Sender to Address Book. That creates a card in Address Book for that recipient with that person's full name (if it's accurate in their email headers) and their email address. You can then switch to Address Book and edit the card to add more information, if desired.

Dealing with Junk Mail

Mail has the built-in ability to deal with junk mail by automatically moving it from your Inbox to a special Junk folder. You can then separate out much of your junk mail so that you can sift through it more quickly and delete it on a fairly regular basis.

If that's sounds interesting, you can proceed. You do that by finding a message in your Inbox that you think is junk mail, highlighting it in the message list, and clicking the Junk button in the toolbar. The first time you do that, you'll see a dialog box appear that tells you about the Junk Mail system built into Mail. Click OK. You're in training mode.

What happens in training mode is simple—messages that Mail *thinks* are junk mail will be turned brown in the message list; if it misses one, you can highlight it and click the Junk button in the toolbar. If Mail accidentally codes a good message as junk, highlight that message in the list and click the Not Junk button in the toolbar. (It's the same button; it just changes when you highlight something that Mail already thinks is junk.) Now proceed this way for at least a few days.

When you feel strongly that Mail is doing a good job sifting between the real messages and the junk mail, choose Mail, Preferences and click the Junk Mail icon. Now, click the Move It to the Junk Mailbox option to turn it on; that takes Junk Mail out of training mode and starts automatically moving anything that Mail thinks is junk. Notice that in this dialog box (see Figure 9.7) you have plenty of other options, including some key options that can help you automatically get around problems with junk mail identification.

TIP

Is your sister's email constantly moved to Junk for no good reason? Well, if you can't convince her to change her name from "No Fee Mortgage" (just a little joke, there) then another solution is to put her in your Address Book and make sure the option Sender of Message Is in My Address Book is turned on in the Junk Mail tab of Mail Preferences.

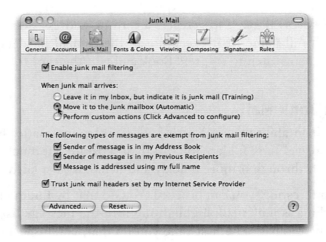

FIGURE 9.7
The Junk Mail portion of Mail Preferences offers a number of options for managing incoming junk.

If you find that Mail's junk filter doesn't work for you, remember that the Junk Mail tab in Preferences gives you the option of turning off Enable Junk Mail Filtering.

Managing Your Accounts and Mailboxes

So far we've been focused mostly on reading and creating messages. But one of the things that you'll probably want to do with your messages is manage them and file them away—at least, some of them. You'll do that using the Mailbox list.

One of the most interesting things Mail does in my opinion is the way it handles multiple email accounts. Each account that you create within Mail gets its own inbox; you can click the main Inbox icon to see all messages in all inboxes at once, or you can click an individual inbox to see only the messages that have come in for that email account. Right away, this can help you to pare things down and focus on messages that are important to you precisely because of the account to which they were sent.

The next step in organizing things is to create your own mailboxes (which, recall, is what Mail calls "folders" for mail messages). Choose Mailbox, New Mailbox to create one or click the plus ("+") icon at the bottom of the mailbox pane. A dialog sheet appears, where you can give the mailbox a name and choose where you want it to appear. You'll put most mailboxes you create under On My Mac if you want to store the messages that you move to this mailbox on your hard disk. With .Mac and IMAP accounts, you also have the option of creating the mailbox as part of that account, meaning you'll have access to it anywhere that you have access to the account, including via the Web.

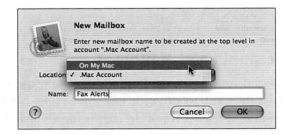

Type a name, click the OK button, and a new mailbox will appear in your mailbox list. You can drag messages to it or you can select messages in the message list and choose Message, Move To, and then the mailbox that you want the message to be moved to. (You can also choose Message, Copy To if you'd like to leave the message in the inbox at the same time that a copy is made in the designated mailbox.)

To delete a mailbox, select it in the list and choose Mailbox, Delete. You'll be asked if you're sure; click Delete again if you are.

TIP

At the bottom of the mailbox pane is the small gear-like Action menu icon; click it and a menu appears with various actions you can take including creating a new mailbox, creating a smart mailbox and deleting a mailbox.

In Mac OS X 10.4, Apple has introduced the Smart Mailbox in Mail. A Smart Mailbox is really nothing more than a standing search result; to create such a mailbox, you'll designate certain characteristics that you'd like to see in the messages that get stored there. Then, Mail will go gather messages that meet your criteria and they'll be accessible via that mailbox icon.

This may not seem like a big deal, but it actually makes a lot of sense—sometimes more than the traditional mailbox does. If you get a lot of email (I've got thousands in my inbox) then you may be overwhelmed by any attempt to move them to different folders. However, a Smart Mailbox allows you to leave thousands of message in your inbox, yet still sort them in ways that make important messages easier to find. To create a Smart Mailbox, choose Mailbox, New Smart Mailbox. A dialog box appears, as shown in Figure 9.8.

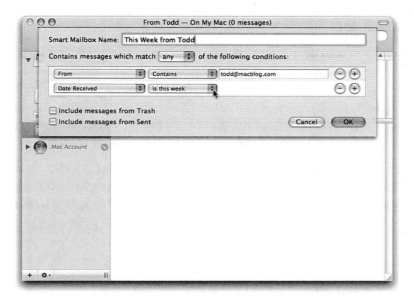

FIGURE 9.8

Creating a Smart Mailbox enables you to view and manage messages that are placed in the mailbox automatically in response to specific rules.

At the top of the dialog sheet, give the mailbox a name. Now, you can use the first criterion line to make a choice about what this smart mailbox will collect. When you've made that decision, you can click OK, or you can add another criterion line by clicking the plus icon next to the first line. Note that you can include messages from the Trash or Sent folders if you'd like to; otherwise, click OK to create the Smart Mailbox. It will appear in the mailbox pane along with all your other mailboxes and it's ready for use.

The sheer number of options you have makes it impossible to characterize everything you can do with smart mailboxes, but there are many permutations. You can whittle things down based on the subject line, any recipient, who the message is from, when it was last viewed, and so on.

Using Rules

Not to be outdone by all the smart searching and Smart Mailboxes and smart whatnot found throughout the Mac OS, Mail offers the ability to run your incoming messages through Rules, which can then be used to do things automatically to those messages. (If you've ever wondered why messages from Apple look different in your message list, you can blame Rules.)

A rule is actually similar to a Smart Mailbox. It begins life as just a query that's applied to a message—who is the sender, when was it sent, to what account and so on. But, the difference is that the query is followed by an *action* that Mail takes on messages that match the initial criteria. So, you can say that any message with a certain From email address should appear in a different text color in the message list, for instance, or that messages with attachments be sent to another mailbox, and so on.

To create a new rule, choose Mail, Preferences and click the Rules icon. You'll see a list here of the rules currently in force; the only one may be the one that turns Apple's email messages blue in the message list. Here's how creating a rule works:

1. To create a new rule, click Add Rule on the Rules tab of Mail Preferences. A dialog sheet appears.
2. In the Description entry box, give the rule a name.
3. In the first menu, choose whether the rule will be satisfied if *any* of the criterion are met or only if *all* the criteria are met. It's an important distinction.
4. Now, set the first criterion. It can be anything from the sender's (From) email address to something found in the message contents. Use the entry boxes and menus to form a sentence such as **From Is todd@macblog.com** or **Any Attachment Name Contains .jpg**.
5. If you want multiple criterion lines, click the plus icon and add another sentence.
6. Now, in the action section, you can choose the actions that you want to take place on messages that meet your criteria. Again, you can build a sentence doing anything from changing the message's color in the message list to moving it directly to the Trash (see Figure 9.9). When you're done, click OK in the dialog sheet. The rule is created and you're asked if you want to apply the rule to messages already in your inbox. Choose Yes or No.

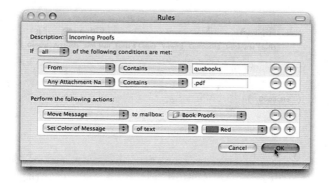

FIGURE 9.9

Creating a rule means building a search and then choosing some actions for the messages that match.

Back on the Rule tab of Mail Preferences, you can turn a rule off by clicking to remove its check mark; click again to turn it back on. (A rule that is "on" is compared against every incoming email message to see if the criteria you specified match.) You can also highlight a rule and click Edit to change it or click Remove to delete it. The Duplicate button can be used to duplicate a rule so that you can edit it to do something similar, but perhaps slightly different.

When you're done, close Mail Preferences and wait for some incoming matches to reach Mail and be processed by the rules.

Using iChat AV

iChat AV is, at its core, Apple's entry into the Internet chat market, working with the AIM (America Online Instant Messaging) network to allow you to chat with people who have either AOL or .Mac usernames and chat accounts.

iChat AV is also very versatile—not only can you "chat" by typing messages to others, you can also send files to one another via iChat, you can "chat" using the microphone and speakers built in to (or attached to) your Mac, or, if you have a compatible camera, you can even accomplish some video conferencing using iChat. And, one last cool feature is that iChat works with Bonjour technology to enable you to chat with others on your network automatically, without special sign-in steps and such. If you both have iChat turned on and you're connected to the same network, you can chat. More on that in a minute.

NOTE

Don't let the names fool you. Apple tends to call this application "iChat AV" in its marketing material, but the name of the program when you're dealing with it in the Finder and the Dock is simply "iChat." I'll refer to it as iChat in the rest of this section, but if you're working in Mac OS X 10.4, you're dealing with the full "iChat AV" set of capabilities.

Setting Up iChat

To begin working with iChat, you should, ideally, have a compatible chat account. If you already have a .Mac account, you can use that—in fact, if your .Mac information is entered into the .Mac pane of System Preferences then iChat will pick that up automatically. If you don't have a .Mac account then an AOL account will work if it's been set up to work with the AIM server. If you have neither of those, you can sign up for a special .Mac iChat account that doesn't cost anything.

NOTE

iChat opts for the AIM service over other chat networks such as the Yahoo! chat servers. You can only use iChat to chat with people who are connected to AIM via AOL or .Mac or to an open-source Jabber server; for other services, you'll need to download a compatible chat application.

To set up iChat to work with your account, launch it. (It's in the Dock by default.) You'll be greeted by the iChat assistant, which will walk you through the steps. After reading the introductory page, click Continue and you should see the Set Up iChat Instant Messaging screen. You can enter info from your .Mac or AIM account or, if you don't have those, click the Get an iChat Account button. You'll be connected to the Internet and allowed to sign up for a free iChat account. Once your iChat account is entered, click Continue.

TIP

If all you want to do is chat on your local network using Bonjour technology, you don't have to set up an iChat account. Instead, simply click Continue to move to the next screen of the assistant.

On the next screen in iChat, you can set up a Jabber account if you have one on your local network. Jabber is an open-source alternative to networks such as AIM, so you may find that your larger organization or institution offers its own Jabber server that you can log in to for chatting on your wide area or "enterprise" network. If you have such an account, enter a name and password; otherwise, just click Continue.

On the screen that follows, you can opt to turn on Bonjour messaging. If you do then other Macs that have Bonjour turned on and that are connected to the same network will be able to see your iChat account and attempt to contact you—that's true whether you're on your office network or a wireless network in a café. (It might be a fun way to get a little flirting done, if you're into that kind of thing.) Otherwise, you can leave it off if most of your chatting happens over the Internet as opposed to over a local network. Make your choice and click Continue.

On the Set Up iChat AV screen, you'll see a small bar that reacts to any noise you make—it's proving to you that you have an audio connection. (If you don't see the line move when you talk or tap the Mac, you may need to dig into the Sound pane in System Preferences and set up your microphone.) If you have a camera connected to your Mac, you'll also see an image in the window. If you don't and you suspect that you should, you need to troubleshoot your camera by seeing if it's turned on and connected. When you're convinced that your Mac is connected to the AV equipment that it should be, click Continue.

NOTE

Pretty much any camera that connects via FireWire and is Mac-compatible will work for iChat, including, of course, Apple's own iSight webcam, but extending to devices such as external DV camcorders. Connect your camcorder, remove the lens cap, and turn it on to see if iChat recognizes it. iChat can also work with a number of USB-connected webcams, as long as they're otherwise Mac-compatible.

You're ready to start using iChat. Click Done and you'll see one or two windows appear. If you signed in to a .Mac or AIM account then you'll see the Buddy List; if you connected to Bonjour, you'll see the Bonjour list; and if you opted for both, you'll see both (see Figure 9.10).

FIGURE 9.10

Here I'm connected to both Bonjour and the AIM service, as evidenced by the appearance of my Buddy List; you can see some other folks on my local network have popped up in the Bonjour list.

Once the windows are up and running, you're connected. You can disconnect from a particular service by choosing iChat, Log Out of AIM or by choosing iChat, Log Out of Bonjour. Or, when you're done completely with iChat, choose iChat, Quit iChat to quit the program and close your connections.

> **TIP**
>
> Want to change your personal iChat icon? You can click the icon itself in a Bonjour, Jabber, or Buddy window and you'll see options to choose other images; choose Edit Picture (or the menu command Buddies, Edit My Picture) to bring up a window that enables you to get different pictures from the Finder, or, if you have a camera connected, you can use the camera to take a snapshot of yourself.

Chatting by Typing

To begin a chat session, all you have to do is double-click the name of a user in one of the iChat windows. If you have Bonjour active and there's anyone else on your local network, you'll see names in the Bonjour window. If you don't see any names at all in the Buddy List, though, you'll need to populate that list with some buddies before you can chat. To do that, click the plus ("+") icon at the bottom of the Buddy List window or choose Buddies, Add Buddy from the iChat menus. You'll see a dialog sheet appear that looks somewhat like an interface to Address Book. If you have people in your Address Book who have iChat or AIM accounts, you can select one of those people and make them a buddy by highlighting their name and clicking Select Buddy (see Figure 9.11).

FIGURE 9.11
In order to chat with people using the AIM service, you add them as "buddies" and can then track when they're online.

Now, when you're looking at your Buddy List, you'll see that person's name dimmed in the list if he or she is not online; when your buddy is online and connected to the AIM service, you'll see his name colorful and bold, and you'll be able to double-click that name to initiate a chat.

TIP

There's another way to initiate a chat—via Mail. You can double-click the small icon that appears in the iChat column in the Mail message list when Mail recognizes a recipient and sees that she's connected to the AIM service. Note that this only works if iChat is also open on your Mac—Mail is checking in with iChat to see if the message sender also happens to be available on iChat.

When you initiate a chat, you'll see a new Chat window, which has your personal icon in the window, the time and an entry box for you to type a message. Type your message and press Return to send it to that person.

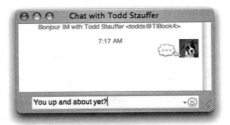

On the other end of that connection, the user will see an alert window from iChat that enables him or her to Decline or Accept the message. If the message is accepted, the other person's icon will appear in your message window and you can start chatting. You can chat away from there by typing a line and pressing return.

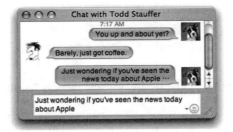

Chatting is pretty simple in this way; if there's anything else to worry about, it's that you can add emoticons (sometimes called "smileys") by selecting them from the small smiley-face menu that's next to the entry box for typing. Just click that menu and choose an emoticon that matches your mood. They're funny and fun to interject into conversation every so often.

When you're done with a chat, say "bye" to the other participant (or whatever you feel like saying) and then click the Close button in the open chat window. That ends the chat and returns you to the iChat buddy and/or Bonjour (or Jabber) windows.

TIP

In the View menu, you can change the look of your chat window using a variety of options; try View, Show Names or View, Show As Text to get a different look from the default. There's also View, Set Chat Background if you'd like to change the background of the text window to something a little different. Note that these changes only affect your window, not the window of the people you chat with; their windows are dictated by their own options.

Sending and Receiving Files

In many cases, you can use the AIM service (and, as far as I know, in all cases with Bonjour) to send files back and forth. There are two basic approaches. One is to drag-and-drop a file from the Finder to the listing for a person in the Buddy or Bonjour window. When you do, you'll see a dialog box that asks if you want to send that file; click Send if it's the right thing to do. Now, on the other side of that transaction, your buddy will see a window appear that enables him to download the file to his Mac. It's the same window that you'd see if someone sent a file to you; you click Save File to accept the file or Decline if you don't want it. You can also click and drag the file's icon out of the Incoming File Transfer window to the Finder or desktop.

The other way to transfer files is while you're chatting with the other person. With a chat window open, simply drag a file to the text entry box and drop it; when you do, a small representation of the file appears along with any text you've written. Press Return and the file appears in the chat window, where your recipient can click it (as if it were a web hyperlink) to download it.

TIP

In iChat Preferences, on the General tab, you can set the default location for downloaded files using the Save Received Files To menu.

iChat's AV Features

Of course, text-based chatting is all the rage and it can be handy for a variety of reasons, not the least of which is being able to manage projects in real-time, ask quick questions, and send files to friends and colleagues. Where iChat really sparkles, though, is its ability to offer audio chats and, if you have a camera connected, video chats.

For audio, all you *need* is built in to most modern Macs—an internal microphone and the speakers that came with your Mac work fine. (The only modern Macs that need a little help out of the box are Power Macintosh minitowers and Mac mini models, which don't have the built-ins that iMacs, eMacs, PowerBooks, and iBooks do.) You should have set up audio when you first launched iChat. If you need to check your connection, choose iChat, Preferences and click the Video icon; there, you'll see the audio indicator that reacts when it hears you make noise. (You can also use this screen to set up a connection to certain types of headsets if you have a compatible model. For best results, USB or Bluetooth headsets are preferable to the built-in audio jacks and microphones.)

If you're able to audio chat with someone in your Buddy or Bonjour list, you'll see the audio icon next to her name. To initiate an audio chat, click that icon.

Your recipient should see a window appear on his or her computer that offers an Accept or Decline button. If the chat is accepted, you'll see the audio chat window appear and you should hear the person on the other end of the connection. You'll even see the audio indicator light up when it hears you speaking (or singing or whatever it is that you decide to do).

That's it—just chat away. Note the small microphone icon: If you need to mute your side of the conversation, you can do that by clicking that icon; you'll see the audio indicator light up red to remind you that you're currently in mute mode. Click the icon again if you're ready to start chatting again.

When you're done, you can say "bye" and click the Close button on the window.

A video chat is essentially the same, except that you need to have a camera set up and connected to your Mac. When you do, you'll see a camera icon appear next to your own name at the top of the Bonjour and/or Buddy window; anyone in your list who is also video capable will likewise have a camera icon. Click that camera icon for one of your buddies and you'll see the video window appear; when they accept the chat, you should see them in the window. Now, chat away, wave, smile, and enjoy the conference. You can click the mute button to cut audio or choose Video, Pause Video (or Option+click the Mute button) to freeze the current video image *and* mute audio at the same time.

Again, when you're done with the video chat, click the Close button.

NOTE

If you have problems with your connection, choose Audio, Connection Doctor or Video, Connection Doctor to see if iChat can help with error messages and other reporting.

251

Create a Group Chat

In Mac OS X 10.4, iChat offers the option of group chats, which can include more than two participants, even for video conferencing. To initiate a group chat, choose File, New Chat.

You'll see a slightly different iChat window, which includes a drawer that will show chat participants. In the drawer, click the plus ("+") icon to add participants to the group; you can add them from your Buddy List or you can choose Other to enter the AIM address for the participant.

Now, enter text and send it off. If others participate, you'll have a group chat up and running (see Figure 9.12). This chat works pretty much like a two-way chat, except you'll see more icons and entries since there are more people. To leave the chat, say "bye" and click the close button.

FIGURE 9.12
In order to chat with people using the AIM service, you add them as "buddies" and can then track when they're online.

> **NOTE**
> What about audio and video? If everyone is running Tiger, a group chat in audio and video is possible. Highlight people in your Buddy list, then click the audio (telephone) or video (camera profile) button at the bottom of the Buddy List window. If your Mac is capable of hosting a chat—be warned, a PowerPC G5 processor is recommended—you'll see the chat window appear and people in your group will be able to accept and begin chatting.

Chapter 10

Browsing the Web: Safari and Sherlock

Of course, the Mac is capable of browsing the Web. It goes without saying. What is worth saying is that Apple doesn't rely on Microsoft for its web browser as it once did—Apple has produced its own browser, called Safari, which is based on a popular open-source web-browsing engine. The result is a fast, capable, and almost completely compatible browser that's a lot of fun to work with. In Mac OS X 10.4, Safari has been improved in ways that make it more pleasing to use with news sites and weblogs, among other features. And, it works well with the plug-ins that make it possible to view multimedia files—movies and sound— that go beyond the basic web page.

Along with Safari, Mac OS X offers a special application designed for accessing certain types of information over the Internet. Sherlock is Apple's own creation, with different "channels" that can be used to gather information on a variety of topics such as movies, stocks, pictures, airline flights, and more. Plus, Sherlock accepts channels written by third parties, making it possible to use Sherlock to search for all sorts of things.

We'll cover both, plus some related services and issues, in this chapter.

Introducing Safari

Safari is based on technology that Apple calls WebCore, which the company makes available as an open source download to application developers. That's partly because WebCore is based on KHTML, a cross-platform library developed as part of the KDE project, which is a graphical user interface for various flavors of Unix.

What all that gobbledygook means is that Safari is both its own animal and a standards-based application that has some close cousins on other operating systems. In fact, some other browsers written specifically for the Mac, such as OmniWeb from the Omni Group (www.omnigroup.com), also use WebCore as the basis for their web browser applications. WebCore is fast, it does a good job of rendering pages, and it has relatively few incompatibilities with poorly coded or non-standard pages on the Internet.

Safari builds on those strengths with some very specific features that make it a pleasure to work with. Safari includes a special Bookmark system that enables you to store links to your favorite websites and get to them easily. Safari has features such as an advanced RSS reader, built-in Google search, tabbed browsing, and some other fun stuff we'll get to in this section.

Browser Basics

You've likely worked with a web browser in the past and, if so, you'll find Safari is relatively familiar. Launch Safari from the Dock or locate its icon in the Application folder and double-click it to launch. When Safari pops up, it'll open a browser window and, if you're connected to the Internet, it may automatically open a web page and display it. That's your *home page*—often, it's set to a special page that Apple hosts. (You can change this, as you'll see in the section "Digging into Safari's Preferences.")

If you haven't worked with a browser in the past, what you need to know is pretty simple. The Web is a series of documents, called *web pages*, that include special *hypertext anchors*. Usually, these are represented by underlined text in a different color, although they can also be images and buttons in the document window. When you click an anchor, that causes another web page to appear; using these links, you can move from page to page and learn or explore quite a bit. Some links will take you to other pages on the same *website*, while others will take you away from one website and lead you to the pages on another.

TIP

In Safari you can hold down the ⌘ key while clicking a hyperlink to see the associated web document in its own, new Safari window. (If you have tabbed browsing turned on, which is discussed later in this chapter, ⌘+clicking opens the linked page in a new tab.) You can also Control+click (or right-click, if you have a multi-button mouse) a hyperlink to see a contextual menu of options that includes opening the linked document in its own window.

Along with the links, special websites called *search engines* collect information about the millions of web pages out there and make it a little easier for you to find them. Google.com, for instance, is an extremely popular search engine—so much so that an entry box is built in to the toolbar of Safari so that you can search Google in one step, without actually loading the Google web page first. (More on Google in a moment, but you can see the entry box in Figure 10.1.)

NOTE

At the bottom of your Safari window is the Status bar, where you'll see information about a page as it's loading and information about links that you point to with your mouse. (You may need to choose View, Show Status Bar to see it.) The top-right corner of the Safari window, however, is where you'll see a small padlock icon when you're accessing a *secure server*—one that is using *encryption* to communicate between your Mac and the server so that data cannot be read if it's intercepted by someone else.

Across the top of the Safari window is a series of buttons and entry boxes. These are the basic controls for Safari; again, they should be relatively familiar if you've worked with a browser in the past. You'll notice that some of them are even similar to buttons in a Finder window. They include

- Back—The back button is used to return to a page that you just left. When you click a hyperlink or enter a new web page address, you create a trail of pages that you've visited; clicking Back takes you backward along that trail.

- Forward—If you ever click Back, you may want to go forward again to a page that you've backed up from; you do that by clicking Forward.

- Refresh/Stop—The third button from the left has a dual purpose. While you're viewing a page that has already completely loaded across the Internet, you can click this button (it will look like a curved arrow) to reload the web page and check for any changes. If the page is currently being retrieved from the Internet, you can click this button (it will look like an "×") to stop the transfer.

- Add Bookmark—The icon that looks like a plus ("+") symbol enables you to add a bookmark for the current page; a bookmark lets you save the web page's address so that you can easily visit it again. More on this in the section "Save and Manage Bookmarks."

- Address box—Each web page on the Internet has a unique address, called a uniform resource locator or *URL*. The URL enables you to go directly to the page in question by typing the URL in the address box and then pressing Return.

- Google box—Safari has a special entry box for searching using the Google.com search engine.

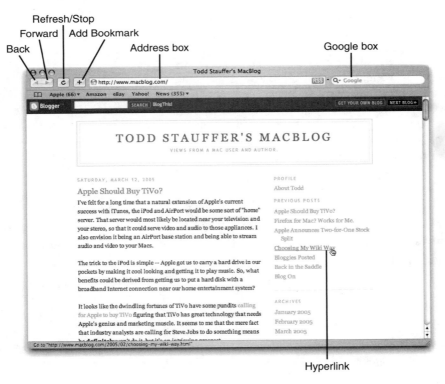

FIGURE 10.1

The Safari window has some basic controls at its top.

TIP

Encounter a page that you need to share with a friend or colleague? Choose File, Mail Contents Of This Page to send the entire page via Mail, or choose File, Mail Link to This Page if you want them to be able to visit the page themselves in their own web browser.

Most of the time, you'll begin by selecting a bookmark or entering an URL in the address entry box and going directly to a page that interests you. Then you'll click around on buttons and hyperlinks to get a look at what web pages and information are available that interest you.

NOTE

If you aren't familiar with URLs, they're addresses that resources on the Internet have to differentiate them from others. For web pages, they begin with the protocol **http://**, followed by an address for the web server computer, and then, finally, the name of the subfolders and pages on that server where a particular document can be found. An example is **http://www.apple.com/** to display the "default" page at Apple's website, or **http://www.macblog.com/about/todd.html**, which is the URL for a very specific HTML document on the Web. (It's also handy to think of the word URL as if it were pronounced like the name royal honorific "earl," at least in this chapter.)

Google Searches

One major way that you'll get to new and interesting web pages is by searching for them. While a number of search engines are available on the Web, Google is likely the most popular, and that's certainly true for Mac users, since it's built into Safari. The Google entry box at the top right of the Safari window also makes it a little more convenient to search with Google, as you can do a trick or two beyond simply searching.

Google is a massive database of information about pages on the Web, which is gathered by small applications called "robots" that move from page to page on the Internet looking for new pages or pages that have changed since the last visit. Google then makes a record of those pages and places them in a searchable database. That database will generally respond to *keyword* searches, which you can initiate by visiting Google.com or by entering keywords in the Google entry box at the top of the Safari window.

Once you've submitted your keywords to the Google search engine, you'll be shown a results list (see Figure 10.2), which is a list of sites that Google thought were relevant to your search. You can then click a hyperlink to see one of the pages that appears as a result. You can click the Next button at the bottom of the Google results window to see more results, or you can use the Google entry box to initiate another search.

FIGURE 10.2
When you search Google using keywords, you end up with a results list that you can explore.

So how do you search? The best way is to come up with a few keywords that really encompass the subject that you're trying to get at—if you need to know what the homestead exemption is for a taxpayer in Wyoming, you might try the keywords **Wyoming homestead exemption taxes**. If you want to see photos of a Tahitian sunset, you might search for **Tahiti sunset photos**.

Google also allows you to use some special codes and symbols to get a little more specific. The plus ("+") symbol can be used to tell Google that the results *must* include a specific term; for instance, **Tahiti sunset +photos** would only include pages that definitely have the term *photos* in them, even if they don't have sunset or Tahiti. (Of course, those with all three in them would be returned near the top of the list.) A minus sign can be used to exclude pages that include a term, such as **Tahiti photos -sunset**, which would return pages that have Tahiti and photos but would ignore pages with the word sunset in them. (This can be particularly useful when you need to exclude a common keyword from a search—for instance, say you were searching for web pages that were about Sammy Sosa, but not about baseball. With the keyboards **Sammy Sosa -baseball** you might have some luck with that.)

Along with the plus and minus symbols, you can use quotes to tell Google that you're looking for a phrase. For instance, **"Sammy Sosa"** is a good way to search for a person's proper name, and it works great with words that are otherwise difficult for Google to stomach, such as **"Mac OS X"**, which Google would prefer to see as "Mac" and "OS" and "X" if it doesn't have quotes around it. Quotes are also good for longer phrases, such as if you'd like to find a reference to **"Oh beautiful, for spacious skies"** or **"Que Sera, Sera"** or anything else you think you might find on the Web.

TIP

Google itself has some other interesting features, such as the ability to look up words in a dictionary or even do basic mathematical equations. Check out Google's help, starting at http://www.google.com/help/ for details.

One other thing to note about using Google with Safari that's kind of cool is that it offers a history of searches, if you click the small arrow menu in the Google entry box. When you click that arrow, a menu appears; select one of those searches and you can relive the results in Safari. (Google also works great with the SnapBack features, discussed in the following section, "Reliving History.")

Reliving History

I mentioned that as you surf, you can use the Back button to return to pages that you've already seen and moved away from. Along those same lines, Safari will actually track every page you visit, giving you the opportunity to return to a page that you've been to recently if you need to. That record is kept in the History for the browser, which is accessible via the History menu. Pull it down (as shown in Figure 10.3) and you can access the sites you've visited in the past few minutes and, in many cases, the past few days.

FIGURE 10.3
The History menu gives you quick access to the sites you've visited recently.

In Safari, the History menu offers a very cool feature called SnapBack. With SnapBack, you designate a particular page as the page that you'd like to "snap back" to. It might be a list of search results in eBay, for instance, or a certain page that has lots of links that you want to explore.

To designate a page as a SnapBack page, simply view it in the browser and choose History, Mark Page for Snapback. Now, you'll see a small curved arrow icon appear in the address bar next to that page's URL—that means the page is now marked for SnapBack. Click the curved arrow at any time and you'll immediately snap back to that page. (You can also choose History, Page SnapBack from the menu.) If at any point you want to change the SnapBack page, go right ahead—view a new page and choose the Mark Page for SnapBack command again.

TIP

Google search results automatically have their own SnapBack icon, which appears in the Google entry box. Click that curved arrow to snap back to the most recent Google results.

Want to clear the history of sites you've visited? You can do that easily using the History, Clear History command. You can also keep Safari from tracking the sites you visit using the Private Browsing feature, discussed later in this chapter.

Managing Bookmarks

As you're surfing along looking at pages, you'll no doubt come across a few that you'd like to refer back to in the future. That's what bookmarks are for. With bookmarks, you can store a reference to any page and get back to it quickly by accessing the bookmark. What's more, you can manage those bookmarks by putting them in folders and subfolders so that they're easy to find and get to.

TIP

Saving bookmarks simply saves a hyperlink to a particular page. Want to save the page itself? Choose File, Save As and choose Web Archive from the Format menu. That will save the page and associated images so that you can reload it in Safari from your hard disk.

Let's start with adding bookmarks. As you're surfing, when you get to a page that you'd like to keep a reference to for later access, just click the plus ("+") icon that appears on the Safari toolbar. When you do, a dialog sheet appears, where you can give a name to the bookmark and choose a folder where that bookmark will be stored (see Figure 10.4).

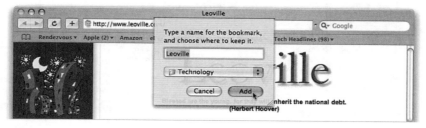

FIGURE 10.4
Click the + symbol to save a bookmark.

In Safari, the weird thing is that if you pick a folder, that bookmark isn't immediately accessible via the Bookmarks menu. (That will seem really weird if you've used other browsers for Windows and Mac; if you haven't, then it actually won't seem that weird at all.) If you'd like to leave the bookmark unsorted so that it appears in the main Bookmarks menu, you can do that—choose Bookmarks Menu from the menu in the dialog sheet.

Another interesting choice is the Bookmarks Bar entry. When you add an item to this subfolder, it appears on the Bookmarks toolbar in the Safari window itself. You can also add pages to that Bookmarks bar by drag-and-drop—simply drag the icon next to the page's URL to the Bookmarks bar.

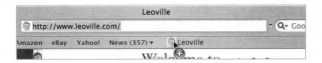

When you drop the icon on the Bookmark bar, you'll see a dialog sheet asking you to name it; you can give the bookmark a shorter name than the page's original name so that you can squeeze more on to the bar.

Otherwise, both to get at your stored bookmarks and to manage them, you have to dig a little further. That digging begins when you click the bookmark icon on the Bookmarks bar; it's the small icon that looks like an open book. That switches the Safari window around so that you see the Bookmark management screen and tools (see Figure 10.5).

FIGURE 10.5

In bookmark management mode you can view your bookmarks and create folders to help you organize them.

In the Collections list, you'll see the different folders that have already been created for you by Safari; you can use those if you like, add to them, or alter them. You'll also see some special "smart" entries, such as the All RSS Feeds collection (select it to see all RSS feeds that are stored, as discussed in the next section) or the History entry, which lets you access the history for your browser. (That's handy for managing bookmarks, too, as you can dig into your history to locate a page that you forgot to bookmark on-the-fly.)

TIP

Do you have bookmarks from another web browser that you'd like to use in Safari? Choose File, Import Bookmarks and you'll see an Open dialog box; now find the HTML document (it should end in .html) that the other application used to store its bookmarks. Often you'll find bookmarks in your personal Library folder, in that web browser's settings folder, which should be located either in Application Support or in Preferences inside your Library folder. If your browser doesn't store bookmarks as HTML files, you may need to launch that browser and export them first.

To create your own folder, click the plus ("+") icon at the bottom of the Collections list. That creates a new untitled folder and immediately makes it highlighted for editing. Just begin typing to give it a name.

With your folders created, you can drag and drop bookmarks around to reorganize them. If you'd like them visible in the Bookmarks menu, you can drag individual bookmarks to the Bookmarks Menu icon in Collections; if you'd like a particular bookmark on the Bookmarks bar, you can drag it there.

You can also drag entire folders to either of those two, and access them as subfolders. Note that this is a little different; select the Bookmarks Menu or Bookmarks Bar item first in the Collections list, then drag a folder from the Collections list into the main window for the Bookmarks menu or Bookmarks bar (whichever is being displayed). That folder is added as a subfolder that you can access immediately.

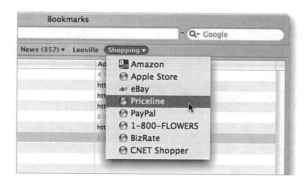

Finally, you'll notice two other things about bookmarks. First, in the main listing area, you can click once on an bookmark's name or address and then press the Return key to begin editing it. (In fact, you can click the plus ["+"] button for the main listing area to create a new blank bookmark and begin filling it in.)

TIP

Open Safari Preferences and click the Bookmarks button to see some interesting options. If you like, you can have Safari automatically include websites from your Address Book on the Bookmarks bar in the Bookmarks menu. Safari can also include Rendezvous links, which are links to web pages that your Mac automatically finds on other Macs attached to your local network.

Second, you can double-click a bookmark to launch it in the browser window and visit that site—after all, that's the point of bookmarks in Safari!

BOOKMARKS AND .MAC

If you're a subscriber to Apple's .Mac online service, you might want to take advantage of a special capability that Safari and Mac OS X have—you can synchronize your bookmarks via the .Mac service so that you can use your bookmarks with more than one computer.

How this works is simple. More than one Mac can be set up to use the same .Mac account—for instance, your laptop and your desktop can both use your .Mac account. And, in that case, you might want to synchronize your bookmarks between the two. To do that, you need to synchronize the bookmarks from those Macs and then register those Macs with the .Mac account.

To set up your Mac to synchronize its bookmarks with your .Mac account, you'll need to open the .Mac pane of System Preferences and select the Account tab. Make sure your .Mac account information is entered properly. Next, select the Sync tab and turn on the Bookmarks option. That makes it so that the bookmarks on this Mac will be stored at the .Mac site and accessible to your other Macs.

To register a Mac and allow it to be synchronized via .Mac, open the .Mac pane of System Preferences and select the Account tab, then make sure the correct .Mac account has been entered. Now, choose the Advanced tab and click that Register This Computer button. You should see it added to the list of computers that are synchronizing Safari bookmarks via that .Mac account.

Reading RSS "Newsfeeds" in Safari

A new feature in Safari with the release of Mac OS X 10.4 is support for RSS news-feeds. *RSS* stands for *Real Simple Syndication*, and it's a method of publishing the head-lines and short blurbs from a website so that others can view those headlines without specifically visiting the site in question. Using RSS, you can quickly take a look and see what's changed at your favorite website without going to the trouble of loading it.

In order to offer its headlines to others, a website must specifically publish an RSS feed, which is a special document, generally called "index.rss" or "index.xml," that is made available via the site's interface; you'll see a link that says Syndicate This Page or Access RSS Feed or something similar.

> **NOTE**
>
> If you want to type a feed's URL into Safari's address bar directly, you need to begin the URL with **feed://** to make sure it's displayed using Safari's feed reader interface. Otherwise, you'll probably see the raw XML code for the document.

Safari, on its own, can detect many sites that have RSS feeds. When Safari finds one, it places an RSS button in the address bar. You can click the button to view the RSS feed or, once you're viewing it, you can click the button to return to the main page.

View a Feed

So, what does an RSS feed look like? In Safari, you'll see a very basic listing of head-lines and stories, along with the time the story was posted (see Figure 10.6). After each story, you'll see a Read More link, which, when clicked, takes you to the site that this RSS feed references, enabling you to read the entire story.

Along the right side of the feed reader window is a toolbar that you can use to orga-nize the stories and make choices about how you view them. The slider enables you to change the length of the blurb that's shown beneath a story, while the other links let you search the stories, sort them, or determine how many recent stories to show (all of them, only today's, only yesterday's, and so on). At the bottom of that list, you can click the Mail Link to This Page button if you'd like to mail the feed's URL to someone using Mail. Click the Add Bookmark link if you'd like to add this feed as a bookmark in Safari.

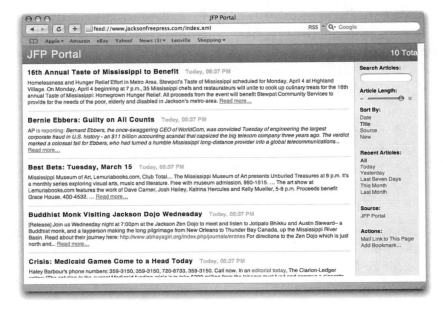

FIGURE 10.6
The RSS feed reader in Safari makes any RSS feed look a little like a weblog.

> **TIP**
>
> As was mentioned in the earlier section on bookmarks, one of the default Collections in the bookmark management interface is All RSS Feeds, which you can use to quickly view all of the RSS feed documents that you have created bookmarks for. (Safari comes with a lot of bookmarked RSS feeds already, so you'll see tons whenever you click this button unless you've deleted them.)

View Multiple Feeds

One of the reasons that people like RSS feeds is that they enable you to view articles from more than one source at a time. At first blush, Safari doesn't seem to do that, but there is a way to make it happen. Here's how:

1. Bookmark the RSS feeds that you'd like to see together on the same page.
2. Switch to the bookmarks screen and collect those bookmarks in one folder.
3. Move the folder to the Bookmarks bar interface.
4. Click on the new folder's menu on the Bookmarks bar and choose View All RSS Articles.

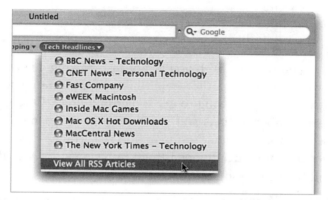

The result will be the same feed reader interface, but with access to the different feeds all in the same window. You can sort by source to see each individual feed's articles consecutively, or sort by other criteria to see them mixed and matched together.

Automatically Check Changes

Another reason savvy web surfers like RSS feeds is that they can be used to quickly notice when a website has been updated and new articles have been posted. With its built-in feed reading, Safari can automatically check for changes to your favorite feeds. Here's how:

1. Choose Safari, Preferences.
2. Click the RSS tab.
3. Click to place a check mark next one or both options in the Automatically Update Article In section. Choose Bookmarks Bar if you want to see the RSS feeds on your Bookmarks bar updated when new articles are posted; choose Bookmarks Menu if you'd like feeds that have been added specifically to your Bookmarks menu to be updated.
4. Optionally, you can turn on Color New Articles if you'd like to see the new articles appear in a different color.
5. Close the Preferences window when you're done.

With your preferences set, you should see small numbers begin to appear next to your RSS feeds and any menus that hold them. That tells you that new articles have been detected.

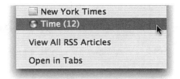

Using Tabs

If you're like me, as you surf the Web you're not just clicking a hyperlink and viewing a new page, and then clicking another hyperlink and continuing to surf a topic like that—at least, not when you're trying to get something done. Often, you'll be looking at a page that has a number of links and you'll want to try many of them before you settle on the page you want to view. You may find that you're holding ⌘ and clicking hyperlinks in order to automatically open them in new windows so that your original page of links is still back there somewhere.

Tabbed browsing is a new feature in Safari, designed to give you another approach for that sort of surfing. With tabbed browsing, you have the choice of opening more than one page within a given browser window. Safari does this by putting each page on its own *tab*, which is just a small clickable indicator toward the top of the Safari window. When you have tabbed browsing activated, you can click a link in one page and have it load in a tab within that same Safari window, which is handy if you get sick of new windows popping up all the time.

To enable tabbed browsing, simply choose Safari, Preferences and click the Tabs button. Click the check box to enable tabbed browsing. You can then choose the other options if desired; if you leave Select New Tabs As They Are Created turned off, then the contents on new tabbed pages will not be displayed until you switch to them, which can be handy.

TIP

If you're a die-hard eBay shopper like me, you may find that not only is the tabbed browsing feature handy, but specifically leaving the Select New Tabs feature turned off makes shopping easier. These features enable you to ⌘+click a link (a product auction, for instance) and continue to view the listing. ⌘+click a few more links before you *then* start checking out the new tabs to see the auction pages once they've loaded.

The Tabs screen in Preferences shows you some of the keyboard commands you can use for opening tabs; with tabbed browsing on, you can also Control+click a hyperlink and choose Open Link in New Tab.

As the contents of a tabbed page load, you'll see a small spinning wheel on that tab; when it disappears, that indicates that the page is loaded. Simply click tabs to switch back and forth between them. Note also that each tab has its own "×" icon, which can be used to quickly delete the tab and dismiss the page (see Figure 10.7).

FIGURE 10.7
Click a tab to switch to it; click its "×" icon to delete it.

Otherwise, when you're viewing a particular tab, it works just like any page in Safari. Click the Refresh button to reload the page; you can use the Forward and Back buttons and so on. Just to be a little more advanced, note that you can Control+click a tab to see options such as closing the tab, closing other tabs, reloading the tab, or even creating a new, blank tab that you can switch to in order to use the address bar to launch a new page.

TIP

Want to open a bunch of bookmarked pages in Safari at once—in their own tabs? You can do it if the bookmarks are in the same folder in the Collections list. Simply Control+click the folder and choose Open in Tabs from the contextual menu that appears. Or, you may notice that bookmark folders in the Bookmarks Bar collection include an Auto-Click option; turn on that option for a given bookmark folder and you can click that bookmark folder once in the Bookmarks bar to open all its bookmarks in separate tabs.

Digging into Safari's Preferences

You've already seen some of the preferences that Safari has to offer. You can open the preferences window using Safari, Preferences. Before you do, however, notice that the Safari menu itself has some commands on it for convenient access, including

- Block Pop-Up Windows—When this command has been selected and is turned on (a check mark appears next to it in the menu), websites aren't able to force windows to "pop up" on the screen automatically while a page is loading or when you leave a web page. Select the command again to turn it off.

- Private Browsing—When this option is turned on (by selecting it in the menu), Safari will not maintain a history of the sites you're viewing, items are removed from the Download list, the AutoFill feature doesn't save data that you enter into HTML forms, previous searches aren't added to the Google entry box, and all cookies accepted during the private session are deleted immediately after you turn Private Browsing off again by re-selecting it in the Safari menu. This is ideal if you work on your Mac in a shared environment and don't want others to have access to your personal data or if you don't want to share your web browsing history with them.

- Reset Safari—This command will "sweep" your personal information out of Safari (aside from your bookmarks). Choose this option to automatically delete your browsing history, empty the cache (HTML documents and multimedia files that are stored on your Mac so that you can more quickly access pages you've already viewed), clear the Download window, remove cookies, and delete saved names and searches from the Autofill feature and Google entry box.

- Empty Cache—Use this command to delete the HTML and multimedia files that Safari stores in its cache.

NOTE

The *cache* is a limited amount of storage space that's used to quickly rebuild pages that you've visited recently so that at least some of the elements that were downloaded previously don't have to be re-downloaded when you access the page again.

The other command on the Safari menu is, of course, the Preferences command, which opens up the Preferences window. From there, you can choose an icon at the top of the window to change different settings. Here's a look at those icons:

- General—On the General preferences screen, you can choose the default web browser that is used for launching web pages from your other applications (note that you can set it to something other than Safari if desired). You can also set a *home page* for your browsing, which is the site that is loaded when you choose

History, Home or click the Home icon in the toolbar. Along with a home page, you can set the new window behavior—I like to set new windows to open with an empty page, but you have other options. From the Save Downloaded Files To menu, you can choose a folder where your downloads will be stored, and you can tell Safari whether or not to launch downloads when they're finished. Finally, you can decide whether links from your applications will open a page in a new window or on a new tab in the current window.

- Appearance—On this screen, you can choose the fonts that are used to display text in the browser, and you can turn on and off images on your pages. (If you opt not to display images, pages will usually load much more quickly.)

- Bookmarks—The Bookmarks screen is used to add some automatic bookmarks to various locations in Safari; you can also start and stop bookmark synchronization from this screen. (See the section "Managing Bookmarks," earlier in this chapter)

- Tabs—Set tabbed browsing behavior here. (See the section "Using Tabs," earlier in this chapter.)

- RSS—Here you can set options for the display of syndicated headlines in Safari. (See the section "Reading RSS 'Newsfeeds' in Safari," earlier in this chapter.)

- AutoFill—On this screen, you can make choices about how the AutoFill feature gets and stores the information that it uses to automatically fill in your name, address, and other information on HTML forms. You can click the Edit button next to each type of data to change it or see what is stored for a given website. And by unchecking all of the options, you can turn off AutoFill completely.

NOTE

AutoFill is an feature in Safari that fills in HTML entry forms from your previous input and/or from sources such as your own Address Book. These HTML entry forms are pages with text entry boxes (and sometimes check boxes and radio buttons and other controls) that are used for things such as ordering products or sending information about yourself to the site in question.

- Security—In the Web Content section of this screen, you can opt to turn on or off the display of various types of multimedia and scripting. You'll likely want plug-ins, JavaScript, and Java enabled, although each carries with it a slight security risk. In the Accept Cookies section, you can decide when and how you'd like to accept cookies; click the Show Cookies button if you'd like to see the cookies that are stored for your user account. At the bottom of the screen, you can turn on the Ask Before Sending a Non-Secure Form option, which lets you know when you might be sending important information over a connection that isn't encrypted. You'll also see the Enable Parental Controls option at the bottom of this screen if you'd like to set the sites that this user can access in Safari. (This only works if the current user is not an Admin-level user.)

- Advanced—On the Advanced screen, you can set a minimum font size (to make pages easier to read) and you can turn on an option that causes the Tab key to select any clickable item on the page; press Tab a second time to move to the next item, and so on. In the Style Sheet menu, you can choose a Cascading Style Sheets (CSS)-formatted style sheet. If you specify such a style sheet, it will be used in addition to any styles that are specified by the websites you visit; this can be handy for increasing the size or readability of text if you have certain visual impairments. (Or, you might just like to have your team's colors behind every page you browse.) Finally, the Proxies button gives you a convenient link to the Proxies tab in the Network pane of System Preferences.

NOTE

Want to know more about CSS and style sheets? Visit www.w3.org/Style/CSS for information on how it works and how you can create your own style sheets.

When you're done setting preferences, click the Close button in the Preferences window. Your changes are saved and implemented immediately.

QuickTime and Streaming Multimedia

As you're surfing the Web, you'll occasionally come across multimedia files that go beyond the basic text and images that comprise the typical web page. Digital audio and movies are popular options available via the Web, and they're becoming increasingly more popular thanks to broadband connections that can transfer the volume of data that's required for web-based video. In many cases, that data is *streamed* over the Internet from a multimedia server to your Mac for playback; in order to keep up with the stream, your Internet connection needs to be quick and efficient.

NOTE

Generally speaking, there are two ways that you deal with audio and video on the Web—either you download a file to your Mac for playback or you initiate a stream of multimedia data, which can begin playing soon after data starts arriving at your Mac. Downloading takes longer—sometimes much longer—but tends to result in better playback; streaming is a little more like turning to a new channel on your television, in that the picture begins to display much more quickly, although compared to downloading the image, it's often smaller and choppier. (That said, streaming technology is getting better all the time.)

The key to dealing with most audio and video on the Web is knowing the format of the data file or stream. For Mac users, the most natural format is QuickTime, because it was created by Apple, provides exceptional video quality, and is built in to the Mac. It's not the only choice, though, as both RealMedia and Windows Media are popular options.

As I said, which one you end up using to view something depends on the format that the data is in. At C-SPAN.org, for instance, all of the feeds are in RealMedia or Windows Media—QuickTime isn't even an option. So, in order to view a C-SPAN feed (see Figure 10.8), you'll need to download a free player from RealNetworks (www.real.com) to play RealMedia feeds or the Windows Media Player (www.microsoft.com/mactopia/) to play back Windows Media on your Mac. Once downloaded and installed, you should be able to view or listen to a good proportion of the multimedia documents or streams that are available in those two formats. You won't be able to see all of them, because some videos use *codecs* (software designed to compress the stream for transport and then decompress it for playback) that only work on Windows-based PCs.

NOTE

All of the technologies we're talking about—QuickTime, RealMedia, and Windows Media—have their own standalone players as well as *plug-ins* that make it possible for you to play back multimedia in the browser window itself. In my experience with Windows Media and the Mac, the plug-in doesn't often work, but in those cases you generally launch the multimedia item in the standalone player.

With QuickTime built in to the Mac OS, the support for QuickTime movies is most complete, even with Safari. What you'll find is that QuickTime movies just work in almost all cases and, if necessary, there's a pane in System Preferences that you can access in order to set options for QuickTime. Open the QuickTime pane and you can choose how QuickTime interacts with Safari, including whether movies are played automatically and how they're stored in the disk cache, by selecting the Browser tab. On the Streaming tab, you can tweak preferences to determine how streaming video will work by setting your connection speed in the Streaming Speed menu. You can also turn on and off the Enable Instant-On option if you're having trouble with the quality of streaming playback.

FIGURE 10.8
Here I'm viewing a QuickTime movie that's streaming from Apple's .Mac server and playing back using the QuickTime plug-in.

Playback of any movie or audio file is pretty straightforward; you'll find that each type of media—QuickTime, RealMedia, and Windows Media—have similar player interfaces that include VCR-like controls for play, pause, fast forward, review, and so forth.

If there's a distinction to be aware of, it's that a downloaded multimedia file can generally be started, stopped, played over again, and even fast-forwarded or reviewed. A stream, however, is more like a live TV broadcast; you can stop or pause the playback, but when you start the streaming again, it will be at the current moment in the stream, since it's "live." That's not the case for all streams, but it's certainly true of live events such as C-SPAN's live broadcasts, called *webcasts*.

TIP

Often, when you initiate a streaming session, it creates a small file on your desktop (or in your downloads folder) called play.rm or play.asx or something similar. These files can be saved and relaunched to access the stream in the future, if necessary, or you can toss them in the Trash when you're done watching a particular stream. The files don't have movie data in them; they're simply pointers to the stream's location online.

Explore Sherlock

Safari is full-featured, but isn't the only web application included with Mac OS X. Sherlock is something of a web-retrieval program; it's designed to work with specially designed web applications—called *channels* in Sherlock's lingo—that are designed for very specific tasks. To get a sense of what Sherlock does, launch it from the Applications folder on your Mac. Figure 10.9 shows Sherlock in action.

One thing you might notice about Sherlock is an occasional redundancy with the tools that come with Dashboard. That's probably true, and I'm not sure what that means for the future of Sherlock; it was really cool technology a few years back for Apple, but the Dashboard widgets might win out for their minimalism. That said, the one difference (at least so far) is that Sherlock channels tend to offer considerably more detailed results than most Dashboard widgets, and Sherlock is still handy for special searches, such as those it offers for eBay and Apple's support documents.

Working with Sherlock is fairly intuitive; choose a channel's icon at the top of the window—Internet is for search engine access, Stocks accesses Lycos's stock ticker, eBay is a search tool for online auctions, and so on. With a channel selected, enter the data that's asked for and make choices; for instance, on the eBay channel, enter a search term and choose a Category to narrow things down. You can then click the Track Listing button to add a listing to your personal tracking within Sherlock.

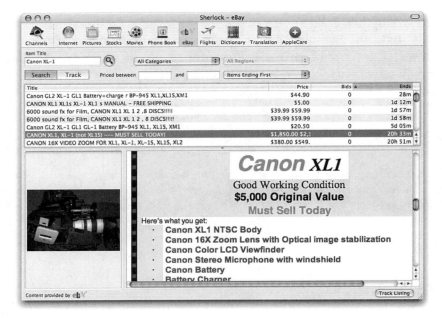

FIGURE 10.9
Sherlock is a web-based information retrieval tool.

Click the Channels button in the top left of the window and you'll see the interface change slightly to a Collections listing and a viewing window. On the Collections list, you'll see some folders and groupings of channels, including some that don't show up on the toolbar. For instance, select the Other Channels folder to see a long list of third-party channels that you can access within Sherlock. To use one of those channels, simply double-click it.

If you find a channel you like, drag it from the Other Channels list to the My Channels folder, or you can create a folder within the Collections list. You can also add a channel to the toolbar by dragging it's icon from the listing are to the toolbar.

> **TIP**
>
> You'll occasionally find Sherlock channels available on the Web, often in collections such as those found at www.sherlockchannels.info. When you come across a channel, look for a link that enables you to add or subscribe to that channel. When you click that link, you'll see a dialog box in Sherlock asking if you want to add the channel; if you click Proceed, the channel should be added directly to your copy of Sherlock.

Chapter 11

Build a Home or Office Network

No Mac is designed to work in a vacuum, and if you've got more than one Mac, you may find that you've got a good reason to connect them together. Macs on a network can share files; they can share printers; they can even share an Internet connection. And when you create a local network of Macs, you can have iChat discussions, play networked games, share iTunes, share Address Book contacts, and otherwise take advantage of tons of different resources thanks to the networking prowess built in to many of Mac OS X's included applications.

How Networks Work

The idea behind a local area network, or LAN, is to get your Macs (and PCs, if that interests you) hooked up so that they can share files and services. Built in to your Mac is the capability for it not only to connect to other Macs, but to allow them to log on to your Mac, via a user account and password, and then access the files on that Mac, either opening them directly or copying them to their own drive.

To create such a network, you need to do a few things. First, you have to decide if your network is going to be wired or wireless. All Mac OS X–compatible Macs feature built-in Ethernet, which is a standard port for wired network connections.

FIGURE 11.1
The Ethernet port on the side of my iBook makes wired network connections simple.

Most modern Macs also support AirPort, usually via an add-on card, which enables your Mac to talk to others via a wireless network. So, if you'd like to go that direction, you likely can.

> **NOTE**
>
> As you may have gathered if you read Chapter 8, "Get on the Internet," AirPort is Apple's implementation of the IEEE 802.11 standard for wireless network communications. Others call this Wi-Fi or "802.11" but they're all generally compatible. Earlier AirPort-enabled Macs support the slower 802.11b standard; later AirPort Extreme-enabled Macs support 802.11g, which is faster, but can drop back into a compatibility mode with 802.11b if you need to network your newer Mac with an older Mac or Macs. Just beware that any network operates at the slowest speed when mixing old and new technologies.

Here's a quick comparison:

- Ethernet. Ethernet connections tend to be faster than AirPort (or wireless) connections and much less prone to any sort of electronic interference. Ethernet is relatively inexpensive to implement, since all modern Macs have Ethernet ports built in. For connections between more than two Macs, you'll need an Ethernet hub or switch, which will add slightly to the cost; depending on the number of Macs you have, you should be able to find an inexpensive router/hub combination that will enable you to connect your network and share a single broadband Internet connection, if desired.

- AirPort. Wireless AirPort connections require that your Mac have an AirPort card, or, if it doesn't support such a card, you'll need some sort of Wi-Fi adapter. (You can get USB-based Wi-Fi adapters, for instance, and some PowerBook models support 802.11-compatible PC Cards for expansion.) Once you've got a card, you can connect a limited number of Macs together if one of them serves as a "hub," although it's best to get a dedicated wireless hub to support computers as they come and go on your wireless network. The AirPort Extreme Base Station and AirPort Express are two examples of wireless hubs that can serve multiple wireless computers at once; they're also routers, making it easy for those wireless computers to access a single broadband Internet connection. Wireless, overall, is a little pricier, because you have to buy the cards for your Macs and, usually, the hub/router to complete your network. They're also a bit slower and less reliable than wired connections; of course, they make all that up in flexibility.

Of the two, Ethernet is more secure when it comes to whether or not unauthorized people can access your network, since they need to be physically connected to it; with wireless, it's possible for people in your immediate vicinity to attempt to access the network, although you can generally come up with a password scheme to keep them from getting very far.

Once you choose a connection type, you then need to configure the *protocol* that you're going to use for the network. The protocol determines how your Macs will connect to one another and the standard language they'll use for swapping packets of data. In almost all cases on a modern Mac network, you'll use TCP/IP, the same protocol used for Internet connections. TCP/IP isn't the only option, though—Mac OS X supports AppleTalk, an aging Apple standard that's still useful for connections to network printers and other devices that support the AppleTalk protocol. And, it's possible to use

AppleTalk for networking and file sharing, which can be handy if you also have much older Macs on your network.

Once a protocol is decided on—don't worry, we explain protocols in much more detail later in this chapter—the third step is to activate *services* on top of that protocol. The most obvious of these is File Sharing, which allows others to log in to your Mac over the network and access files stored on it. Others include everything from Printer Sharing, to Web Sharing, and even using applications such as iChat and network-capable games. All of those applications work on top of the protocol that you choose in order to move data along the connections—wired or wireless—that you've set up and configured.

Connecting Your Macs

So, the first step, as we saw in the previous section, is to connect the Macs that will make up your network. You can do that with Ethernet cables, with wireless connections or with a combination of the two. We'll start this section discussing Ethernet and then we'll move on to AirPort connections.

BROADBAND AND THE LOCAL AREA NETWORK

Does your Mac currently have a broadband Internet connection? Those of us with cable or DSL modems or other high-speed connections, such as in apartment buildings or small business offices that are wired for Internet, may find that we have to solve a small problem when we decide to build a local network. If you have such a connection and you're currently working with a single Mac, more than likely you're using your Mac's Ethernet port to connect to the Internet. But what if you want to use Ethernet for a local network? Unfortunately, your Ethernet port is already taken up by the modem connection. So, if you want to add your Mac to a network that uses Ethernet, you need to take an extra step.

The most common solution is to get a router/hub combination, so that the Ethernet cable for the broadband Internet service is connected to the router, instead of your Mac. Then, Internet data can be routed to any computer that's connected to the router's built-in hub. (Routers and hubs can also be separate devices.)

We'll discuss all this in more detail in the section "Internet Access for Your Networked Macs" that comes later in this chapter. For now, though, know that you'll either need to use a different port for your local area network and your broadband connection (use AirPort for networking and Ethernet to connect to your cable modem, for instance) or you'll need a router of some kind so that you can use that Internet service to offer a connection to everyone on your network.

Connecting via Ethernet

If you have two Macs that you'd like to connect, you can do that with a just an Ethernet cable; depending on the Mac models, it may need to be a special type of Ethernet cable, called a *crossover* cable. (Crossover cables are very similar to regular Ethernet "patch" cables, except that they're usually brighter colors than regular Ethernet cables and labeled "crossover" on the plastic sheath of the cable itself.) Any Mac that has Gigabit Ethernet can be connected to any other Mac using a regular Ethernet cable, which is generally called a *Cat 5* cable; otherwise, older Macs and consumer Macs designed without Gigabit Ethernet need to be connected using a crossover cable.

If you're connecting more than one Mac via Ethernet, you'll need to use a switch or a hub (see Figure 11.2). These devices are similar—a switch is generally a bit "smarter" and more expensive than a hub—and they do what their names imply, connecting computers together by connecting to each of them, in turn, via an Ethernet cable. Using a hub or switch, you run a cable from your Mac's Ethernet port to an available port on that hub or switch; you then do the same for each of the computers that you want to connect.

FIGURE 11.2

Here's an example of a switch, used at the center of Ethernet networks. (Photo courtesy of Asanté—www.asante.com.)

There's no particular trick to configuring an Ethernet network—the only real problem is getting enough cable (and long enough cables) to reach from your computers to the hub. If you have Macs on different floors in your home or office or otherwise rather far from one another, you might start to see why a lot of people like to build Ethernet cabling into the walls of their offices and homes.

> **NOTE**
>
> Hubs and switches often have at least one port that's labeled differently—if you see an uplink port, that port is generally designed to connect the hub to another hub, switch, or router—meaning you're connecting this small network to a larger one. A router is a device that connects two different networks to one another by routing *some* data from one to the other. For example, connecting your entire local network to the Internet requires a router, because only *some* of the data that bounces around your network is bound for the Internet, and vice versa.

One thing that's nice about Mac OS X is that it tends to recognize when a cable has been connected to your Mac and when it appears to be properly connected to your local network. You can get a sense of that by launching System Preferences (Apple, System Preferences) and clicking the Network pane's icon. On the Network Status screen, you'll see an entry for Ethernet that shows you've connected a cable to your Mac's Ethernet port, along with the status that your Mac has detected for that connection (see Figure 11.3).

FIGURE 11.3
The Network Status screen is handy for seeing whether a connection appears to be recognized.

Set Up AirPort Connections

Unlike an Ethernet connection, an AirPort connection—that is, getting your wireless Mac to talk to other wireless computers—has to be a bit more flexible, since many such Macs are mobile. To establish such a connection, you'll need an AirPort-equipped Mac—or you'll need to grab an AirPort (or other Mac-compatible wireless) card and install it in your Mac. (If you have an AirPort-capable Mac, the thin manual that came with your Mac includes step-by-step instructions on how to install an AirPort card. If you don't have the manual then I suggest you head to www.apple.com/support/airport/ and locate the online instructions specific to your Mac model.)

The other thing you're going to need is some sort of wireless base station or access point. AirPort-enabled Macs, you probably won't be surprised to learn, work best with Apple's own AirPort Extreme Base Station or AirPort Express base stations, which are combination routers and hubs. But they can work with other wireless hubs/routers as well, as long as they conform to the 802.11b and/or 802.11g standard.

TIP

You can also connect two or a few wireless Macs to one another without a wireless hub, as discussed in the upcoming "Computer to Computer" sidebar.

If you have an AirPort Extreme or AirPort Express (or any earlier AirPort base station), you'll find that all you have to do is plug it in and it will automatically be able to serve as a hub for your wireless Macs, so that they can share data among themselves. If you also want to set up that AirPort base station for Internet routing and security, you'll need to use the AirPort Setup Utility for that particular base station model. (You'll find the AirPort Setup Utility in the Utilities folder inside your main Applications folder.)

With your base station configured (or anywhere that you have a wireless hub available), your next step with an AirPort-enabled Mac is to ensure that the AirPort card is turned on. You do that by accessing the AirPort menu that appears in your menu bar by default when an AirPort card is recognized. If AirPort is not turned on, choose the Turn AirPort On command.

NOTE

If you don't see this menu, you'll need to open the Network pane of System Preferences, choose to edit AirPort settings, and turn on the menu on the AirPort tab.

Once AirPort is turned on, you can return to the AirPort menu and check to see if any base stations (or wireless hubs of any sort) are recognized. If they are, you'll see the hub's name appear in this menu; select the hub you want to connect to.

After you connect to the hub, you may find that you're asked for a password; many wireless hubs and base stations have a single network password to keep out intruders. Otherwise, anyone in close enough proximity to pick up the signal can log in and use the network. If you see such a password dialog box, you'll need to enter the password for the network to which you're connecting. (If you click Add to Keychain, your Mac will consult your personal Keychain for this password in the future. See Chapter 14 for more on the Keychain.)

That's it—you've got a connection. To break the connection, you can return to the AirPort menu and choose a different hub or base station, or you can turn AirPort off. In most cases, though, you can simply put your Mac to sleep or shut its case (if it's a portable) to take your Mac off the network. AirPort and Wi-Fi connections are forgiving—the next time you power up or arrive back in the area, you'll have the option of signing on again.

If you do move your Mac around a bit, you'll find that Mac OS X is actually designed to "remember" wireless networks it's connected to before and connect to them again when you come in their vicinity. You can manage that via the Network pane in System Preferences; choose AirPort from the Show menu, then click the AirPort tab. In the

By Default, Join menu, you'll see Automatic selected; that's the default. If you prefer, you can choose Preferred Networks, which then gives you a list of networks that you designate as those to which you would like your Mac to connect automatically (see Figure 11.4). Now, whenever you get in the vicinity of a wireless hub or base station that isn't on the list, your Mac will ask you if you'd like to connect to it; if it is on the list, you'll connect automatically.

FIGURE 11.4

On the AirPort tab of the Network pane, you can decide which are preferred networks. Use the plus ("+") icon to add one or highlight a network and click the minus ("−") icon to remove one.

COMPUTER TO COMPUTER

To complete an AirPort connection, you don't need to have a wireless hub or base station, because your Mac can act as a base station on its own. The downside is that you've got to keep your Mac running for others to access it, and a real base station is more efficient. Still, in a pinch, you can use your AirPort-enabled Mac to create a network that other AirPort-enabled Macs can access.

(continues)

(continued)

To do that, open the AirPort menu and choose Create Network. In the dialog box that appears, enter a name for the network, and, if desired, choose a channel (most of the time the default or Automatic setting is best, but you may be told to try different channel by a support technician or system administrator). If you'd like to require a password, click the Show Options button, then turn on Enable Encryption and enter a password for your network. (With encryption enabled, communications between your two Macs is done in "code," such that data can't be intercepted by another wireless computer.) Finally, choose an encryption level from the WEP Key menu—128-bit is stronger, but 40-bit works best with a variety of computer types—and click OK. Encryption and password protection are described in more detail in Chapter 14, "Securing Your Mac."

Now, on the other Macs you want to connect together, open the AirPort menu and choose your newly named network from the Computer to Computer section. Now you're connected and ready to configure services, share files, and play networked games.

Configuring the Protocols

Getting your computers connected to one another—wired or wireless—is a third of the battle. The next step is to configure the protocol(s) that will be used to transmit data between your Mac and other computers on your network.

As was mentioned, the dominant protocol for local networking with Macs is the same protocol used for accessing the Internet—TCP/IP. The Transmission Control Protocol/Internet Protocol is a protocol suite that enables computers to find one another and then transfer packets of data from one to another. In a practical sense, it's like English or Spanish for computer networking hardware. It's how computers say "hi" to one another and discuss the weather.

To configure your network connection to use the TCP/IP protocol, you need to launch System Preferences and choose the Network pane. You should see a list of the ports that your Mac thinks are available for networking on the Network Status screen.

Set Up TCP/IP

To begin setting up TCP/IP for a particular port, you can double-click it on the Network Status screen or you can choose it from the Show menu. Options for the selected port will appear in the Network Status dialog.

Now, you will see the TCP/IP tab for that port; click it if it isn't already active. Here you can decide how you're going to configure your Mac to access the network, choosing among three basic choices:

- Manually. If you select this option, you're going to need to enter the IP address for your Mac as well as the addresses of any routers or DNS servers that your Mac needs to connect to. I'll define those in a moment.
- Using DHCP. If you want to assign your IP addresses automatically, you'll do it by choosing Using DHCP. This is the setting most often used when you have a router on your network that is capable of assigning IP addresses dynamically. (DHCP stands for Dynamic Host Configuration Protocol.)
- Using BootP. You won't often use this protocol on a small home or office network, but it is used sometimes for networks that have dedicated server computers.

How you opt to set up TCP/IP depends on your network. If you have a router that includes a DHCP server, and that server is active, then you should choose Using DHCP. If you *don't* have any sort of DHCP server or router, you can also choose DHCP, and your Macs will self-select IP addresses. You can then use File Sharing and Bonjour-enabled services—such as local-network iChat—but you probably won't be able to access the Internet via your network.

NOTE

With an Airport network, you're almost always going to use DHCP for the TCP/IP numbers, because you'll usually be using either an AirPort base station or a similar router. That said, you don't *have* to use DHCP; if you prefer to specify IP addresses manually because you want certain Macs to always have the same local IP address, you can opt to enter them manually as described in this section.

If you prefer, you can set up TCP/IP manually in one of two ways. The "semi"-manual approach is to specify Using DHCP with Manual Address; you will need to have a DHCP server on your network, but the address for your Mac will not be assigned dynamically (meaning your IP will not be different every time you connect to the network). You can enter a fixed address on your subnet so that your Mac is always available at that particular IP address. (More on subnets in the next few paragraphs.)

The other approach is the Manually option. You accomplish this by entering an IP address, a subnet mask and, if appropriate, router and DNS server addresses. The advantage in setting up manual IP addresses is that they remain fixed on your local network, which can be handy for some applications. You can use manual addresses whether or not you have a router on your network. If you do, you should enter the router address as well; if you don't, you can still use manually entered IP addresses to build a TCP/IP network.

Here's what each term means and some hints for choosing them if you go the manual route:

- IP Address. This is the series of four numbers that represent a particular computer's address on the network. On a *closed* network, like the one you're likely creating for your Macs, it's common to use a standard addressing scheme, usually in the 192.168.x.x. range, as in 192.168.0.1, 192.168.0.2, 192.168.0.3, and so on. If you have just a few Macs, you can enter their IP addresses in just that way to get them to talk to one another on an Ethernet network.

- Subnet Mask. The subnet mask is a special number that's used to tell your Mac how to interpret the size of the *subnet* that you want to create. (A subnet is, essentially, your local network, as opposed to any networks to which your local network is connected.) The typical subnet mask is 255.255.255.0, which tells the Mac that any computers found on the local network that have the same first three numbers in the series are on the same subnet; so 192.168.0.1 and 192.168.0.9 are on the same subnet, while 192.168.0.1 and 192.168.2.9 are not. If your subnet needs more than 254 different nodes for your computers, you can go with the subnet mask 255.255.0.0—which, clearly, is uncommon for small home and business networks.

- Router address. This is the IP address for the router, if your network has one. The router address is necessary for receiving Internet data (if an Internet connection is plugged into your router) or for otherwise reaching network assets that are outside of your subnet. If all you've got is an internal network with no outside connections, you don't need a router address.

- DNS Servers and Search domains. These are generally used for accessing Internet sites as discussed in Chapter 8; DNS servers turn word-based Internet addresses (such as apple.com or yahoo.com) into the IP numbers that are necessary for computers to talk to one another on the Internet. You can specify a domain name that will be automatically added when you only type one word into the address bar in a web browser. If your network has a local domain, like leoville.com, then you could enter that as your search domain. Then, if you entered text such as leo1 in a web browser's address bar, the browser would automatically search for a site at leo1.leoville.com.

When you're done configuring one of your Macs manually (see Figure 11.5), you'll need to move on to the others. As long as they're on the same subnet (both in terms of the IP addresses that you choose and the subnet mask that you specify), they should be able to connect with one another, regardless of whether or not you have a router.

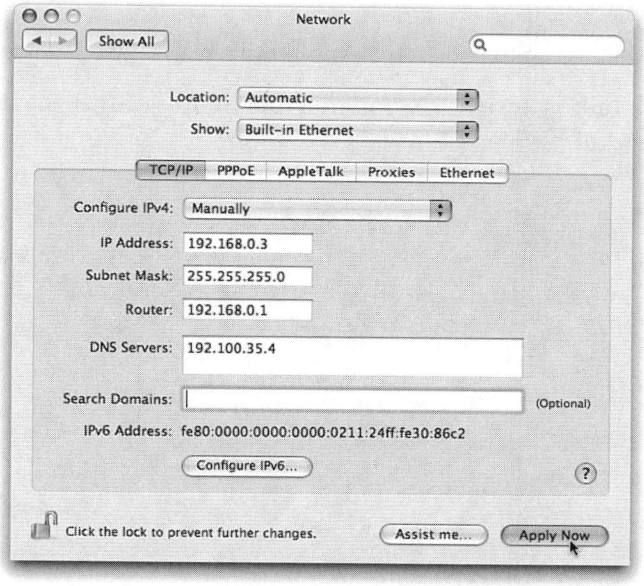

FIGURE 11.5
You can configure your Mac manually for network access.

Turn on AppleTalk

Mac OS X has another protocol built in for networking purposes, although it isn't often used for File Sharing. (In fact, as of Mac OS X 10.4, it can't be used for file sharing, although Mac OS X 10.1 through 10.3 could use AppleTalk for File Sharing.) AppleTalk is an aging proprietary Apple protocol that was very popular in earlier versions of the Mac OS. With the advent of Mac OS X, however, Apple switched wholesale to the use of TCP/IP as a protocol.

Still, you can turn on AppleTalk for one port on your Mac at a time in order to use it to send print jobs to older AppleTalk-compatible network printers. AppleTalk and TCP/IP can be active for that one port at the same time, so you'll continue to be able to access network services that require TCP/IP as their protocol.

Here's how to turn on AppleTalk:

1. Open the Network pane of System Preferences.
2. Choose the port (Ethernet or AirPort) that you want to use for the AppleTalk connection from the Show menu.
3. Click the AppleTalk tab.
4. Check the check box next to Make AppleTalk Active (see Figure 11.6).

With that, AppleTalk is turned on for that port and you can use it for AppleTalk-compatible networking services.

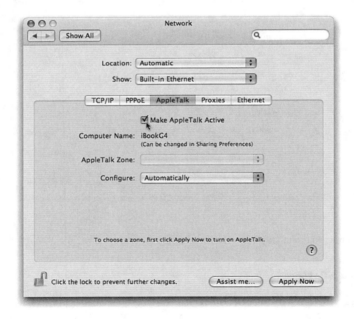

FIGURE 11.6

Turning on AppleTalk for a particular port is a simple matter.

Turn On Services and Share Files

Once you've gotten your computers connected and a networking protocol established and configured, you're ready to *use* your network. How do you do that? By turning on services on some or all of your Macs and then accessing those Macs from other Macs or PCs on your network. In this section, we'll take a look at the different services that you can activate, starting with the main one, Personal File Sharing, as well most of the others that are built into Mac OS X.

Turn On Personal File Sharing

Personal File Sharing is the service that enables others to log in to your Mac in order to work with or copy files to and from that Mac. In order to do so, that person must have access to the user account name and password of a valid account on your Mac; or, if you prefer, they can have limited guest access.

CAUTION

If your Mac has a direct connection to the Internet—meaning it is not behind a *firewall* for Internet security—then turning on Personal File Sharing will make your Mac available to anyone who finds it on the Internet. That's a vulnerability in terms of Internet security and you most likely will not want to have Personal File Sharing on under those circumstances. See Chapter 14 for more on security and firewalls.

To turn on Personal File Sharing on your Mac, open System Preferences and select the Sharing pane. On the Services tab, you'll see a list of services that you can access; one of those is Personal File Sharing. Click the check box next to Personal File Sharing to turn it on (see Figure 11.7).

To turn off Personal File Sharing, simply open the Sharing pane and click the check box again, or, with Personal File Sharing selected in the list, you can click the Stop button that's also shown in Figure 11.7.

TIP

When you're looking at the Network pane with Personal File Sharing selected, note that the bottom of the screen shows two different ways that your Mac can be accessed—either via the afp:// protocol or by browsing for the computer's name, as we'll discuss in the next section.

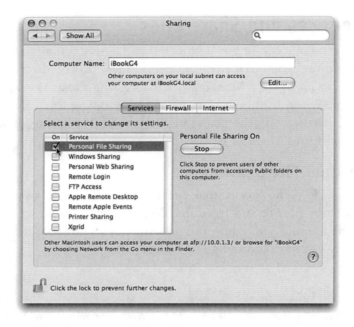

FIGURE 11.7
Turning on Personal File Sharing offers others access to your Mac via your network.

Note that if you turn off Personal File Sharing while others are connected to your Mac, you'll see a dialog sheet that warns you of that fact. In the dialog sheet, you can set the number of minutes before Personal File Sharing is disabled and you can enter a message to those users; when you click OK, that message will appear on those users' screens, warning them that they have a limited amount of time to finish up their networking tasks.

Accessing Networked Macs

Once Personal File Sharing is enabled on your Mac, you're allowing two different types of user access. First, anyone who has an account on your Mac—with a username and password—can log in to that account and access the files in it remotely; once logged in, that user can also gain access to any files that are in the Shared folder in the main Users folder on your Mac.

Second, anyone who has access to your network at all can access your Mac as a Guest. When you log in as a Guest, you have more limited access to the Mac. You can only access the Public folders of the user accounts on that Mac, you can place files in the Drop Box within that Public folder, and you can access any files that have been placed in that public folder by the user himself or herself. Figure 11.8 shows me accessing Todd's Public folder.

> **NOTE**
>
> When you're logged in to your account on your Mac and working normally, you'll find that the Public folder is one of the default folders in your home folder, right next to the Sites, Movies, Music, Documents, and other home folders.

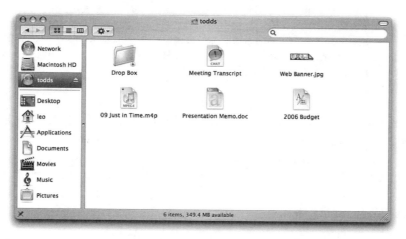

FIGURE 11.8
Here's what it looks like to access a public folder over a network connection.

So, how do you go about logging in? The easiest way is to open a Finder window and click the Network icon in the top-left corner. When you do, you should see any file-sharing Macs that are available to you over the network. Double-click the name of one of those Macs. The result should be the Connect to Server dialog box.

TIP

If you know the name of the Mac that you want to log in to, you can choose Go, Connect to Server in the Finder, and, in the Connect to Server window, enter **afp://*computername*. local** where *computername* is the name of the Mac you want to log in to. (This also works if you know the address of a Mac that's available with a public IP on the Internet.) Click Connect and you should see the Connect to Server dialog box appear.

If you have a user account on the remote Mac, you can select Registered User and enter your Name and Password on that machine. (You can also turn on the Remember Password in Keychain option if you want to store your password for accessing this server again later.) If you don't have an account on the Mac, you can click the Guest option and you won't have to enter any additional information. With those choices made, click the Connect button.

Once you've clicked Connect, you should see another window, assuming the remote Mac accepts you as a user; that window shows you the items that you can *mount* from the remote Mac. If you're logging in to an account with a username and password, you'll be able to access your own home folder, other users' public folders, and, depending on whether or not you're an administrative user on the remote Mac, you may have access to the remote Mac's main hard disk or any other mounted disks.

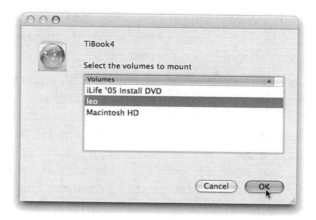

Double-click one of the volumes in that window and you'll see it appear in the Finder. Depending on the options you've set, it may appear on your desktop as a mounted volume; it will definitely appear in the Finder window's Sidebar, where you can access it as you would any mounted volume such as an external hard disk or an inserted data CD or DVD.

Once you're done moving files to and from the volume, you can eject it. If it's mounted on the desktop, select its icon and choose File, Eject, or Control+click the icon and choose Eject from the contextual menu. (You can also drag a volume from the desktop to the Trash.) Or, in the Finder window's Sidebar, you can click the small Eject icon that appears next to the volume's name.

User Accounts and File Sharing

As I mentioned, you can use a valid username and password to sign on to a remote Mac and access files. If you trust your family members or colleagues, you can always give them your username and password so that they can log in to your Mac and access files that are in your personal home folder or on your desktop; that's not totally uncommon. It isn't terribly secure, though, so if you're a little more interested in keeping everyone's files separate, you can either create accounts on your Mac that others can log in to or you can allow them to have Guest access only, which means you'll need to place any files that you want them to be able to access in your own Public folder.

Note that user accounts are also used to allow other users to log in to your Mac using either FTP or Remote Login services. In other words, if someone is supposed to have access to your Mac, they should have a user account.

Creating a user account is covered in Chapter 4, "Configuring the Mac OS X Interface." It's worth noting here, though, that when it comes to File Sharing and some other features, the difference between an administrator user account and a regular one is significant. When an admin user logs in to your Mac via File Sharing, he or she has direct access to most of the volumes on your Mac, including your internal hard disk and any mounted external disks or CDs/DVDs. The admin user won't have access to your personal files in your home folder (except those in the Public and Sites folders), but that's the only real limitation. So, when you're setting up user accounts in Chapter 4, give some consideration as to whether or not you want the users to be administrators if they'll be accessing your Mac via File Sharing. Likewise, when you have Personal File Sharing turned on, remember that any administrative users can access attached disks and CDs/DVDs as well as most anything on your Mac's hard disk.

Share Your Printer

If you have a printer connected to your Mac via USB, you can share it with others, making it automatically available in their Printer Setup Utility application. To do that, all you have to do is open the Sharing pane of System Preferences and click the check box next to Printer Sharing to turn it on.

Now, any printer to which your Mac can connect will automatically be available to other users on your network, even if the printer itself isn't designed for network access. The only caveat is that in order for others to print to your printer, your Mac is going to need to be turned on.

NOTE

If you have a printer that's specifically designed for network access, you'll configure it slightly differently, as detailed in Chapter 5, "Work Those Peripherals."

Enabling Other Sharing Services

If you've been following along in this chapter then you've seen Personal File Sharing and Printer Sharing in the Sharing pane of System Preferences. You may also have noticed a number of other services that you can turn on for use over a local network. I'd like to take a brief look at those in this section.

> ## CAUTION
>
> As I mentioned in the section "Turn On Personal File Sharing," turning on these services while your Mac is connected directly to an Internet connection—particularly if your Mac is not situated behind a firewall—can be a security hazard. See the section "Internet Access for Your Networked Macs" and Chapter 14 for more.

Windows Sharing

One great compatibility feature is Mac OS X's built-in Windows Sharing service. Windows Sharing is like Personal File Sharing except that it enables your Mac to be accessed from a computer that's running Microsoft Windows. It also enables Windows users to gain access to a printer that's connected to your Mac.

Note that in order to enable Windows Sharing, you must specifically enable one or more accounts on your Mac to be accessed from Windows; in fact, when you turn on Windows Sharing in the Sharing pane, you'll see the Enable Accounts button appear (see Figure 11.9). This is because the password for a Windows-enabled user's account has to be stored in a different format than Mac OS X generally uses.

Once you have Windows Sharing active, a user can log in to one of the Windows-enabled accounts from a Windows-compatible PC that's on your local network. To do that, you begin by opening the Start menu and choosing My Network Places. Next, click Add a Network Place. In the Network Wizard that appears, walk through the process of adding the network connection. You'll need to specify the IP address of your Mac and the user name that you want to connect to, in this way: **\\192.168.0.23\leo** as specified back in the Sharing pane on your Mac. (There's also a Browse button that you might be able to use; open it up, choose Windows Networks, and then the Workgroup option. You may see your Mac appear there.) With the connection created, you should be able to add the connection and access it from the My Network Places window in the future.

Once you're connected to your Mac from Windows, you'll have access to the entire home folder for the user account that you've signed in to.

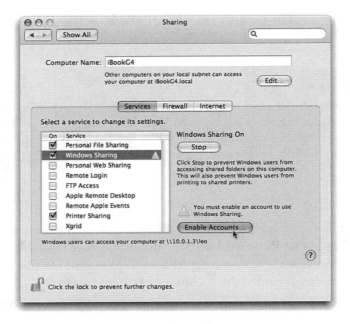

FIGURE 11.9
When you turn on Windows Sharing, you'll also need to enable one or more users for Windows access.

Personal Web Sharing

When you turn on Personal Web Sharing, you are turning on the built-in web server application that's included with Mac OS X. This means that anyone who has access to your Mac—whether over a local network or via the Internet—will be able to use a web browser to connect to your Mac and view any web pages (or other web scripts and applications) that you decide to publish.

> **NOTE**
> The web server application built into Mac OS X is Apache, which is the same industrial-grade server that's used by the majority of sites on the Internet. So, if you decide to dig deep into web server configuration, know that you can access the **apache.conf** configuration file from the Mac OS X command line (via Terminal) just as you can in most Unix installations.

Although it's called Personal Web Sharing, when you turn this option on, both the personal web pages for your account (which are stored in the Sites folder that's in your home folder) and the Mac's main web server documents, which are stored in /Library/WebServer/Documents/ on your Mac, are shared. In fact, turning on Personal Web Sharing will instantly share *everyone's* Sites folder on your Mac, so be aware of that before making the decision; you might want to confirm with any other users who have accounts on your Mac that they think turning on the web server is a good idea.

Once you turn on the web server, your Mac is accessible via the **http://** protocol, which is used mostly in web browsers. To connect to your Mac, you can use a number of addresses; on your local network, you can use the computer's name and the local domain, as in **http://iBookG4.local** in a web browser that's on any computer on your LAN. Or, you can use the specific IP address for your Mac to access its pages; note that the address is different for the Mac's main site than for your personal pages that are stored in the Sites folder—it uses the tilde character (~) and then the short name of the account to specifically access the files in that account's Sites folder.

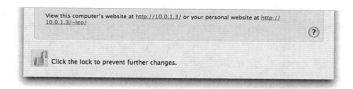

Another cool way to access other people's websites on your LAN is using Bonjour, which is built in to Safari in Tiger. On the Safari Bookmarks bar, locate the Bonjour menu; click it to see its contents, and you should see a listing of all users on your network who have Personal Web Sharing turned on. Select a user to see his or her personal web pages.

Other Services

Along with File Sharing and Web Sharing, you can initiate a number of other services on your local network that you may or may not find useful. Here's a look at the remaining services that appear in the Sharing pane of System Preferences:

- Remote Login. Turn on Remote Login and you or others with accounts on your Mac will be able to log in to the Mac using an SSH client. SSH is generally done at a Unix or Linux command line; from a Mac OS X machine, you can access SSH via the Terminal application. Once you've connected to a Mac via SSH, you can run command-line programs and scripts and perform other low-level tasks using the Darwin commands built in to Mac OS X. (For more on Terminal and the command line, see Chapter 12.) You probably won't use this service much unless you want others using Macs or other Unix-based computers to connect to your computer and run command-line applications.

> **NOTE**
> *SSH* stands for *Secure Shell*, and it's a method of remotely accessing computers that can support it. It's commonly used on Unix-based computers to connect from one to the other for file sharing and for launching programs remotely, somewhat like File Sharing except that you can run applications on the remote machine and view the results on yours.

- FTP Access. The File Transfer Protocol is a popular service on the Internet, as it's designed specifically to move files across a TCP/IP network from one computer to another. On your local network, you'll probably find that Personal File Sharing is more convenient to use than FTP, but turning on your FTP server can be handy when you're dealing with a network that has multiple PC and computing platforms, such as a mix of Windows and Unix/Linux machines along with Macs. Once FTP access is turned on, other Macs can use an FTP client application or the FTP application from the command line (via the Terminal application) to log in to your Mac (they'll need a valid account or they'll log in as Guest and only have access to Public folders) and retrieve files.

> **NOTE**
> On the Internet, you'll often find "anonymous FTP" (similar to Guest access in File Sharing) sites for public access to files for downloading; on your local network, however, FTP requires a valid user account and password on the host computer. If you want people to be able to access your personal files, have them use your own login and password; otherwise, you'll need to create accounts for them just as you would for Personal File Sharing.

- Apple Remote Desktop. If you'd like to allow others who have the Apple Remote Desktop software to access your Mac, you can turn on that service. Remote Desktop is an Apple application that enables you to observe or even control another Mac via a network connection. When you turn on the Apple Remote Desktop service, you'll need to configure the access control options that appear in the dialog sheet; consult the Apple Remote Desktop documentation for more information.

- Remote Apple Events. Turn on this service if you want to allow AppleScripts on other Macs on your network to perform automatic tasks on your Mac. This is generally considered a security risk, so it's best to do this only in a production environment or similar computer lab scenario where the Macs are overseen by a knowledgeable administrator.

- Xgrid. Xgrid is a technology that allows individual Macs to be used together under certain circumstances to run very computer-intensive applications. If you happen to have a Mac OS X Server on your network, you can configure it as an Xgrid controller. Then you can set up your Mac to work in conjunction with that controller by turning on the Xgrid service in the Sharing pane and then clicking the Configure button to configure Xgrid.

You can generally turn these services on and off at any time; note that services other than Personal File Sharing won't always warn your users that the service is going offline, so if you suspect that someone is connected to your Mac and you don't want to toss them off, you should consult with them before turning off a service (or, for that matter, before restarting, disconnecting from the network, or shutting down your Mac, if you can help it).

Internet Access for Your Network

So you've got a network of Macs (maybe a PC here and there) and you'd like them all to get Internet access. As I mentioned earlier, that's generally done with a router of some kind; for home networks and small offices, you should be able to get an inexpensive router from any office warehouse or electronics retailer that offers computer equipment. If you already have a good hub or switch, you can get a standalone router that plugs into that hub. If you're just putting together your local network, you can find some great hub/router combinations that will get your Internet connection to all your connected Macs.

TIP

In fact, you can find router/hub/wireless combos that will connect your computers via Ethernet or Wi-Fi/AirPort, offering both file sharing and Internet access to all machines.

As you may have gathered, a router is a device that knows how to connect to another network—in this case, the Internet—and then route data from the Internet to the appropriate computer on your local network. Using the capabilities of the router, a single Internet connection can be shared by multiple Macs, since the router knows how to send data from the Internet to the internal IP address of any of the computers that are on your LAN. In fact, it keeps track of the requests made by each particular computer, so that it can retrieve the correct information and send it back to that requestor. (If you don't have a server computer on your network such as one that runs Mac OS X Server, you can probably rely on your router to provide DHCP services to your Macs so they can be assigned.)

AIRPORT BASE STATIONS AS ROUTERS

It may go without saying that the easiest way to get up and running with an AirPort-based network is using Apple's own AirPort base stations. The AirPort Express is relatively inexpensive, and it's designed as both a router and a wireless hub for networks that are exclusively wireless. (It also includes a special feature that enables you to send iTunes music from your Mac across the wireless network to your home stereo or entertainment system.)

The AirPort Extreme Base Station has two Ethernet ports—one that can accept input from a broadband Ethernet connection, and one that can route that data to a wired Ethernet hub or switch. Along with that capability, the AirPort Extreme Base Station is, of course, a wireless router and hub for your AirPort-enabled Macs. So, it does double-duty as both a wired and wireless hub, redirecting Internet data to your wired switch or hub if desired.

In either case, you can use the AirPort Setup Assistant (found in the Utilities Folder inside your Mac's main Applications folder) to walk you through setting up your base station to connect to the Internet. Then, for more in-depth configuration, launch the AirPort Admin Utility in the Utilities folder; using that utility, you can configure your base station for a variety of purposes, add password protection, and customize its ability to share an Internet connection.

Set Up Router Hardware

In a practical sense, a router is a set-up-and-go proposition. You need to install it, and then access its configuration software so that you can tell it how it will connect to the Internet and how you want it to manage your local network. Once you've got it running, though, the router will generally be able to handle the interaction with your ISP and network relatively automatically.

How you set up the router depends, in part, on the type of Internet connection that you have. If you already have a DSL or cable modem then you can generally plug that modem directly into the uplink port on your router. Similarly, if you have some other type of broadband connection that comes into your home or office via Ethernet, you should be able to connect that to the broadband port of your router as well (see Figure 11.10).

TIP

Because routers vary from manufacturer to manufacturer, this is definitely a case where you should read the manual included with the router if you're unfamiliar with its configuration. You should also find instructions on how to connect to that router and configure it via a web browser in that manual. (For the simplest setup, I'd recommend an Apple-branded AirPort base station, discussed in the sidebar, since the setup software is included with Mac OS X.)

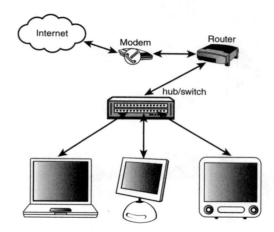

FIGURE 11.10

Here's a sample configuration; the router connects to the broadband modem and to the hub or switch.

In other cases, though, you may opt to buy a router that includes a DSL or cable modem built in to it—that can eliminate the need for an broadband modem, and you can use the router itself to connect to your Internet service, as long as it's compatible with that service.

Set Up the Software

Once you have your router situated between your Internet connection and your network, you're ready to configure it. In most cases you'll do that using a web browser to connect to a special IP address, which is the address served by the web server built in to that router. Consult your router's instruction manual to learn the specific address and any login information you need. Figure 11.11 shows the interface for one of my routers.

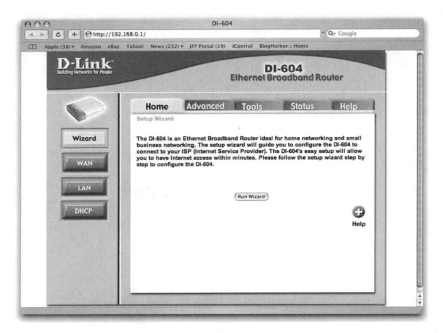

FIGURE 11.11
Here's the configuration landing page for a router on my network.

The major configuration that you need to accomplish is telling the router how it will complete its Internet connection (for the D-Link router shown in Figure 11.11, that's the WAN button), which will likely include choices such as Dynamic IP Address, Static IP Address, PPPoE, and so on. Generally, if your router needs to connect to a cable modem or DSL modem, you'll have choices that can cover that. (PPPoE is often used for DSL connections, for instance.) Make those choices and configure the router to connect to the Internet using the instructions from your ISP and the router's manual as a guide.

NOTE

In some cases you may need to use your router's configuration tools to "clone the MAC address" of the computer that was initially connected to the Internet via your broadband modem. (A MAC address is a unique address given to Ethernet or AirPort hardware—confusingly enough, it has nothing to do with your Macintosh per se, as the Ethernet card in a PC has a MAC address, too. It stands for *media access control address*.) You should also know that some ISPs don't allow you to connect a network of computers to a broadband modem without paying an additional fee.

Next, you'll configure your local network—in Figure 11.11, that's the LAN and DCHP buttons. This configuration covers things such as the IP address for the router itself and the domain name that's been assigned to your public IP address (if one has been assigned).

You can also set up your router to assign DHCP addresses if you'd like your Macs to get their addresses automatically from the router. (This is the most likely scenario.) Turn on the DHCP server and choose a range of addresses that you'd like to use for your network; for instance, if the router suggests 192.168.0.x for the addresses, you might choose a range between 192.168.0.2 and 192.168.0.10, just to limit the number of computers that can connect to this router. (The limit isn't mandatory, but it can be a useful step to make your router a little more secure.) Now, if you set your Macs to Using DHCP in their respective Network panes, as we discussed earlier in the section "Set Up TCP/IP," they'll be able to automatically retrieve an address from the router.

You may need to reset your router once all of its settings are in place. Once that's done, there may be one more step to take on the TCP/IP tab of the Network pane on all of the Macs that you have connected to your network, but only if you've opted for setting them up Manually and if your router is *not* set up as a DHCP server. In that case, you may need to enter the router's IP address in the Router entry box and then save changes. That's what makes it possible for your Mac not only to share data on the local network, but to access the router for Internet access.

What's left? Test it. Open a web browser on a connected Mac and see if you've got Internet access. If you do, then you're set—if not, check your connections and configuration again, and check with your ISP to see if you need to enter a DNS address on your Macs so that you can access web servers by name.

305

NOTE

Your router most likely has a number of other options built in to it, including a firewall and other security options. We'll touch on those in Chapter 14.

iChat AV and Bonjour

One last thing I wanted to touch on in this chapter is iChat AV, which has increasingly become a tool for local network communications and even file sharing. Coupled with Bonjour technology, iChat AV is actually an easy way for an office full of Macs to stay in touch with one another.

Using iChat AV couldn't be simpler. If you have a network configured and protocols established, simply launch iChat AV on all of the Macs that you want to be able to communicate between. If it's the first time you've launched iChat AV, you'll encounter a setup assistant. Whatever else you configure, you should make sure you turn on Bonjour networking. (If this isn't the first time iChat has been launched, you can turn on Bonjour chatting by choosing iChat, Log In to Bonjour.

When the assistant is finished, you'll end up with at least one window open in iChat AV—that should be the Bonjour window. (You may also see a Buddy List and/or a Jabber window if you're configured for Internet-based chat or chat served by a organizational server.) In the Bonjour window, you'll automatically see everyone else on your network who has a network connection, iChat AV active, and Bonjour activated within iChat AV (see Figure 11.12).

To chat with someone via text, you can simply double-click her name in the Bonjour list. When the chat window appears, type your introductory message and press Return to send the message; on the other end of the connection, she can opt to accept the incoming message and carry on the conversation. When you're done chatting, you can click the Close button to close the window.

FIGURE 11.12

iChat AV uses Bonjour technology to automatically locate everyone on your network who also has iChat AV running.

iChat AV can also be used to transfer files—or folders of files—from one person to another. This is handy when you want to send a file but don't want to have to log in to his Mac; instead, you can simply drag a file to someone's name in the Bonjour list. When you drop the file on that person's name, you'll see a dialog box asking you if you want to send the file. If you do, click Send.

If the other user accepts the file, then it will be transferred to him or her.

TIP

You can drag a file from the Finder to the text entry line in the iChat AV chat window while you're chatting with someone. When you press Return, he'll see a link to the file, which he can then click in order to download that file.

Aside from transferring files, you can also use iChat AV as an intercom system in your home or office; if you see a user who has a small telephone icon next to her name, you can click that icon to initiate an audio chat with her. If She accepts the audio chat, you can begin speaking into your Mac's microphone and you'll hear her respond through your Mac's speakers (or you can use an external mic or headset if you have one configured). Likewise, if you both have cameras connected to your Macs (such as the iSight FireWire camera that Apple makes for video conferencing), you can start a video chat by clicking the small camera icon next to one of the people in your Bonjour listing. To me, that's a cool way to use your local network!

Part IV

TROUBLESHOOT, RECOVER, AND SECURE

Chapter 12

Swiss Army Apps: Mac OS X's Utilities

Mac OS X comes complete with a number of utility applications that you can use to accomplish a variety of tasks, ranging from checking your hardware, software, and log files for problems to managing your internal disks and erasing rewritable CDs and DVDs. In this chapter, we'll be digging into the Utilities folder of Mac OS X, taking a look at some of the different applications you'll encounter for testing, maintaining, and getting the most of your Mac.

The heart of it all is the Utilities folder, found inside the main Applications folder on the root level of your Mac's internal hard disk. Open Utilities and you'll see a number of the applications that are discussed both here and in other chapters throughout the book.

Using System Profiler

The System Profiler (originally called Apple System Profiler) made its debut many years ago in the Classic Mac OS, although initially it seemed to be designed more as a tool for getting troubleshooting help over the phone from Apple's tech support than it was a utility for public consumption. Back then, if you called the help line, the person you reached could walk you through the System Profiler to generate reports that helped them troubleshoot. That's still a wonderful way to use the System Profiler, but it's now such a versatile tool that it can be used for a variety of troubleshooting tasks.

To launch the System Profiler, locate it in the Utilities folder and double-click its icon. Alternatively, you can launch System Profiler in a unique way; choose Apple, About This Mac, and in the About This Mac window, click the More Info button (see Figure 12.1). That opens System Profiler, which is designed to offer "more info" about what's inside your Mac than the About This Mac window, which just tells you the processor speed and amount of memory installed.

FIGURE 12.1
The About This Mac window gives you a little information and a button that launches System Profiler.

Once System Profiler is launched, you're ready to dig in and get a sense of what's connected to and loaded on your Mac. The System Profiler isn't totally dissimilar to many of the applications that Apple writes these days. On the left is a column called Contents, where you can make choices about the items that you'd like to explore; on the right is a "viewer" area that gives you the results that you're looking for (see Figure 12.2).

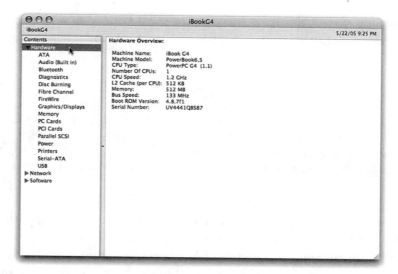

FIGURE 12.2

The System Profiler is handy for getting a sense of what's installed in—and recognized by—your Mac.

Click an item in the Contents list of the System Profiler and it offers an insight into a number of different things about your Mac, including these items under the Hardware header:

- **ATA.** In most Macs, ATA (Advanced Technology Attachment) is the data bus that's used to connect internal hard disks and removable media drives, such as optical (CD and DVD) drives. Click ATA and you should see the devices that your Mac recognizes as installed, along with a little information about them.

- **Audio.** This item refers to the audio input and output devices that are built in to and attached to your Mac; if you have external speakers or a microphone attached, you can check this tab to make sure they're recognized.

- **Bluetooth.** Check this item to see not only whether or not your Mac is enabled for Bluetooth (many modern Macs have a small optional card installed) as well as the services that are currently recognized; if you're trying to get a Bluetooth device or service to work, you can check here to see how that's going.

- **Diagnostics.** Click this item to review the power-on diagnostic test that your Mac goes through when it starts up—if your Mac is encountering any minor errors in its startup process, those will show here.

- Disc Burning. Select this item and you can see if your Mac is configured to burn optical discs, what drive is installed for that purpose, and what sort of discs it can write.

NOTE

Many Macs are compatible exclusively with the DVD-R and DVD-RW formats for burning discs—that's as opposed to the DVD+R and DVD+RW formats that are popular with the Windows-compatible PC but were originally unsupported on Macs. Some later Macs will burn to both; the Disc Burning item can let you know whether or not your Mac is one of them.

- Fibre Channel and Serial-ATA. These two items are used for Macs that offer high-end hard disk and RAID interfaces; at the time of writing, only a few Macs ship with fibre channel, although SATA is becoming more popular for mission-critical and high-end creative endeavors. These interfaces are faster and a bit more reliable for data-intensive applications than standard ATA.

- FireWire. Click this item to see the speed of your FireWire bus.

- Graphics/Displays. This one tells you what graphics card you have installed in your Mac and a little about what it's capable of, including whether Quartz Extreme technology is supported. (Macs that support Quartz Extreme have more sophisticated graphics and animation in the Finder and elsewhere.) You can also see what display(s) are connected to your Mac and their current resolution and color depth, which can be handy for troubleshooting situations where multiple displays or external displays for presentations don't seem to be working correctly.

- Memory. On this item you can see not only how much RAM is installed in your Mac, but *how* it's installed, in terms of what size memory modules have been recognized, the technology that they use, and whether your Mac has any free memory slots available. This can prove handy if you don't think your Mac is recognizing all of the RAM that you've installed.

- PC Cards and PCI Cards. If your Mac supports PC cards (PowerBooks exclusively) or PCI cards (mostly desktop Power Macs, although some iMacs and eMacs register internal devices as PCI cards) then you'll see information about them on these two tabs. That info can be particularly handy if you're attempting to install cards that aren't showing up in the Finder or that, for some reason, don't seem to be recognized by your Mac and/or the driver software you've installed. You can at least check here and see whether the card is recognized.

- Power. Particularly on a PowerBook or iBook, this entry can be handy for checking the current settings that have been stored for when the Mac is on battery power as opposed to when it's connected to an AC adapter. You can also test to see other settings that have to do with power, such as whether the Mac recognizes when an external AC adapter is plugged in (useful if you're having trouble charging your portable) and what settings you have regarding power savings and other options in the Energy Saver pane of System Preferences.

- Printers. Click this item to see the printers that have been recognized and configured for this Mac. If you have a printer connected and wonder if your Mac knows it's there, check here.

- USB. Select this item to see the various USB buses that are a part of your Mac's circuitry and to get a sense of what's connected to them. If you've connected something via USB and it doesn't seem to show up, you can check here to see if your Mac at least thinks it's been attached successfully.

More items are found under the Network header, including information specifically about your AirPort card, your built-in firewall settings, the locations that you've set up on this Mac, the modem that's installed, and any network or remote volumes that you're connected to.

Under the Software heading, you can view the applications that are installed on your Mac and the kernel extensions that are recognized by your Mac. (This is something to check if you've installed a kernel-level driver that doesn't seem to be working—usually such a driver is something installed by an Apple installer, although you'll find that some specialized utility software will add kernel extensions.)

Also under the Software heading you'll find the Fonts, Frameworks, Preference Panes, and Startup Items that are installed or specified on your Mac, all of which can be handy for troubleshooting. A really special entry, though, is the Logs entry, which can be used to access a number of the behind-the-scenes log files that your Mac keeps up with on a day-to-day basis. Click Logs and you'll see the window rearrange slightly so that you can click a specific log file at the top of the window and then see its results below (see Figure 12.3). This can be very handy for troubleshooting printer problems, user logins, problems with installations, networking, and more.

Feel like System Profiler is overwhelming you with items? You can choose View, Mini Profile or View, Basic Profile to cut down on the number of hardware, network, and software items that appear.

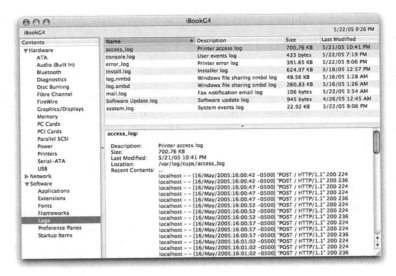

FIGURE 12.3
The Logs entry in the System Profiler can be handy for tracking down problems.

It's also worth knowing that you can choose File, Save to save a report of your Mac's current status in terms of hardware, software, and network settings. In the Save dialog box, you can choose to save the report in System Profile format (which you can then load again later using the File, Open command) or as a Rich Text or Plain Text document.

Digging into Disk Utility

If you get acquainted with only one of Mac OS X's utilities, this should be the one. Disk Utility is something you'll want to dive into every so often, as it holds some of the important diagnostic and repair tools that Mac OS X relies on. At the same time, it's useful for a variety of other reasons, not the least of which is its ability to erase optical discs, reformat hard disks, and create disk images.

Disk Utility is sort of a hodge-podge of different utility programs that Apple has offered through the years and over a span of many versions of the Macintosh operating system, from the early Drive Setup utility through Disk Tools, Disk First Aid, and many others. If you're new to the Mac game, you probably don't care. (In fact, even seasoned Mac users may not care.) What you should care about is that Disk Utility can help you do some pretty cool stuff with your Mac's internal and removable media, including some troubleshooting that may recover data when things start to go wrong.

For starters, let's look at the interface. Disk Utility is arranged so that any hard disks, external disks, or mounted optical discs will appear in the listing at the left; you'll often see a representation of both the physical disk and the mounted *volume* (or multiple volumes) that are stored on that disk. For instance, you'll probably see an icon that represents the actual, physical disk in your Mac, then you'll see a volume under it called Macintosh HD or something similar.

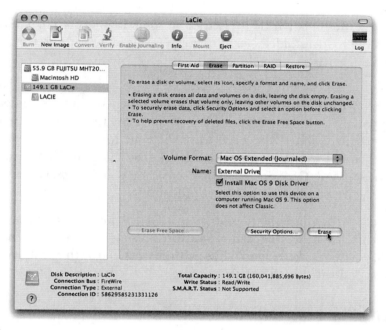

FIGURE 12.4
Select a disk on the left and you can then work with it on the right.

To begin working with Disk Utility, you'll select a volume and then click a tab on the right side to choose the toolset that you want to use.

First Aid

Disk Utility offers two tools on the First Aid tab—Permissions First Aid and Disk First Aid. You can verify and/or repair permissions on your startup disk or any others at pretty much any time; with the volume selected on the left, simply click the Verify Disk Permissions or Repair Disk Permissions button, depending on which you want to do.

(Verify is a bit quicker, but there's usually *something* to repair, so I usually just go ahead and click Repair Disk Permissions.)

When you repair disk permissions, your Mac searches the drive for any items or folders that don't have their read, write, and execute permissions set correctly given the folder that the item is stored in or, in some cases, the purpose of the file. When disk permissions are wrong, this can sometimes result in odd behavior, such as applications that won't start up or that crash when attempting to launch or access a particular file. Permissions can often get a little messed up in some low-level folders on your Mac—even some of the hidden folders—and that can result in everything from instability to serious problems getting things done.

The other option is Disk First Aid, represented by the buttons Verify Disk and Repair Disk. In order to use these commands, you need to be working with a disk other than the one that you used to start up your Mac. At most any time, you can repair an external disk, for instance, but if you need to repair your Mac's internal hard disk, you'll need to either restart from an external hard disk that has Mac OS X installed on it, or start up from your Mac OS X installation disc. When you do that, you can choose Disk Utility from the Installer menu to launch it from the disc.

Repair Disk combs through the files on your hard disk looking for those that have lost or corrupted information that can be restored using the utility. When trouble is encountered, you'll be asked if you'd like to attempt to repair the problem; click Repair and Disk First Aid will attempt to fix the file.

> **NOTE**
>
> It's worth noting that Disk First Aid can't do every repair that's possible—and when it can't, it will often tell you that. For more complex disk-fixing solutions, you'll need a third-party application such as Norton Disk Doctor or Alsoft DiskWarrior.

Erase

Select a disk or volume in Disk Utility and click the Erase tab to see your options for erasing the selected item. Obviously this isn't something you want to take lightly—you definitely want to be sure of what you're doing if you're considering erasing a hard disk. Of course, the decision to erase a rewritable CD or DVD is usually a little easier, and if your Mac has write/rewrite capabilities for discs, you may find yourself erasing those discs fairly often.

CAUTION

If possible, before you erase a disk, you should back up any important data files and make sure you're not losing anything that you want to hold on to. Depending on how you go about it, choosing the Erase command will make it difficult or impossible for you to recover the files from the volume you've erased.

Erasing is also called *reformatting* a disk, because you have the option of giving the disk a new format as part of the erasure process. With the volume selected, choose the format that you'll want the new disk to use in the Volume Format menu. Then give that volume a name.

NOTE

Generally, you'll choose Mac OS X Extended in the Format menu; that's the standard method for formatting a disk for use in Mac OS X. The Unix File System is also an option, and Mac OS X can run from it, but it's usually only a good idea if you have a good reason to do it—for instance, for compatibility with other computers that are running Unix or if you need to boot your Mac into another Unix operating system that supports UFS. Otherwise, Mac OS X Extended (Journaled) is best for the internal disk for your Mac, or you can choose Mac OS X Extended if you need this disk to be compatible with older Macs as well.

Now, you can choose the Security options (see Figure 12.5). When your Mac erases a volume, by default all it really does is tell the Mac that space that was previously reserved for files is no longer reserved, and it's free to overwrite the disk with new files; what it doesn't do is actually remove the data that's there. That makes it possible to recover the old files, at least until they're overwritten by new files. To *securely* erase the files, so that they cannot be recovered, you need to make some additional selections. Click the Security Options button. In the dialog that appears, choose the number of times to write over the current data with zeros—that makes the data that currently exists on the volume nearly impossible to recover using third-party tools.

Finally, click the Erase button. You'll be asked if you're sure that erasing the disk is what you want to do; click Erase again. Now the erasure process takes place. Depending on the security options you've chosen, it may be over in less than a minute or it may take a while. When you're done, you should have a blank volume, ready for you to copy new data to it.

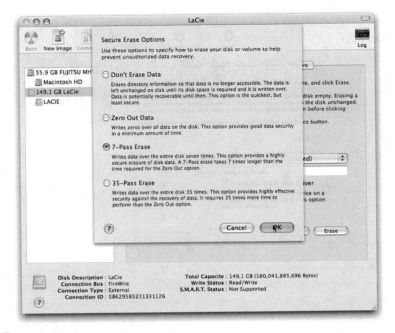

FIGURE 12.5
The Security options enable you to erase the data on the volume securely so that it cannot be recovered using third-party tools.

On the Erase tab, you may notice another option, the Erase Free Space button. This securely erases the space on your disk that isn't currently being used by files, but that may still have loose data from previously erased files on the disk such that they could be recovered using a disk-recovery tool. When you click the Erase Free Space button, you'll see a dialog asking how many times you'd like to overwrite those old, deleted sectors of the disk (7 passes is very secure, 35 passes is extremely secure). Make your choice and click Erase Free Space. This process will take a little while, but, when you're done, your old files will be almost impossible to recover.

CAUTION

Realize that choosing 7 passes—much less 35 passes—can take an extremely long time to clear off a hard disk. That's not to say that the security might not be important to you, but you'll likely need to give the process many hours to complete.

Partition

If you choose a hard disk in the Disk Utility list (and not just a volume on that disk), you'll see another tab appear in the window, called Partition. On that tab, you can choose to create more than one volume for that disk. This can be handy for a variety of reasons—for instance, you might want to create a volume that you use exclusively for one large, ongoing project, such as a volume you share from your Mac that has your desktop layout files or your stored digital images.

Another common reason to partition is to use part of a large disk as a "scratch" area for editing video clips in an application such as Final Cut Pro. This can be handy because when you're done with a project and have exported or backed up the final project, you can erase that partition completely and start over again. The erased partition will then be less *fragmented*, since it won't have files on it, and it'll be ready for your next project.

WHAT IS DISK FRAGMENTATION?

A disk becomes fragmented when many files have been written and deleted and written again to it. After this has taken place over time, there's less *contiguous* space for larger files, because the disk becomes a little like a library shelf that was once filled with books, but now has some of those books removed. You could fill in those gaps, but if you planned to add, say, an entire collection of encyclopedia volumes, you'd have to break up (fragment) the set and fit it into available spots.

The Mac OS has the ability to break up large files into fragments and write them to any available sectors on a disk, including sectors from which files have previously been deleted, and it usually keeps track of the different fragments rather easily.

However, that fragmentation can slow down the retrieval of files. That's why it's handy to have "scratch" partitions for operations such as image manipulation or video editing, because those operations involve creating and deleting files continuously and rapidly, causing fragmentation fairly quickly. And slower file retrieval in something like video editing can lead to problems with quality.

That's also why some companies offer third-party defragmentation (or "speed disk") tools, which work by reordering the files that are on your disk so that they're once again written contiguously. The easiest way to keep your files contiguous, however, is to erase the volume occasionally and start over; this isn't always practical for the volumes that hold the Mac OS and your regular documents, but it can work great when you have multiple volumes.

The catch when it comes to partitioning a disk that you're already using is that the act of partitioning a disk will destroy all of the data on it. So, this is something you want to do with a new disk (such as an external hard disk) or with a disk that you're reformatting and reinstalling items to anyway.

To partition a disk, choose a physical disk in the list and click the Partition tab. Now you'll see the partition tools; in the Volume Scheme menu, choose the number of partitions that you'd like to have (see Figure 12.6).

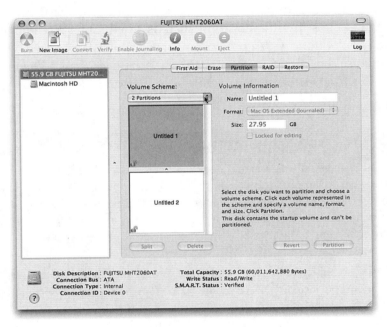

FIGURE 12.6
Here I'm partitioning a disk into two different volumes.

Now you can name each volume; select it in the graphical representation and type a name in the Name entry box. In the Size box, you can enter a size for each partition if you don't want them to be exact mirrors of one another. (You can also drag the small bar that appears between two partitions to resize them relative to one another.) In the Format menu, choose a disk format that will be used to create the volume.

When you've done the naming and sizing and made the format choice for each partition, you're ready to create those partitions. Click the Partition button. You'll see a dialog asking if you're sure of what you're doing. Click Partition again to continue with your plan. Once you do, Disk Utility will start the process of partitioning the disk into volumes and formatting those volumes according to your choices. When it's done, you'll have two (or more) new disk icons in the Finder, representing those newly formed volumes.

RAID

The RAID tab in Disk Utility is useful for special circumstances. A RAID, or Redundant Array of Independent Disks, is a way to take multiple identical hard disks (or volumes on different hard disks) and turn them into either a single, faster hard disk or a hard disk that writes the same data to two drives for the sake of redundancy. Some RAIDs are managed in hardware, but Mac OS X makes it possible to create a RAID in software, as well.

A striped RAID, which is one that uses both drives to make the read/write operation faster, is ideal for things such as video editing, where you need quick response from your drives to get the most out of them. A mirrored RAID is one that creates redundancy, which is a good idea for a server or a computer that stores mission-critical information.

A concatenated disk enables you to use multiple disks as one volume, giving you access to what appears to be a very large drive. This isn't really a RAID, as such, but Apple places the tools here in the same place.

To create a RAID, you'll first need to install two or more drives that have the same or similar capacities. You should see them in the listing in the Disk Utility window. Now, on the RAID tab, enter a name in the RAID Set Name entry box and then choose a Volume Format. Next, you need to choose a RAID type from among striped, mirrored, or concatenated disk.

Now, drag the disks or volumes that you want to use for the RAID into the window area. Note that you can't do this with your startup disk—you'll need to drag in two additional volumes, and you're going to be formatting them, so you want them to be clean of any important data (or that data should be backed up).

With the volumes set, you can click the Options button to make some additional choices. The RAID block size is used to set the size of the file blocks that will be created on the drives. Smaller blocks are important if you'll be storing a lot of files on the drives, particularly smaller files. Larger blocks can make the drives a little faster when you're dealing with large files such as multimedia, photos, and so on. If you're setting up a mirrored RAID, you can use the Raid Mirror AutoRebuild option to automatically rebuild the RAID in case of a failure of some kind; the practical upshot is that you can replace one of the drives in your RAID setup and the data will be mirrored to it automatically.

With the options chosen, click OK. Next, click Create. You'll see a dialog asking if you're sure this is what you want to do, and then you're off to the races. When you're done, your two drives or volumes will appear as one in the Finder, and you should experience the benefit of faster or redundant operation if you've chosen a RAID setup or a larger disk if you've selected concatenated disk.

Restore

The final option in Disk Utility is an interesting one—the Restore tab. On the Restore tab, you can use a backup disk or disk image to mirror its contents onto your Mac's main hard disk in order to restore your Mac to good condition if and when something bad happens. This is handy for situations where, for instance, you want to move from one Mac to another with an exact copy of your files and you have access to an external hard disk with enough capacity. This is also a potentially interesting method for creating complete archives of your Mac's hard drive so that you could recover files that you accidentally delete, overwrite, or whatnot.

> **NOTE**
>
> Note that a disk image should be scanned before it's used to restore for best results; we'll discuss that in the upcoming section of creating disk images.

To restore from a disk or disk image, first realize that you'll need to boot from a volume other than your Mac's hard disk if that's the one you're going to restore. (You can boot from your Mac OS X installation CD or DVD, for instance, and then run Disk Utility to restore your internal hard disk from an external disk.)

Then, open Disk Utility and select the volume on the left side of the Disk Utility window, or, if it's an image that isn't mounted, click the Image button. Now, drag a volume to the Destination box—this is the volume that you're going to restore. Finally, you have a *very* important decision to make: You can choose to turn on Erase Destination if you'd like to have your destination drive fully restored to the image or volume that you're using as a source. If, however, you'd prefer simply to have the source replace missing files on the destination volume, you can leave the Erase Destination option off (see Figure 12.7).

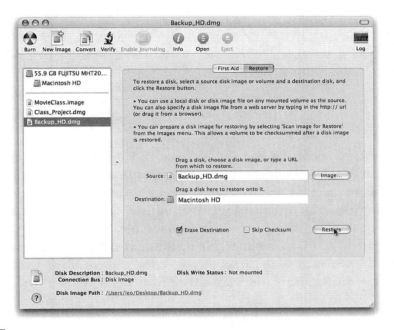

FIGURE 12.7
I'm set up to restore the destination drive from the backup disk image I've created previously.

CAUTION

You don't want to confuse these two options. Leave Erase Destination turned off if you don't want to delete all the files on your destination volume and replace them with the files on the source disk or volume.

The Skip Checksum option can be turned on if you don't want your Mac to double-check things once the restore process is finished; you may have to leave this checked if your backup disk image hasn't been scanned by Disk Utility.

With your decisions made, click Restore. You'll be nagged by the Mac OS to make sure this is the right decision; click Restore again if it's something you really want to do. When it's done, you should find yourself with a newly restored volume, ready, once again, to compute.

TIP

Disk Utility's restore function is interesting, in that you can *almost* create a "clone" of your Mac's hard drive to an external drive. The only issue is that the external drive will likely not be bootable, at least not without some tweaking. I suggest if you're trying to create a bootable drive that you use a utility such as Carbon Copy Cloner (http://www.bombich.com/software/ccc.html), which is specifically designed to create bootable clones from your internal drive to an external drive.

Creating Disk Images

A disk image is a computer file that can be "mounted" in the Finder in such a way that it acts as if it were a disk. Disk images have come to be an increasingly important part of the Mac experience, if only because Apple and many application developers now make their downloadable installers available using disk images. A disk image offers some flexibility, since it can be treated like a typical file, but then opened in the Finder and worked with as if it were a removable media drive of some sort. Plus, disk images have hidden talents, such as the flexibility to grow and shrink and the capability to encrypt the disk images so that files are secure from prying eyes.

Use Disk Images

To work with a disk image that's already been created, all you have to do is double-click its file. When you do, a disk icon for that image appears on the desktop and/or in the Finder window's Sidebar (see Figure 12.8), so that you can access it as you would any connected disk. In some cases, the mounted disk image is in a read-only form, meaning you can only copy files from it, not to it. Other than that, though, the mounted disk image works very much like a removable disk that's been inserted or connected to your Mac.

Now, if the image is read-only, you can simply copy items from the disk; if it supports read-and-write then you can copy items to and from the disk, with the only limit being the upper size that was created for the disk image.

To eject the disk image, select it in the Finder and choose File, Eject or, in the Finder window's Sidebar, click the small Eject icon that appears next to the disk image's name.

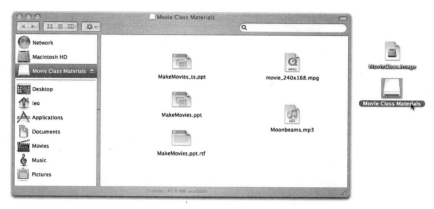

FIGURE 12.8

A mounted disk image appears in the Finder just like a connected external disk.

Create Disk Images

Ready to build your own disk image? I find them handy; you can use them for project work, for instance, saving them in sizes that happen to fit on a recordable CD. Then you can burn that image to CD when it's filled and you know the data will fit. Also, disk images are *great* for storing all the files from a given project and sending them to another Mac user, who can then mount the disk image and access the files. You may even find it handy to clone data CDs to disk images, so that you can store them on your Mac for easy access when you need to reinstall something or play a game. And you can use a disk image to back up a disk so that you can use the Restore feature in Disk Utility.

You can create disk images in a few different ways. The first method is to simply create a blank image to which you can then copy items. To do, that, launch Disk Utility and, without selecting anything in the list of volumes, click the New Image button in the toolbar or choose File, New, Blank Disk Image. That brings up a dialog box, shown in Figure 12.9, which you use to set the specifics of your disk image.

Enter a name in the Save As entry box. This will be the name of the disk once mounted; Disk Utility will give the disk image file itself a slightly different name. Then choose where on your Mac you want the disk image stored; you can click the down arrow icon to get a full Save As dialog boxes.

FIGURE 12.9
The New Blank Image dialog is used to configure a disk image that you create.

The other options dictate the size and features of your disk image. Choose a size from the Size menu—you'll see some preset options, or you can choose Custom if you'd like to enter your own size. In the Encryption menu, choose a type of encryption if desired; you'll then need to set a password once you've begun creating the disk image.

On the Format menu, you'll see at least two choices: Read/Write and Sparse. Read/Write means that anyone can copy files to and from the disk image (or delete them) as desired. A sparse disk image is special; it simply means that the disk image file will only take up as much space as it has files to hold, as opposed to taking up the entire 100MB (or whatever size you specified) immediately upon being created. A sparse image can be filled up to the limit that you set in the Size menu, while a regular image is created at that size from the outset.

> **NOTE**
> You can't create a read-only blank disk image because it wouldn't make sense—you've got to be able to "write" to a blank image in order to put something on it. You can, however, convert a read/write image to read-only using the Convert command, as discussed later in this section.

With your choices made, click the Create button. If you've opted for encryption, you'll be asked to enter a password for this image; you'll need to use the password (or have it stored in your Keychain—see Chapter 14) in order to mount the disk image in the future. Now, the disk image will be created with a .dmg filename extension for a regular disk image file or a .image extension for a sparse disk image file.

The other way to create a disk image to select something first and then create the disk image from that volume or folder. There are two different approaches:

- To create a disk image from a volume in Disk Utility, simply select that volume in the listing and click the New Image button in the toolbar. You'll see a dialog sheet appear that's similar to the dialog box in Figure 12.9, the only differences being the lack of a Size option (the image will be the size of the volume you're cloning) and the addition of Read-only and Compressed options to the Image Format menu. A compressed disk image takes up less space on your hard drive when it's not mounted, which can be handy for archiving disk images and/or sending them to others.

- To create a disk image from a folder in the Finder, choose File, New, Disk Image from Folder. Choose the folder in the Open dialog box that appears and click Image. A dialog box appears that's identical to the dialog sheet used to create an image from a volume. Make your choices and click Save.

Convert Disk Images

If you have a disk image in one format that you'd like to see in another, you can use the Convert command. First, select the disk image file in the list in Disk Utility. (If you don't see it there, you can choose File, Open Disk Image and locate it using the Open dialog box.)

Next, with the disk image selected, choose Images, Convert. The Convert Image dialog box appears, giving you pretty much the same options as you've seen for creating disk images elsewhere; of course, these choices, particularly Compressed and Read-Only, may not have been available to you the first time around. Make your choices and click Save. That creates the new, converted image.

TIP

You might also have noticed the Burn command in Disk Utility, which can be used to quickly burn a disk image to an optical disc such as a CD-R or DVD-R. Just select the image in the Disk Utility window and click Burn or choose Images, Burn. You'll be prompted to insert a blank disc; once it's recognized, you can begin the burn process.

Scan Image for Restore

If you have an image that you've used to create a backup or "clone" of another volume on your Mac, you should use the Scan Image for Restore command so that Disk Utility can scan the disk image and make note of the files that are on the image. It then builds a *checksum*, which is a special number that's used with the Restore command to better ensure that all files that need to be copied are copied correctly during the restore process.

To scan an image, select it in the Disk Utility window and choose Images, Scan Image for Restore. Then, follow the dialog prompts until Disk Utility successfully scans the image.

Manage Performance with Activity Monitor

To me, Activity Monitor is one of the most fun of Apple's utilities, because, while it's a great troubleshooting tool, it also has colorful graphs and fun little charts. The idea is twofold—Activity Monitor shows you all of the currently running "processes" on your Mac, including open applications, background services, system processes, and so on. Using Activity Manager, then, you can find and kill errant processes, which at least sounds adventurous.

The other thing you can do with Activity Monitor is check in on the efficiency of your system in terms of how the processor, RAM, disks, and network are being used. This will often give a clue to any performances issues you're having with your Mac, if you're having them, and is certainly interesting if you'd care to know a little more about what's going on under the hood with your Mac.

Managing Processes

Before there was Activity Monitor, which was new in Mac OS X 10.3, there was a separate application called Process Manager, which is about half of what Activity Monitor does these days. When you first launch Activity Monitor (double-click its icon in the Utilities folder), you'll see a listing of active processes at the top of the application's window (see Figure 12.10).

The way the process window works is straightforward—by default, the processes that you're viewing are arranged by Process ID number, although you can change that by clicking a column heading, much as you might in the Finder. (You could click the % CPU heading, for instance, to see which applications are taking up the most of the processor's attention.)

FIGURE 12.10
The Activity Monitor shows active processes at the top of its window.

To learn more about a particular process, highlight it in the list and click the Inspect button. There you'll see a dialog box that's a touch complex, but can give you a little insight into the RAM that the application is using and various statistics that may (and, then again, may not) be of interest. Click the window's Close button to dismiss it.

TIP

You can choose View, Columns to change the columns that you're viewing in the process window. Note also that you can choose View, Update Frequency to change how often Activity Viewer checks for new activity. Be aware, though, that the more frequent the checks, the more processor time Activity Viewer will take up itself.

At the top of the window is a menu where you can choose the processes that you want to view; by default, you'll see My Processes, and you'll be viewing items that have been started by your user account on the Mac. You can also choose to view All Processes, Administrator Processes, and so on. Most of the time when you're troubleshooting, you can stick to My Processes, but you may occasionally find reason to delve into the others.

The other thing you can do in this window is quit (or *kill*) a process. Generally, you only need to do this when a Force Quit operation has already failed to work or when you need to force something to quit that doesn't show up in the Force Quit window. (Force Quit is discussed in more depth in Chapter 13.) For now, know that you can highlight a process and click Quit Process to shut it down. In the dialog sheet that appears, first try the Quit command, which is a bit gentler; if that doesn't work, invoke the command again and choose Force Quit in the dialog.

TIP

Want a list of your active processes (you know, to pass around at parties)? Choose File, Save and, in the Save dialog box, choose whether you want to save the list as a Process List, which can be opened in an application such as TextEdit, or as an XML property list, which can be read by a number of XML editors.

Checking Activity

At the bottom of the Activity Monitor is a series of tabs that give you a more aggregated view of what's going on with all of the processes, as well as to give you some clues about performance issues if you feel you're experiencing slow-downs or other problems. Here's a look at those tabs:

CPU

On the CPU tab you're shown the percentage of CPU time that's being used by user processes, system processes, nice processes (certain server processes that have scheduling priority), and the percentage that's idle. You can also see the number of open processes and threads.

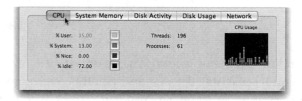

This screen can tell you when certain types of processes seem to be monopolizing activity. For instance, if you aren't running any background applications that are doing hard math such as rendering video or adding filters to photos, it would be a little odd if the CPU showed no idle time at all. That might suggest that some process is creating problems, using all of the available CPU time because it's caught in a loop or somehow has stopped responding. If that's the case, you can comb back through the process list and see if there's a process that's either using an inordinate amount of processor time or that is red in the display, which suggests it may be crashed or non-responsive.

TIP

Activity Monitor has a standalone CPU monitor that you can put on the screen even when the Activity Monitor application isn't open. Choose Window, Show Floating CPU Window and either Horizontally or Vertically to see the window onscreen. A small color-bar indicator will appear on the screen showing your CPU activity.

System Memory

Click the System Memory tab and you can quickly get a sense of whether or not you have enough RAM installed in your Mac. If you see some inactive memory and some free memory, you may be in good shape; if all your memory is used, you may find that closing a few applications will help.

Virtual memory is simply a portion of your hard disk that is reserved by the Mac OS so that it can "swap" data from system memory to the hard disk when it's not in use. (For instance, if you switch away from Mail, the data that was active in system memory when you were working in Mail might be quickly written to the swap disk area, so that other applications can have access to system memory.)

A large number of Page in/Page Out requests—in the hundreds of thousands—can sometimes suggest that your Mac is experiencing memory fragmentation, and that too much is being swapped to disk. The more swapping, the slower your Mac is, because it's slower to retrieve something from your hard disk than it is to retrieve it from system memory. So, if it's taking a little while for your Mac to switch between applications or if you're experiencing other slow-downs, you might be experiencing memory

333

fragmentation. Fortunately, memory fragmentation is easy to fix; you just restart your Mac. System memory is wiped clean and you can start over.

Disk Activity and Disk Usage

On these two tabs, you can dig a little further into how much data is being written and read from the disks that are mounted on your Mac. On the Disk Activity tab, you can see the total amounts that have been moved this session (since you restarted your Mac), how many reads and writes have taken place, and how quickly that data is moving. On the Disk Usage tab, you can see how much space is in use on your Mac's attached drives and how much space is free.

Network

Lastly, on the Network tab, you can once again see how much data is being moved over your network and how quickly it seems to move.

It's Terminal, But It Won't Kill You

As you probably well know by now, Mac OS X is built on top of a Unix-style platform (FreeBSD, to be exact), which is part of how it gets its sophisticated technological underpinnings—at least, some of them. But what that also means is that for pretty much the entire twenty-first century so far, the Macintosh operating system has had a *command line*, something for which snooty Mac experts used to have nothing but contempt. Joke's on them.

Actually, the best part for many Mac users is that you can completely ignore the fact that the command line is there at all. It doesn't really have to play into your daily life of clicking and switching and working in your applications. But, it's there if you need it, which is rare, although it may come up in Chapter 13 once or twice.

> **NOTE**
>
> Apple calls its particular hybrid of the open-source FreeBSD and a number of other technologies *Darwin*, so, when you launch the command line you'll see the somewhat cryptic phrase "Welcome to Darwin." Darwin is actually a complete operating system that can run on Macintosh or Intel-based PC hardware. In fact, because Apple is using open source software as part of Mac OS X, it makes the source code and an installer for the Darwin portions of the operating available for free at http://developer.apple.com/darwin/. So if you've ever had a strong desire to experiment with a command line Unix-style operating system on your Mac (without the Mac's signature interface, that is), then downloading and installing Darwin is one option.

For now, I'm not going to talk much about the command line interface itself. (If you know anything about Unix or Linux, you might be interested to know that Mac OS X offers the bash shell at the command line and can handle typical scripting and so on.) Instead, let's focus on getting you *to* the command line using Terminal. It's actually pretty simple.

Terminal is found in the Utilities folder along with the other programs I've discussed in this chapter; double-click its icon to launch it. When you do, you'll see the Terminal window and the command line, shown in Figure 12.11.

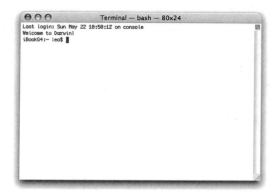

FIGURE 12.11
The Terminal window is how you can access the Darwin command line.

As you can see, getting to the command line is simple; once the Terminal window is open, you can start typing. If you don't know what to type, start with these commands:

- **ls**, which means to list a directory's contents.
- **pwd**, which shows the path to the current directory.
- **cd** */path/*, which means to change directories, as in **cd /Applications/Utilities** or **cd /users/leo/documents**. Feel free to experiment.
- The **help** command, which shows you some commands, and the **man** command, which can be used to explain commands, as in **man ls** or **man pwd**.

The Terminal window itself offers some interesting commands, such as the Font menu, which you can use to change the font face and size in the window. The Scrollback menu gives you options such as Scroll to Top and Page Down to play with different quick moves within your Terminal session. And File, Save Text As (or File, Save

Selected Text As) can be used to save a text record of this Terminal session on your Mac.

When you're done working within a Terminal session, it's best to type **logout** at the command line before closing the window. You can then choose File, Close Window or click the Close button on that Terminal window to end that session. (If you close the window without typing logout, you'll see a dialog sheet asking if you want to terminate the session; click Terminate to do so.)

TIP

One little trick is worth telling you about if you're going to experiment at the command line. In the Mac OS, you'll encounter many folders that have spaces in their names—you've probably created a few of them yourself within the hierarchy of your home folder. At the command line, you can access a folder with a space in its name using single quotes, by typing something like **cd /users/leo/documents/'my movie'** and then pressing Return. And while I'm on the subject, it's also cool to know that your home folder has a special symbol, ~, such that the command **cd ~/ documents/'my movie'** would accomplish the same thing.

Chapter 13

Common Problems and Solutions

Chapter 12, "Swiss Army Apps: MacOS X's Utilities," covered some of the key utility applications that are included with your Mac which can be used for some basic troubleshooting. The System Profiler can help you determine whether peripherals and installed upgrades are recognized. Disk Utility enables you to fix permissions and some corruption problems on your disks, and the Activity Monitor is handy for detecting some of the performance issues that may occasionally cause your Mac to feel like it's crawling.

In this chapter, I'd like to build upon that introduction to these tools by looking at some more specific problems and how we can use those tools—and others—to troubleshoot and solve some of the major causes of consternation when it comes to working with your computer.

Application Crashing and Freezes

Mac OS X is designed from the ground up to be a very robust, modern operating system. Unlike the "Classic" Mac OS, Mac

OS X is extremely difficult to crash on an operating-system level—there are a number of redundancies and protections designed to keep that from happening.

That said, that doesn't mean your Mac won't ever experience "crashes"—errors, unexpected quitting, or even *hangs*—but rather that most of the time those problems occur within the *applications* that run on top of the Mac OS, not the Mac OS itself. In fact, the Mac OS might even contribute to an application's problems if the application tries to do something unauthorized, since the operating system's primary responsibility is to keep the Mac OS itself running and prevent applications from interfering with one another.

Applications can encounter a number of different types of problems that cause them either to behave erratically or to quit functioning. Those include

- Bugs. A bug is a problem or mistake in the way the program was coded by its programmer. When the bug is encountered, the application crashes or otherwise fails to do what's expected of it.

- Corruption. Applications generally work from the assumption that the files they open to work with—documents, fonts, preference files, application support files—will be formatted in certain uniform ways and have the particular set of data needed to function. When a file is saved wrong, encounters garbage data, or otherwise becomes *corrupt*, the application may choke on that input, resulting in an error or crash.

- Compatibility or conflicts. Sometimes when an application attempts to connect to a printer that has a problematic driver, or the Mac itself begins to run out of hard disk space or available system memory, an application may fail simply because it doesn't get the right feedback or it has a conflict with driver software that's either a part of the Mac OS or a third-party add-on. Conflicts tend to arise with software written as low-level utilities (a virus protection application, a firewall, or a peripheral driver, for instance), which sometimes have problems with subsequent Mac OS X versions beyond the one that they're tested for.

So those are the basic reasons why applications crash. Now, knowing that, it's also interesting to know that applications can crash in a variety of *ways*, and which way an application crashes can sometimes give you a sense of the problem it's encountering:

- Error message. An application that fails to complete a command and offers you an error message is one that hasn't crashed, but, instead has recovered nicely from a problem. That doesn't mean the problem isn't something to troubleshoot. If the problem is loading or printing or saving a document, that might suggest corruption; if it's a problem with an external device then you may need to troubleshoot for a conflict or compatibility issue. If the error message happens when you've given the application good data and invoked a command that you expect should work, that might suggest a bug.

- Unexpected quit. What's commonly referred to as a "crash" is an unexpected quit, where your application simply gives up and quits running, perhaps with a dialog box from the Mac OS telling you that the application has unexpectedly quit. Again, this can be for any of the variety of reasons, but what you were doing prior can provide clues. Were you opening or printing a document? Then that document might be corrupt. Did you access a particular command? That might be a bug in the program. Did the application crash while you were working with a different application or accessing a item in the Finder? That might point to conflict or resource issues.

- Hang. A hang is an error that causes the application to become unresponsive. This is usually due to some sort of endless loop that the application falls into—it's attempting to modify a file or open a resource and can't, so it sits and waits until it can. But, perhaps it never will be able to. When this happens, you generally have to force the application to quit so that you can restart it or otherwise get on with your computing. Hangs can happen as the result of corruption or a bug, but they'll often happen because a resource is unavailable or the application conflicts somehow with a system-level component.

A hang is different from a *freeze* in that the hang is generally something that happens within an application, while a freeze is something that happens either to the Mac OS or to the user interface. With a hang, you can probably move the mouse and access the Dock; if not, you may be able to press ⌘+Tab and move from application to application. In a freeze—which should be considerably more rare—you may have to restart the Mac with a hardware reset in order to get some response from it.

Of course, the most immediate need you may have when dealing with an application that has hung is getting back to work. But, at the same time, you don't want to do anything hasty—every time you experience a "violent" quit or reset an application or your Mac, you're introducing the possibility of increased corruption among your Mac's open files. The Mac OS and its applications can have tens or hundreds of files open at once for writing data, logs, and preferences, as well as for application support. When you reset, restart, or force quit any of your applications, those files are more likely to be left open with garbage input or closed improperly, which can lead to corruption down the road. We'll look at some approaches to getting past problems—as gracefully as possible—in these next sections.

Hangs, Freezes, and Force Quit

When an application stops responding to input, you can take some steps to try to get a response back from the application and, if that doesn't work, to quit the application and move on to other computing tasks (or relaunch it and try again). Here are a few steps you should take, in order, when you're dealing with an application—or Mac—that won't seem to respond:

1. The first thing you should do is wait, if only for a little while. On older Macs, those with a lot of applications open and running, or Macs with a less than ideal amount of RAM and/or free hard disk space, it can take a while for some tasks to be accomplished. If you can get up and walk around or get a cup of coffee while your Mac is spinning its beachball cursor or otherwise waiting for something to happen, try that first. You should definitely avoid tapping the mouse or pressing keys repeatedly, as that can fill the Mac's input buffer and add to the amount of time it takes for an application to recover.

2. See if you can switch to another application. You can either move the mouse down to the Dock and see if you can change applications there or press ⌘+Tab to move to the next application. If you can, then you know you aren't having trouble with the Mac interface itself. You might even work in one of those other applications for a little while and then switch back to the problem application to see if it frees itself up.

3. If you can't seem to switch to other applications, check your input devices to make sure they haven't become unplugged. A keyboard or mouse that's been kicked or yanked out of its connector port can feel a whole lot like your Mac is frozen, because you're used to getting a response from those devices.

4. Launch Activity Monitor (discussed in Chapter 12) and make a note as to whether the processes for the application in question seem to be taking up a lot of processor time or memory. That can be a sign that the application is hung or having trouble; changes in the amount of process time it uses might suggest it's working through an issue and could pop free with a little extra patience.

5. With the application frontmost, attempt to save any changes in the current document by pressing ⌘+S once. Then, attempt to close any open documents (press ⌘+W once) or attempt to quit the application by pressing ⌘+Q. Again, wait a few moments.

If you still don't get a response from the application after waiting a decent interval, there's a good chance it's frozen. You can proceed to force quit the application. You can open the Force Quit window one of two ways, either by pressing ⌘+Option+Esc or by choosing Force Quit from the Apple menu. (You may have to switch to a different application before you can access the Apple menu.) That brings up the Force Quit window shown in Figure 13.1.

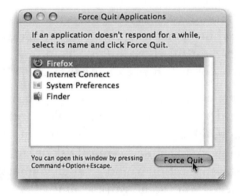

FIGURE 13.1

The Force Quit window is used to quit applications that don't respond to input.

In the Force Quit window, applications that the Mac OS recognizes as hung will appear in red with the message Application Not Responding in the window. This is a good indication that your hunch is right and the application is hung. To force it to quit, select it in the window and click the Force Quit button. That brings up a dialog sheet to verify that it's really a step you want to take. (Remember that any unsaved changes you made in open documents may be lost.) Click Force Quit again and the Mac OS will attempt to force the application to quit.

> **NOTE**
>
> If the Finder ever crashes or hangs, you can use the Force Quit window to Relaunch the Finder, which should force it to quit and then allow it to restart again. Also, note that you will occasionally have to attempt to force quit an application multiple times. If that doesn't work, you can use the Activity Monitor to attempt to stop that application's processes, as discussed in Chapter 12.

Dealing with Errors and Corruption

If a Mac OS X application crashes without a terribly good reason (in your mind), it's always possible to simply start it back up and compute again. Unlike older versions of the Mac OS and many other operating systems, a crashed application doesn't add to the instability of the Mac itself; because each application works in a protected space, the crashing of one should have no affect on the others. So, you can switch to other applications or launch the offending application again and see if you get different results.

If you do then there's little to worry about—perhaps it was a momentary conflict or passing glitch. If you do reproduce the error, however, then you've stumbled upon the key to troubleshooting problems in your computer applications—figuring out when they happen and why. An error that is reproducible, in that it happens every time you do x, is one that you have a better chance of either tracking down or avoiding.

With error messages, the message itself will often give you an indication of what's gone wrong. If the issue is a bad file, a document that can't be read, or a resource that isn't available to the application, the error message may say that. If you can then reproduce the error—you have trouble saving a file to your iDisk or launching a certain command when text is selected in the application window—then you may have stumbled on a bug in the application that means you should work around it by trying something different or contact the application's developer and see if they can fix it for you (or if they plan a future release that fixes the bug).

Applications that crash when certain files are opened—or when the Fonts menu, the Preferences menu, or the Print menu (in many cases) is accessed—may be experiencing corruption. A corrupt document file can crash an application as the document opens; a corrupt font file can crash an application as the application is opening, as a document is opening, or when you attempt to print. A corrupt preferences file can crash the application when it's opening, when you access the Preferences command, or any time you change something that might write to that preferences file.

The closer you get to reproducing when your application crashes, the more targeted your troubleshooting can be. Here are some different approaches for troubleshooting corruption.

Document Corruption

If you encounter a crash every time you open a document, scroll to a certain point, or attempt to save that document, then you may be dealing with a file that's corrupt. Unfortunately, that may make it difficult to deal with in the application that's crashing as a result of it. So, you may want to avoid using the document in that application.

Instead, you should see if another application can open it—preferably one that is less likely to be affected by corruption in the file. For instance, a Microsoft Word document with corruption in its commands might crash Word, but that same file might open in TextEdit (which can read the rudimentary formatting of Word files) and allow you to save the file and at least retrieve the text from it. If you're having trouble getting TextEdit to open the file, a pure text editor such as TextWrangler (www.barebones.com) might be able to extract the content from the file and give you access to it, sans formatting.

If you're dealing with a database or similar sort of document (such as an email inbox) that seems to be corrupt, then you may need to dig into that application's documentation or support website to get tips on how to deal with corruption. In Mail, for instance, you can rebuild a particular mailbox by selecting it in the program and choosing Mailbox, Rebuild. Other applications have the ability to rebuild their databases or indexes as needed—check the documentation of an application that's giving you trouble.

If you don't have that luxury with a particular application or document type, you may simply have to stop using the document in question. If you have a backup of the file, you can restore it and attempt to work with it; otherwise, you may simply need to delete it and start over.

Preference File Corruption

The preference files for applications are relatively prone to corruption because they tend to be written to often. Since they spend a lot of time "open," there's a chance they will be corrupted if their application crashes, unexpectedly quits, or if the Mac itself is powered down improperly. Removing a corrupt preference file is a common step in troubleshooting a crashing application.

So, if your application crashes when it's starting up, you can try moving the preference file for that application out of your Preferences folder. Here's how:

1. Open the Library folder in your home folder.

2. Locate the Preferences folder and open it.

3. Locate the preferences file for the problem application and drag that file to your desktop.

Now launch the application and see if it can get through its startup process. If it does, it will create a new preference file with the same name and in the appropriate place; you can drag the old preference file to the Trash. Be warned, though, that you'll need to reset any of the application's preferences that would have been stored in that corrupt file.

> **NOTE**
>
> Along with preference files, certain applications have other files that can also be the cause of problems if they become corrupt. For instance, Safari stores special cache files that might cause problems; if you experience problems in Safari, you can use the Safari, Empty Cache command to clear the cache. Or, you may have to dig into the Safari folder inside your personal Library folder to delete the files Bookmarks.plist or History.plist if it seems like you hit corruption when you attempt to access one of those.

Font Corruption

Font corruption usually manifests itself with crashes when you select a font or attempt to print a document using a particular font, although some applications will crash on startup when detecting a corrupt font. The solution is to attempt to isolate which font is causing the trouble and then remove it from the Fonts folder, found in the main Library folder on your Mac's hard disk. (Fonts can also be stored in your personal Library/Fonts folder, as well as in the Fonts subfolder inside the Classic System Folder, if you can't seem to find the font you're looking for in the main Library folder.)

One approach to working around a font corruption problem is to open the document in question, quickly choose the Select All command (Edit, Select All or ⌘+A), and then change the entire document to an extremely standard font such as Times New Roman or Arial. That may wipe out references to the corrupt font so that you can keep working with the document in the short run.

If you suspect font corruption but can't isolate the font, you might try a utility application that's designed to fix fonts, such as Font Doctor from Extensis (www.extensis.com). Such utilities will comb your font folders and check for corruption and other issues that can cause problems in applications that use fonts intensively.

Fixing Permissions

Somewhat unique to Mac OS X is the problem of permissions issues, which can be messed up by applications, installers, and utility programs over time. Permissions issues often cause unexplained slow-downs and the occasional hang in an application that can't gain access to a file it thinks it should be able to open, read from, and/or write to.

To fix permissions you'll use Disk Utility. Consult Chapter 12 for specifics.

Kernel Panics

If you ever experience a kernel panic, you'll know it almost immediately—your Mac will freeze up and crash, with your graphical Mac OS display overwritten by plain-text words and command-line text, almost as if the underlying Unix code had seeped out onto the screen. That's a kernel panic—at the lowest level possible, your Mac has shut down and thrown in the towel.

The kernel is the center of the operating system, where extremely basic communication happens between items such as the Mac and its connected disks, video cards, and other peripherals and bus upgrades. When you have a kernel panic, it is almost always after a driver has been altered or added—you installed a device, began to work with it, and encountered the panic. Or, you may have encountered the problem without installing a driver, but simply by connecting something to your Mac that isn't fully compatible—it used to happen to me all the time when I connected a certain external FireWire hard disk to my PowerBook.

The solution is similar to the solution offered by the doctor in that old joke—*don't do that*. (A man tells his doctor, "It hurts when I bend my arm like this," and the doctor says, "Then don't bend your arm like that.") If your Mac crashes when you connect a particular peripheral then head to the Web to find out whether the peripheral manufacturer has come up with a workaround, whether they know about the problem, or whether they're planning a new driver. If it happens after you install a new driver, check out the installer to see whether it has an uninstall option so that you can get the driver out of there. If not, take it up with the manufacturer or check their support offerings for hints and advice.

> **NOTE**
>
> The only time I've seen kernel panics not related to faulty drivers or iffy hardware has been with low-level utilities that install kernel drivers. If you have repeated trouble with kernel panics and you have a disk fixing utility or low-level recovery software running, check its support website to see if it could be causing trouble.

Resetting Passwords

Forget your password? Or did someone else on your Mac forget theirs? Well, there are two stages to this solution—you can either use an administrator's account to change the passwords for other users or you can reset your own password using the Mac OS X startup disk.

To reset other users' passwords, simply log in to your account, if you're an administrator, and open the Accounts pane of System Preferences. You can then change the passwords for anyone who has an account on your Mac and they will be able to log in using the new password.

If you don't have another administrator account that you can log in to, the backup solution is to start up your Mac from the Mac OS X installation CD or DVD. You can do that by selecting the installation disc in the Startup pane of System Preferences (see Figure 13.2).

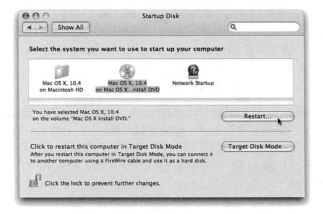

FIGURE 13.2
Start up from the Mac OS X Installation disc in order to reset your password.

Once the Installer has started, choose Reset Password from the Utilities menu. Now, you can use the Reset Password utility to reset the password for one or more of the users on this Mac. When you're done, click Save and then choose Quit Reset Password from the Reset Password menu. Now, choose Utilities, Startup Disk, and choose your Mac's internal hard disk as the startup disk. Click Restart and you should be back to your old tricks.

NOTE

When you reset a forgotten password using either of these methods, the user's Keychain password is not updated. If it's forgotten, the user will need to create a new Keychain via the Keychain Access application that's discussed in Chapter 14.

Using Software Update

Built in to Mac OS X is the capability for the operating system to head out over the Internet to server computers provided by Apple and check for updates to the Mac OS as well as to many other Apple applications and utilities. Often you'll find that this happens automatically, but you can check manually at any time by choosing Software Update from the Apple menu. When you do, you'll see the Software Update window appear; if it's able to successfully connect to the Internet, you'll see a list of the updates that your Mac is eligible to download and install to keep your Mac up to date (see Figure 13.3).

Leave the check marks next to all of the updates that you'd like to install and then click the Install button. For some of the updates, you may have to read and agree to a licensing agreement before the download will start; for others, the download and upgrade process is automatic. When Software Update is finished cycling through and installing all of the updates that you've chosen to activate, you may have to restart your Mac, depending on the items that have been installed. If not, you can quit Software Update and keep working on your newly updated Mac.

To set the automatic options for Software Update, open System Preferences and choose the Software Update pane. On the Update Software tab, you can turn on the Check for Updates option and use the menu to determine how often you want your Mac to check. The Download Important Updates in the Background option can be used if you'd like your Mac to begin downloading important upgrades without your explicit permission as soon as they are recognized as such and then let you know when the download is complete so you can immediately begin installation. The Check Now button can be used to check for updates immediately.

FIGURE 13.3
Software Update can be used to locate updates from Apple.

On the Installed Updates tab, you can see the updates that you've installed on your Mac since you first installed Mac OS X.

Viruses and Virus Protection

The Mac doesn't get many viruses, because there aren't many written for it. But that shouldn't make virus protection an afterthought—getting yourself a virus-protection application is a good idea, because it's always possible that your Mac could be hit with one of the relatively few viruses that are written for the Mac, and there are also other malicious code attacks that the Mac can be infected with—such as Word and Excel macro viruses—and still others that a Mac can be a carrier of, not getting infected itself but transmitting the code on to others. So, it's nice to knock those out when possible.

If you have a .Mac subscription, you can log in to www.mac.com and download Virex, which comes with your subscription. (At the time of writing, Virex hadn't been updated for Mac OS X 10.4, so whether it remains a free benefit of .Mac is currently in question. If you have Panther or earlier, you should be able to use Virex.)

Other options include Intego's VirusBarrier (www.intego.com/virusbarrier, see Figure 13.4) and Norton Antivirus for Mac (www.symantec.com). Both of these have been updated for Mac OS X 10.4 compatibility and sport the ability to download and maintain new virus database files, which keeps them in touch with the latest knowledge on new viruses. (Norton also includes a handy Dashboard widget for checking virus protection issues.)

With one of these applications running and checking periodically, you should be able to keep yourself out of harm's way when it comes to viruses and other malicious code.

FIGURE 13.4
Virus Barrier is a unique-looking application that scans your Mac for viruses.

Chapter 14

Securing Your Mac

The term *security* in the context of your Mac can mean a variety of things. Perhaps put most simply, it means "keeping your files from being accessed by others who are not authorized to do so." From there, we're talking about everything from passwords to encryption to Internet firewalls.

There's no question, however, that computing in general is becoming more "serious" all the time, as we're doing more and more of our personal and public business on the Internet, whether it be for banking, shopping, reading important emails, or accessing our network remotely. Fortunately, Mac OS X continues to take security pretty seriously, too, offering you the option of multiple levels of file and network security that you can take advantage of if it's important to you. And if it isn't important to you, go ahead and read on just to make *sure* that it isn't important to you.

Using Your User Passwords

You're probably not dying to add one more password to your life, let alone the multiplicity of passwords that go with our 24-hour-banking-and-buying lifestyles. But if there's one more that might help more than it hurts, it could be the password for your user account on your Mac.

When you first install Mac OS X and/or begin working with a new Mac, the Setup Assistant has you fill in the account name and password. By default, however, that account will be automatically logged in when you start or restart your Mac, meaning that anyone who gains access to your Mac will have access to your account. While that may not seem like a problem if your Mac sits in your den, spare room, or a small office to which you have the only key, there are some potentially good reasons for you to go ahead and require that password for access to your Mac—just in case it gets stolen or to keep someone from accidentally deleting or changing something personal, financial, or flammable. (Okay, so that last one isn't terribly likely.)

NOTE

If members of your family use your Mac, I recommend that you go ahead and create user accounts and have everybody log in as themselves. This gives you all the freedom to set up your Mail accounts, desktops, preferences, and everything else according to individual taste, and it keeps you from accidentally sending emails from another person's account—with the added bonus that it keeps the kids from accidentally deleting the checkbook file.

So, in terms of personal security, this is a two-part issue. First, I want you to make sure that you have a secure password. (No, your anniversary date is not a secure password, especially since I know you're also using it for your ATM code.) Second, I want you to use that password as often as possible.

Set Your Password

Your password should not be a word found in the dictionary (or on your letterhead), and should include symbols and numbers if at all possible. If it is a word, go ahead and make it two unrelated words that are sandwiched around a number and some symbols—think **bowler496#tire** or something along those lines. The password should be at least eight characters long, and more is usually better. (Mac OS X supports passwords up to 31 characters.)

To change your password, open System Preferences and click the Accounts icon. Next, you'll need to authenticate by clicking the padlock icon at the bottom of the window and then entering your username and password. (This won't work if you aren't an administrative user; if that's the case, you'll need to enter an administrative user's name and password to get past authentication.) In the Accounts pane, choose your own account, then click the Password tab if it isn't already selected. Click the Change Password button and you'll see a dialog sheet (see Figure 14.1).

TIP

If you have trouble coming up with a suitable password, Mac OS X will actually help you when you go to change the password for your account. Next to the New Password entry box is a small key icon; click that and you'll see the Password Assistant appears, which will help you create a password. (The larger the green bar, the more secure the password is that Password Assistant has come up with.)

FIGURE 14.1
Change your password in the Accounts pane if it was too simple to start with.

In the dialog sheet, enter your old password, then enter your new password in the New Password and Verify entry boxes. Then you can enter a password hint if you like; make sure it's only a reminder to yourself and not something that would tip off your password to others. With those entries made, click Change Password.

NOTE

When you change your password, you should see a dialog box telling you that your Keychain password will also be changed, so that your Keychain is opened automatically when you log in to your Mac. Note that if someone else changes your password—another administrator on your Mac—your Keychain password is not changed. (More on the Keychain later in this chapter.)

Use Your Password

Once you've got a good password, you need to start using it. To turn off automatic login, open the Security pane of System Preferences. On the Security pane, you'll see a dividing line between the top and bottom halves. On the bottom half, under For All Accounts on This Computer, click to place a check mark next to Disable Automatic Login. That will make it so that when you start up your Mac, you'll now see the login screen instead of automatically being logged in to your current user account.

While you're in the Security pane, you might want to consider some of these other settings, including the option Require Password to Wake This Computer from Sleep or Screen Saver. This is particularly important if your Mac is in a high-traffic area or if it's a portable; you don't want to go to the trouble of all this logging in and out only to find that people can get access to your Mac simply by waking it from sleep. Turn on the option and you're that much more secure.

TIP

Want to make sure the screen saver is set to turn on? Switch to the Desktop & Screen Saver pane in System Preferences and click the Screen Saver tab. Select a screen saver and choose the amount of time the Mac should wait before the screen saver kicks in.

Storing Items Securely on the Keychain

Perhaps one of Mac OS X's least-understood features is the *Keychain*, which can be interesting to get a grasp of. The Keychain is a database of passwords and secure items that are tied to your user account and protected by a single master password. Your Keychain can be accessed by applications that are aware of it and, in many cases, the Keychain can be used to automatically access a network resource, such as a mail server, secure website, or a File Sharing server.

And even if you can't automatically log in to a site—for instance, some websites don't offer access to Keychain tools—you can still securely store your username and password information in the Keychain, so that you can refer to it to jog your memory. This approach is considerably more secure than jotting down passwords on sticky notes. And once you get to know the Keychain Access utility, you may find that adding things to it becomes second nature.

By default, your Keychain's password is the same as the password for your user account on your Mac and, in fact, your Keychain is "opened" when you log in to your Mac. Otherwise, your Keychain is an encrypted database that sits on your hard drive and can't be accessed without your user password. In fact, that's another really good reason to have a secure user password, as your user password is also the gateway to your Keychain, where many of your other passwords and some personal information can be stored.

Using Keychain Access

To launch Keychain Access, open the Utilities folder inside your Applications folder and double-click the Keychain Access icon. That should open Keychain Access and display the contents of your default Keychain (you can have more than one, if desired), called *login*. Figure 14.2 shows Keychain Access.

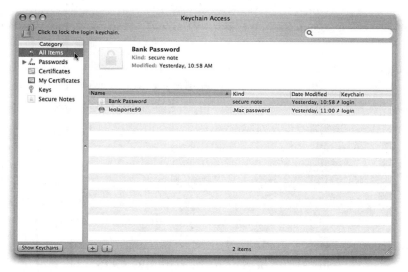

FIGURE 14.2
Keychain Access can be used to change settings for your Keychain or to add items.

Again, Keychain Access has the familiar look of many of Apple's applications, even going so far as to have adopted the iLife "brushed metal" look. On the left side of the application window is the Category list, where you can select the type of item you'd like to see. With All Items selected, you can see everything that Keychain Access is storing for you. Those items include

- Passwords. Click the disclosure triangle and you'll see that you can store AppleShare, Application, and Internet passwords in the Keychain; these are passwords that are added to your Keychain by Keychain-savvy programs such as Safari, Mail, or Disk Utility, or when you're connecting to a File Sharing server.

- Certificates. Certificates are "digital identity" documents that can be used to "sign" messages, encrypt email messages, and perform other security-related tasks in situations where it's important that others know who you are and you know who they are. They aren't used extensively throughout the Mac OS at the present time, but more and more people find them useful, particularly for online business.

- Secure Notes. These are the most fun—particularly if you consider being able to password protect little snippets of info "fun." Any information that you'd like to store on your Mac and password-protect can be saved as a secure note—that can include passwords for sites and applications that don't directly support the Keychain, or it could be credit card information or other personal stuff. You could even create personal diary entries and "lock them up" in your Keychain if desired.

To view an existing item, locate it in the Keychain window and double-click its entry. You'll see a dialog box for that item. To see the secured password, username, or similar information, click the Show Note or Show Password check box (see Figure 14.3).

You may be asked for your Keychain password; enter it and click on Allow Once or Always Allow, depending on whether or not you want your passwords revealed without requiring your Keychain password in the future. (The Always Allow option will make it so that whenever your Keychain is open, you can simply see stored passwords or secure notes without entering your Keychain password again. So think that through—entering your password repeatedly might be worth the peace of mind.)

On certain password items, such as the .Mac password item shown in Figure 14.4, you'll also see an Access Control tab in the window. Click that tab and you can set some options for how this password item gets used, including whether or not applications need to ask you for confirmation before accessing the password item and which applications are allowed to access it. This can be an interesting screen to delve into occasionally, just so that you get a sense of which applications are accessing your network passwords and assets, and how much permission they have to do so.

FIGURE 14.3
Each Keychain item has an information window that you can use to learn about it.

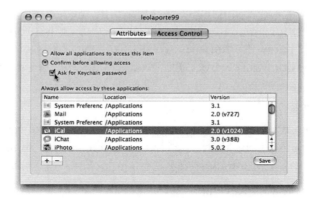

FIGURE 14.4
On the Access Control tab, you can learn which applications have access to a particular Keychain item.

Keychain Settings and Passwords

In Keychain Access, you can change the way your Keychain works as well as change the password. By default, you log in to your Keychain when you log in to your user account on your Mac. The Keychain stays open for the entire time that you're logged in, so that it can be easily accessed without getting in your way. But it doesn't have to work that way, and that probably isn't the most secure option.

To change those settings, choose Edit, Change Settings for Keychain *"KeychainName"* from the Keychain Access menu. Now, in the Change Keychain Settings dialog box, you can turn on the option Lock After ___ Minutes of Inactivity if you'd like your Keychain to automatically lock when you're not working on your Mac. The Lock When Sleeping option is handy, too, because the Keychain is locked even if someone else manages to get your Mac to wake up from sleep.

> **NOTE**
> If you have a valid .Mac account entered on the .Mac pane of System Preferences then you'll see another option available, Synchronize This Keychain Using .Mac. You actually turn this option on in the .Mac pane of System Preferences on the Sync tab. Once you have it turned on, you can synchronize this Keychain with other computers, giving you easy access to the items stored in it.

Aside from changing options, you can also change your Keychain password so that it's independent from the password used for your user account. To do that, choose Edit, Change Password for Keychain *"KeychainName."* In the Change Keychain Password dialog box, enter the original Keychain password (which is probably still your user password) and then enter the new password in the New Password and Verify entry boxes. Once you've done that, click OK. Now your Keychain and user account will have different passwords set.

In either case—whether you've changed your password or changed how often it locks—you've now introduced yourself to a whole new world of responding to queries from your applications about your Keychain. Whenever an application attempts to access a stored password and finds your Keychain locked, you'll see a dialog asking for the password.

Just enter your password and you'll be able to compute again for a while, until your password finds itself locked again.

If you'd like to manually unlock your Keychain, you can do that in Keychain Access. At the top-left corner of the window, click the padlock icon to lock and unlock your Keychain. Even easier is using a menu bar icon; choose Keychain Access, Preferences, and in the Preferences dialog box on the General tab, turn on Show Status in Menu Bar. Now, from the menu bar, you can lock and unlock your Keychain quickly.

The menu bar item also offers an additional security command, Lock Screen. That's a little like invoking the screen saver immediately; it requires that you enter a valid username and password before you're able to get back into the Mac.

Add a Password Item

There are two ways to add a password item that Keychain Access will track; you can type it into Keychain Access or you can add it to your Keychain from within the application itself. To type a password item, choose File, New Password Item from the Keychain Access menu. A dialog sheet will appear; enter a name for the Keychain item, then enter an account name and a password to associate with that account name.

Note that a password item doesn't always work automatically when you access the website or network resource. Instead, it's designed more as a reference; you can open the item back up in Keychain Access and display the password for that username to help you jog your memory. To do that, double-click the item in Keychain Access, then, in the dialog box that appears, click the check box next to Show Password. You'll be asked for your Keychain password and then you'll need to click Allow Once or Allow Always; when you return to the item's dialog, you should see the password you typed.

The other way to add a network username and password is from within an application. Often when you're logging in to websites in your browser, you'll be asked if you'd like to save the login to your Keychain; if you would, click the appropriate buttons and the next time you're at that website, the browser will access your Keychain in order to automatically retrieve the setup information.

Similarly, you can save your login information when you're accessing a File Sharing server. You do that from the Connect to Server window that appears when you're entering your username and password for a particular server. When you're logging in, simply click the Remember Password in Keychain item and, from now on, when you go to access this particular server, you'll see your username and password already filled in.

Add a Secure Note

Secure notes can be used for anything that you'd like to store in your Keychain but that doesn't fit into a Password item, so that the note can't be accessed without your password. To create one, choose File, New Secure Note Item. In the dialog sheet that appears, enter a name in the Keychain Item Name entry box, then enter the text of your note in the Note area. You can type returns, tabs, and all sorts of characters and numbers in your note, if desired; you might want to put a bunch of usernames and passwords in a single note for quick access (as long as you stay on top of your Keychain security). Or, you might just put your innermost thoughts down in pixels. In either case, when you've got something you want to save, click the Add button.

To access the note's contents, find it in the Keychain Access program and double-click it. In the dialog box that appears, click the Show Note item. Now, you'll be prompted for your Keychain password (assuming you haven't accessed this item before and selected Always Allow). Enter your Keychain password and choose whether you want the note's contents revealed just this time or any time it's requested from an open Keychain (see Figure 14.5).

FIGURE 14.5
When you attempt to access a note's contents, you'll probably have to enter your Keychain password.

Securing Your Files

Aside from keeping everything about your user account secure—by taking full advantage of the login and Keychain features of your Mac—you can also use two different tools to encrypt your files, so that if someone does gain access to your Mac, they may still have trouble getting a good look at your files. Plus, in this section, we briefly discuss the Trash's secure emptying option, which is important for making sure that people can't access the files that you throw away—particularly if you want them erased for good.

Encrypting Some of Your Files

One approach to keeping your files secure in Mac OS X is to create an encrypted disk image, which you can mount and use when you're working on your Mac, but which is left in a password-protected state when you're not working with it. This is particularly handy if you have certain files that you want to keep encrypted—such as your Quicken or accounting database or business documents—but you still want quick access to them. Plus, creating a disk image has the added advantage of creating a file that's relatively portable and easy to back up. Your encrypted disk image file can be transported to your iDisk, burned to a CD, or copied to a network drive and left in its encrypted state; when you need it again, all you have to do is enter its password.

To create the disk image, open Disk Utility (double-click its icon in the Utilities folder inside your Applications folder) and click the New Image button in the toolbar, or choose File, New, Blank Disk Image. Now, in the New Blank Image dialog box (see Figure 14.6), give the image's volume a name and choose where you'd like to create it. After choosing a size from the Size menu, choose AES-128 from the Encryption menu. Now, in the Format menu, you can decide between a read/write disk image (which is created at the full size specified in the Size menu) or a sparse image (which will only take up as much space as the files that you copy to it consume).

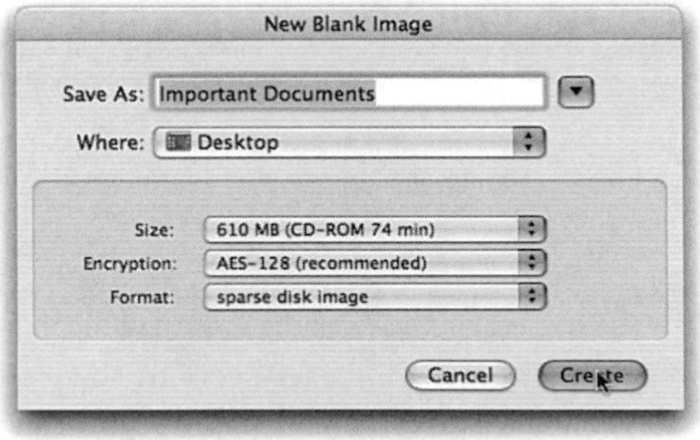

FIGURE 14.6
When creating a blank disc image, you can specify that you want encryption for the image and that it should be sparse, taking up the same amount of storage space that the files you place on it consume.

Click Create and Disk Utility will begin to create the disk image. However, the first question when you get started will be the password that you want to use to encrypt the disk image. In the Authenticate dialog box, enter a password for the disk image twice, once in the Password entry box and once in the Verify entry box. Now, decide whether you want to store this password on your Keychain. Then, click OK. Now the disk image won't decrypt its files or mount in the Finder without the password.

NOTE
So, should you put the password for your encrypted disk image in your Keychain? If you're practicing heightened security with your Keychain (locking it automatically, using a password different from your login password) then, yes, that should be enough security for your encrypted disk image, too. Note that you can always tell the Keychain to Allow Once when accessing your disk image, so that you have to enter your Keychain password every time you attempt to mount the disk image. Of course, if you do opt for a good password and leave it out of the Keychain, that's even more secure, although you risk potentially forgetting the password and losing access to your documents.

In the Finder, you can mount the disk image by double-clicking its icon. If you haven't saved its password in your Keychain, you'll be asked to enter the password for the encrypted image. Do so and click OK.

If you get the password right, you should see the disk image open up on your desktop and/or in the Finder Sidebar, ready for you to access. Eject the mounted volume and you're back to an encrypted disk image file that can't be opened without the proper password.

Encrypting All of Your Documents

The other approach to file encryption takes advantage of a feature in Mac OS X called FileVault. Using FileVault, you can essentially turn your entire home folder into an encrypted disk image, which is managed by your Mac on-the-fly. When you log in to your account, that disk image is expanded and decrypted based on your account password. You then have access to your files and so on as usual. When you log out of your account, however, your files go back into that encrypted state, making it very difficult for someone to gain access to your files if they don't know your password—even if they remove your hard disk and go at it with sophisticated tools.

To turn on FileVault, open System Preferences and click the Security icon. That launches the Security pane. At the top of the Security pane are the FileVault options (see Figure 14.7).

Before you can turn on FileVault, you must first have a master password set on your Mac. To do that, click the Set Master Password button and enter a password. Note that this password will allow you to unlock any account that has used the FileVault feature to encrypt files, so it's very important that it be as secure and private as your own user account password.

FIGURE 14.7
The Security pane offers the FileVault controls, which encrypt your entire home folder.

With a master password set, click the Turn On FileVault button to turn on the feature. You may have to jump through some hoops first—this only works if you're the only person logged in to your Mac and you have enough hard disk space to create a duplicate of your home folder in encrypted form. Once you've satisfied your Mac on those fronts, you'll see a dialog sheet asking for your account password. Enter it and click OK.

Now you'll see a big warning dialog sheet that lets you know what you're in for with FileVault, including the fact that it may take a while. Remember—FileVault is essentially creating an encrypted disk image of your home folder. If your home folder has gigabyte after gigabyte of files stored in it, that process could take a long time.

NOTE
In that warning dialog sheet, you'll see and option called Use Secure Erase, which is used to erase your original files once the disk image for FileVault is created. If you want those files to be relatively difficult to recover then you should turn on the option.

buddy

When FileVault gets started up, you'll see your desktop disappear and the FileVault progress window pop up and take over. Now, you wait. Once FileVault is done, you'll be back at the login window for your Mac. Choose your account, enter your password, and log in. You're set to use your files like there's almost nothing different—only the icon really gives it away. But when you log out again, those files will once more be encrypted and password-protected.

To turn off FileVault, you simply reopen the Security pane and click Turn Off FileVault. Again, you're returned to the FileVault progress screen, your home folder is decrypted, and you'll be returned to normal computing.

Securely Toss the Trash

One other item is worth noting when it comes to file security, and that's the security of the documents that you toss in the Trash. By default, when you delete a file and then empty the Trash, you may be surprised to learn that the Mac OS doesn't actually "delete" that file in an active sense of the word. Instead, it simply decides to no longer track that file's whereabouts on your disk. The upshot is that some or all of that data may still be on the disk, but now it's okay for the Mac OS to overwrite it with other files when it so chooses.

Unfortunately, that's not very secure. Because the files aren't specifically deleted, they can be recovered relatively easily by a third-party file recovery program (which can be a nice thing when you're talking about files that you *accidentally* lose or delete). So suddenly that deleted letter to your ex doesn't look quite as secure from discovery—especially if, you know, your ex ever gets hold of your Mac for some reason.

To get around that little problem, you can use the Secure Empty Trash feature in the Finder. What Secure Empty Trash does is overwrite each data file that you're trashing with meaningless data. That makes the files considerably more difficult to recover.

To securely delete files, place them in the Trash and choose Finder, Secure Empty Trash. Note that it can take a while because overwriting files (especially if you have a lot of them or they take up a lot of space) can require much more time than the typical Empty Trash command takes to delete trash the regular way.

TIP

If you want even more security when it comes to deleted files, launch the Disk Utility, select your disk, and choose the Erase tab. On the Erase screen, you'll see an option for Erase Free Space. In the dialog sheet that appears, you can opt to overwrite the free space on your disk with up to 35 passes of meaningless data. That's a very secure approach, but note that it takes a *lot* of time to accomplish.

Set Your Open Firmware Password

So, in your quest for an extremely secure Mac, you've done quite a bit. You've set up a good user password, you've begun managing your Keychain closely, and you've gone to the trouble to encrypt your home folder and securely delete your trashed files.

It's too bad someone could overcome all that with nothing more than a Mac OS X installation disc! A Mac OS X installation CD or DVD is designed to allow you to recover from a lost password in an administrator's account. But what that means is that it's also relatively easy to defeat some of the security measures on your Mac, since your password can be changed and your account logged in to.

Similarly, Target Disk Mode represents a security risk, as someone could simply connect your Mac to another via FireWire and start it up by holding down the T key. When your Mac starts up in Target Disk Mode, it will appear as a FireWire drive to the other Mac and can be accessed without permissions limitations—in other words, they've got free reign over the Mac. Sure, it's handy, but it also defeats a fair bit of the work you've put into security. (For the record, you can't use Target Disk Mode to get into an encrypted home folder or an encrypted disk image, and Changing that user's password via the Mac OS X Installer is not a good idea if that user has FileVault active, because the new password will not decrypt the FileVault volume.)

So the trick to securing these two problems—restarting from CD and rebooting into Target Disk Mode—is to set an Open Firmware Password. What this does is disable the keyboard commands that make restarting from disc or in Target Disk Mode possible at startup time—instead, you can only change the way your Mac starts up from the Startup Disk pane in System Preferences. That way, you must already have jumped through the security hoops of gaining access to your account and administrative access to the System Preferences before you can change the way your Mac starts up.

To set the Open Firmware password, launch the Open Firmware Password utility, which isn't installed by default in a typical Mac OS X installation. You'll need to copy the application from your Mac OS X installation disc or download it from Apple's Support website.

Once installed, launch the utility. You'll see a dialog box telling you that you need to be an administrative user; if you are, click Change.

Now, in the Open Firmware Password dialog box, turn on the option Require Password to Change Open Firmware Settings. Then, enter the password for Open Firmware and Verify the password. Now, click OK. You'll need to restart your Mac for the change to take effect.

Now, interestingly, this password isn't really necessary to know. All you've really done from a practical point of view is keep the Mac from reacting to the C and T keys when it starts up or restarts. (The password is used if you actually access the Open Firmware command line, which can you can do by holding down [cmd]+Option+O+F. There's no reason to do this in the course of everyday Mac use, so I'd avoid it unless you have good reason.)

To re-enable your Mac's ability to start up differently using keyboard commands, simply open Open Firmware Password again and, after clicking Change, turn off the option Require Password to Change Open Firmware Settings. Click OK, and the next time you restart your Mac, you'll be back to the standard behavior.

367

Exploring Internet Security

The final broad topic I want to tackle in this chapter is the idea of Internet security. Again, we can boil this one down to a simple phrase, something like "making sure that others on the Internet can only gain access to items on your Mac that they're authorized to see." That means keeping unauthorized people from being able to log in to your Mac, keeping your web browser and email private whenever possible, and keeping transmissions of personal data secure, ideally via encryption. In this section, I'd also like to talk about the parental control features for Internet browsing, email and instant messaging that Apple has added to Mac OS X 10.4.

Secure Your Mac from Access

Even a regular, consumer Mac model can be a high-powered *server* computer thanks to Mac OS X. From web serving to File Sharing, to FTP, and even to Unix-style remote access, you can turn on all kinds of servers in the Sharing pane of System Preferences. (Or, if you're really adventurous, you can dig into the Terminal and turn on even more servers at the command line or by editing some of the low-level system files.)

Your Mac is also designed to live on the Internet and, if you're like me, most of the time that you're on the Internet you're in more of a *client* mode—you're using your Mac to get email, surf the Web, or access your .Mac services—that kind of thing. But that's one place where problems can crop up. Whenever you're on the Internet, your Mac may be acting as a server computer, even if it isn't your primary purpose or you aren't thinking about sharing files at the moment.

So, securing your Mac from access is really two different thoughts. First, you need to be vigilant about what services you have turned on. Second, you need to block access to the services that you turn off, which you'll generally do using a *firewall*, which can be software or hardware.

Turn Off Services

The first step in having a more secure Mac is thinking very seriously about whether you want to have certain sharing services turned on when your Mac is connected to the Internet. In particular, it's worth remembering that File Sharing is *designed* to use TCP/IP as its protocol, which is the same protocol that's used on the Internet. So, when you connect to the Internet (or to any public TCP/IP router) and you have Personal File Sharing turned on, you may be opening yourself up to a security risk.

CAUTION

One place this is particularly true where we don't often think about is a café or similar place that has wireless Internet available. When you join that wireless network with your AirPort-enabled Mac, most likely you are sitting behind a router that has either a firewall built-in or at the very least something called Network Address Translation, which makes it a bit harder for others on the Internet to access your Mac. (NAT is discussed in the next section.) However, others *in the café* or otherwise attached to that router are on your local subnet and can see your Mac's services. (In fact, thanks to Bonjour technology, those services may pop right up on their Macs.) So, it's conceivable that anyone in the vicinity could see your Mac and attempt to access it if you have File Sharing, FTP, remote access, or even Windows Sharing turned on.

Whenever your Mac is connected to the Internet—and a direct connection via DSL, cable, or even regular telephone modem counts—you should consider very seriously whether you need to have File Sharing, FTP, remote access, or Windows Sharing turned on. Ideally, those technologies are designed to work when you have a small network that is served by (and protected using) a hardware router, so that others can't access your Mac using a direct IP address.

When you're surfing from a direct connection or in any circumstance where you're accessing a public network, I'd recommend heading to your Sharing pane and turning off absolutely any of the services that you can get away with turning off.

TIP

Want to do some file sharing in a public setting? Turn on iChat. You can drop files between you and others you know, whether you're sitting in a café or working with one another over a direct Internet connection.

Firewalls and Routers

In order to serve data to remote computers, a server computer opens up a *port* that the client application can access to request and receive data. The port is in addition to the IP address for that server. For instance, to request web data from a web server, your browser accesses that server's IP address and then requests access on Port 80, which is the most commonly used port for HTTP protocol services.

A firewall, then, is software or hardware that manages access to those ports, blocking outside requests to ports that aren't currently offering services. That's what the firewall in Mac OS X does—it blocks access to ports that aren't currently in use because you've haven't turned on that service (see Figure 14.8). To turn on the firewall in Mac OS X (or to check to ensure that it's on), click the Firewall tab in the Sharing pane of System Preferences.

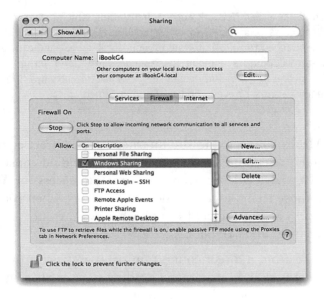

FIGURE 14.8
With the firewall turned on, your Mac will block attempts to access any port that you're not currently using for a service.

Toward the bottom of the list of items on the firewall, you'll see some that aren't grayed out, such as iTunes Music Sharing; if you'd like to allow those requests, you can click on the check box to enable that service. (A service that's enabled *allows* traffic to your Mac on that port; a disabled service will not allow that traffic to get through on that port.)

With the firewall active, you may find out that occasionally a service or application can't be used to access your Mac and you'd like it to. If that's the case, you can click the New button, and, in the dialog sheet that appears, specify a new port by choosing it from the menu or by choosing Other and giving it a name. If you choose an existing service then that service's default port number will be used; if you choose your own service, you can enter the port number. Click OK to save that service to the list for your firewall; you can then turn it on or off.

The Mac OS X firewall has some additional options that you can access by clicking the Advanced button. On the dialog sheet that appears, you can turn on these options:

- Block UDP Traffic. This is simply another type of traffic that can use IP protocols, similar to TCP (Transmission Control Protocol—the standard for most Internet communications) data. UDP is used in specific circumstances for data that needs to arrive quickly and where reliability isn't quite as mission-critical— applications such as online gaming, Voice over IP, and streaming media. If you block this traffic, your Mac is more secure, but you won't have access to many of these types of applications.

- Enable Firewall Logging. Turn on this option if you'd like your Mac to keep a log of the attempts that are made to access it via networking ports. The Open Log button can be used to view that log.

- Enable Stealth Mode. When this option is turned on, any unwelcome data requests that come to your computer go unanswered, which is meant to suggest to the sender that there's no computer at the address that it's attempting to reach.

Make those choices and click OK to dismiss the dialog sheet.

Aside from the built-in firewall, you've got two other options as well. First, if you'd simply like more features in a software router, you can opt for an application such as Intego's NetBarrier (www.intego.com), which offers a variety of services that replace those offered by the built-in firewall, along with other, more comprehensive options. For instance, NetBarrier enables you to more actively monitor traffic to and from your Mac, allowing you to even capture and block requests from your Mac to other servers on the Internet. You can check detailed logs, protect against "Trojans" and other malicious code, and permanently block certain IP addresses from attempting to access your Mac. In fact, NetBarrier will "sniff" the data that is sent *out* of your Mac and it can alert you if it notices personal information that fits certain patterns—such as credit card or bank account numbers—being sent over the Internet.

Similar applications are offered as shareware that can be downloaded and registered online, such as FireWalk X2 (www.pliris-soft.com). FireWalk X2 is very full-featured, offering the ability to set up rules that automate firewall behavior, to block access to particular applications via the network, and to receive real-time alerts when something suspicious or interesting is going on.

What's the other option? A hardware router. This is usually something that's built in to the Internet router that you use to provide Internet access to your local network, if you have one. Your router will likely provide some rudimentary security just by virtue of its being a router, such as

- Network Address Translation. With NAT, you have a "private" IP address on your local network, and the "public" IP address you're using to access the web is actually your router's address. So, when someone tries to access the address that's reported to the world as your IP address, they get blocked by the router.

- Port Mapping ("virtual servers"). Any router should also include the ability to map a port from the router to a particular Mac on your network, allowing you to route traffic to a specific computer designed for the task. For instance, if you want a particular Mac on your network to respond to requests for web pages, you can map port 80 to that particular Mac's private IP address using your router's port mapping table.

- DMZ. The "demilitarized zone" service on some routers is designed to give access to a particular computer outside of the NAT firewall so that it can be used for hosting, particularly in situations where streaming multimedia or gaming isn't working from behind the firewall.

- Access logging. Many routers will keep track of the requests coming into and out of the router so that you can get a sense of the traffic that's being requested and whether you need to block access or certain IP addresses that may be causing problems.

Secure and Private Browsing

Another issue of security and privacy is two-fold—knowing when you're accessing a server that offers security for certain transactions, such as accessing your bank account, and knowing where personal data about your web surfing is stored so that you can delete it when necessary.

Secure Browsing

The Web uses a special protocol, secure HTTP, for transactions that need to be encrypted between your browser and the remote host. You access a secure server using an URL that begins with **https://**. You'll notice that you often switch to a secure server when you opt to purchase something using a "shopping cart" on many e-commerce sites. When you do, you should also see another indicator in your browser. In Safari, you'll see a small padlock icon that shows up in the top-right portion of the window.

In other applications you should see a similar indicator.

Private Browsing

When you're working in your web browser, such as Safari, there's generally quite a bit that goes on in the background. In particular, most web browsers maintain a browser *cache* file (either a collection of files or a database) designed to store the pages that you've recently visited. This cache of data makes it quicker for you to return to those pages; if a page is in your cache then only the changes, if any, need to be downloaded before the page is displayed.

Most browsers also maintain a history of sites that you visit so that you can return to them quickly using the Back button in the browser. In modern browsers such as Safari, a record of the sites that you visit is also kept so that URLs can be "auto completed," and a record of downloaded files is kept in the Downloads list so that you can quickly download them again or access them in the Finder.

Other items are also stored on your Mac when you're browsing. *Cookies*, for instance, are small data files that a website can store on your Mac so that when you return to the site, it can remember information about you (items ranging from the fact that you're a registered user to what was in your "shopping cart" the last time you visited the site). Cookies are mostly harmless, since they're designed specifically not to give a remote website *any* access to your Mac's other files or file system. Still, that is a little bit of personal information that you may not want stored on your Mac for the long term.

In Mac OS X 10.4, Safari includes a special mode called Private Browsing, designed for situations where groups of people use the same Mac. When Private Browsing is turned on, none of these records are kept in a permanent way—instead, history and cache files are only kept for the duration of the current session. When you turn off Private Browsing, close the current window, or quit Safari, the cache, cookies, history, and so on are all deleted. This is ideal for a computer lab or Internet café, so that information about that person's webmail login and items such as user info for accessing .Mac services (or an online bank account) aren't stored beyond the duration of the session. Likewise, if you ever visit a friend's Mac to check your email or surf the Web, you can turn on Private Browsing so that you don't leave a trail of where you've been or leave your settings for online services associated with their application.

To turn on Private Browsing, choose Safari, Private Browsing. You'll see a dialog asking if you're sure. Clicking OK places a check mark next to the option in the Safari menu, which is your indication that it's in force. To turn it off and return to normal, choose Safari, Private Browsing again and close any windows that you were working in.

> **TIP**
>
> Safari also includes the Safari, Empty Cache command, which can be used to quickly clear your Safari cache of its currently stored files. Now, all of the sites you visit will have to be completely downloaded again, including items that haven't changed since they last time you visited the page. Clearing the cache can be handy sometimes for troubleshooting pages (particularly pages with scripts or Flash movies, or online application interfaces such as webmail site) that don't seem to update correctly.

Most other web browsers offer similar commands to clear the cache, history, and other items where records are stored—check out the preferences for those browsers and look for Privacy or Advanced settings.

Parental Controls

In Mac OS X version 10.4, Apple has introduced support for Parental Controls, which give you a little more control over what some of the user accounts on your Mac can see and access. To set the Parental Controls, open the Accounts pane of System Preference. Then, select a user account that is not an Admin user—you'll need to select a Standard user account in order to set Parental Controls for that account. (If the account you want to set is currently an administrator account, simply select it, and, on the Password tab, turn off the option Allow User to Administer This Computer.)

To set Parental Controls, click the Parent Controls tab. There, you'll see the different applications that enable you to set Parental Controls. For Mail, for instance, click the check box next to its icon, then click the Configure button (see Figure 14.9).

When you click that button, in the case of Mail, you'll see a window where you can add the people with whom this account is allowed to exchange email messages. Then, turn on the Send Permission Emails To option and enter your own email address, and you'll be sent email notifications when someone attempts to contact this user (or when this user tries to send out a message). You can then decide whether or not to let the message through.

FIGURE 14.9

Turn on an application that you want to use with Parental Controls and you'll then be able to configure those controls.

The iChat option works in a similar way; you simply build a list of people with whom this user can chat. Also, by simply turning on the Dictionary parental control, you keep the user from being able to access certain words.

The Finder & System options offer a bit more depth. Using them, you can turn on the Simple Finder, if desired, which limits the user to only the applications that you want them to use—you can dig in and put check marks next to the applications that should be available for them. (This is ideal for a young child or in some computer lab situations where you want to offer limited access to applications, utilities, and settings.)

If you leave Finder & System options set to Some Limits, then you can go in and specify those limits, including whether the user can open System Preferences, modify the Dock, and so on. Make your choices and click OK to update them.

Setting Parental Controls for Safari is a little different. First, you turn them on here in the Accounts pane. The next step, though, is to log in as this user (you can use Fast User Switching if it's enabled) and launch Safari. When you do, you'll see a special interface that enables you to set up parental controls in the browser (see Figure 14.10).

FIGURE 14.10

With Parental Controls turned on, this user account is only able to access websites that are already book-marked.

The way it works is simple; the user can surf to any site that already has a bookmark. When a site is encountered that doesn't have a bookmark, a page comes up as shown in Figure 14.10. Now the user can either click the Go Back button and continue surfing approved sites.

The other option that appears when an unauthorized site is accessed, the Add Website button, requires an administrator's account and password. Click that button and enter your username and password. Now you, as the administrator for this user, have approved this site as an addition to this user's approved bookmarks.

That's Parental Controls. If you decide not to have them on for a particular user, just dive back into the Accounts pane of System Preferences, select that user, and turn off the Parental Controls that you no longer need set. Or, you can make the user an Admin user and the Parental Controls are immediately all turned off.

After all, they all have to grow up sometime. (Sigh.)

Index

G-H

J-K

Jabber accounts, 245
junk mail, 237-238

kernel panics, 345
keyboard
document navigation, 101
function keys, 104-105
shortcuts, 99
text, 100
closing, 99
copying, 96
cutting, 96
force quitting, 341
hiding applications, 99
menu commands, 100
opening documents, 99
pasting, 97
printing, 99
quitting applications, 99
redo, 99
saving, 99
selecting all, 99
toggling applications, 101-102
undo, 99
zooming, 100
Keyboard & Mouse pane, 33, 115
Keychain Access, 357
Keychains
locking, 358
passwords, 356-358
screen locks, 359
viewing, 356
launching, 355
password items, adding, 359-360
secure notes, 360

Keychains, 354
disk images, 362
locking, 358
passwords, 355-360
screen locks, 359
secure notes, 360
viewing, 356

L

labeling files/folders, 57-58
LANs (local area networks), 277
launching
Address Book, 152
applications, 26, 75-77
Automator, 108
bookmarks, 264
Dashboard, 106
dial-up Internet connections, 208-210
documents, 77-78, 86, 99
DSL connections, 212
email contacts, 157
FileVault, 363
Finder window, 44
iChat, 157, 244
Internet Connect, 208
iTunes, 179
Keychain Access, 355
.Mac, 219
Mail, 223
Music Store, 182
Open Firmware Password utility, 367
Safari, 254
Sherlock, 275
System Preferences, 29, 110
System Profiler, 130, 312

LDIF (LDAP Interchange Format), 162
Library (iTunes)
interface, 179
playlists, 186-188
songs
importing, 180
searches, 185-186
List view (Finder window), 50, 52
local area networks (LANs), 277
locking Keychains, 358
Log Out command (Apple menu), 39
logging in/out
networks, 293-294
Remote Login, 299
Terminal, 336
users
accounts, 121-123
passwords, 354
Logs entry (System Profiler), 315

M

.Mac, 14
bookmark synchronization, 264
contacts, 163-164
iDisk, 220-221
launching, 219
pane, 113
services, 219
Mail Account Type menu, 224
syncing Address Book/iCal, 174-175
MAC (media access control) addresses, 305
Mac OS X
compared to classic, 11-15
history, 9-10

Q-R